Petter Gottschalk

**Corporate Control of White-Collar Crime**

Petter Gottschalk

# Corporate Control of White-Collar Crime

A Bottom-Up Approach to Executive Deviance

DE GRUYTER

ISBN 978-3-11-153678-1
e-ISBN (PDF) 978-3-11-098668-6
e-ISBN (EPUB) 978-3-11-098686-0

**Library of Congress Control Number: 2022940034**

**Bibliographic information published by the Deutsche Nationalbibliothek**
The Deutsche Nationalbibliothek lists this publication in the Deutsche Nationalbibliografie; detailed bibliographic data are available on the Internet at http://dnb.dnb.de.


This volume is text- and page-identical with the hardback published in 2022.
Cover image: Atstock Productions/iStock/Getty Images
Typesetting: Integra Software Services Pvt.

www.degruyter.com

# Contents

# Introduction

Traditionally, control in organizations is concerned with top-down approaches, where executives attempt to direct their employees' attention, behaviors, and performance to align with the organization's goals and objectives. More recently, the control perspective has extended to include customization and transmutation of control mechanisms, where transmutation captures the idea that organizational units implement control regimes that are different from the mandated control mechanism from management (Chown, 2021: 711):

> Researchers are now beginning to bring these literatures together, marrying the top-down managerial perspective with the lived experiences of employees throughout the organization.

This book takes a new approach by turning the problem of control upside down as it focuses on control of executives who find white-collar crime convenient. The bottom-up approach to executive compliance focuses on organizational measures to make white-collar crime less convenient for potential offenders (Haines et al., 2022). Compliance refers to obeying the formal rules and regulations in force at a given time and place (Durand et al., 2019). Some deviant executives apply creative compliance (Nurse, 2022: 69):

> Creative compliance involves the use of techniques which can be argued to be 'perfectly legal' despite the purpose and impact of such techniques being to undermine the whole purpose of reporting and regulation and in practical terms using the letter of the law to defeat its spirit, arguably 'with impunity'.

Control is concerned with a negative discrepancy between the desired and current state of affairs. Control mechanisms attempt to reduce the discrepancy through adaptive action in the form of behavioral reactions (Direnzo and Greenhaus, 2011). Control mechanisms attempt to influence and manage the process, content, and outcome of work (Kownatzki et al., 2013). Control involves processes of negotiation in which various strategies are developed to produce particular outcomes. Control is therefore a dynamic process that regulates behavior through a set of modes, rules, or strategies (Gill, 2019).

There are various types of control mechanisms with various targets (Chown, 2021: 752):

> For example, prominent frameworks delineate controls based on whether they are formal or informal, coercive, normative, peer-based, or concertive. Controls are also divided based on whether they target employees' behaviors by implementing processes or rules that ensure individuals perform tasks in a particular manner, target their outputs by assessing employees based on measurable items such as profits or production, or target the inputs to the production process by controlling the human capital and material inputs utilized by the organization.

https://doi.org/10.1515/9783110986686-001

Corporate white-collar crime control is mainly focused on attempts to prevent, detect, and reduce negative discrepancy between desired and current state of executive affairs. Control attempts to influence the process of work in normative ways. Control targets executive behavior to ensure that executive individuals perform tasks in a legitimate manner. As argued by Kownatzki et al. (2013), behavior control relies on subjective, organizationally relevant criteria to assess executive activity and measures performance in the context of long-term progress toward the development of a particular way of doing things. Behavior control not only provides checks and balances for executive performance, but also provides a common vocabulary that facilitates dialogue among stakeholders and fosters the creation of ambitious behavioral norms. When behavior rather that outcome is the focus, controls may provide a buffer for external short-term pressures.

Within an organization, struggles are about conceptions of control (Yue et al., 2013). Control mechanisms have to satisfy a number of requirements to be successful, such as fairness perceived by controlled individuals (Long et al., 2011). Social control is based on attachment, commitment, involvement, and belief, where a control mechanism is informal punishment in the appearance of shaming (Amry and Meliala, 2021).

Research has documented the failure of the traditional top-down approach to executive compliance, in particular control of chief executive officers (Bosse and Phillips, 2016; Galvin et al., 2015; Khanna et al., 2015; Pillay and Klubers, 2014; Williams, 2008; Zahra, 2005; Zhu and Chen, 2015).

Some CEOs will employ illegal or objectionable means in striving to reach goals. This type of behavior is not necessarily different from the behavior of others in positions of power and authority (e.g., politicians, officers of universities, church officials, heads of major philanthropies, etc.), but the degrees of freedom enjoyed by many CEOs make the CEO position nevertheless very special in terms of convenience. For example, a CEO may conveniently cheat and defraud owners (Khanna et al., 2015; Williams, 2008; Zahra et al., 2005) because there is lack of oversight and guardianship in the agency relationship (Bosse and Phillips, 2006; Pillay and Kluvers, 2014).

While there is considerable variance in narcissistic tendencies across CEOs, many CEOs have narcissistic personality traits such as self-focus, self-admiration, a sense of entitlement, and a sense of superiority (Zhu and Chen, 2015: 35):

> Narcissistic CEOs tend to favor bold actions, such as large acquisitions, that attract attention. They are less responsive than other CEOs to objective indicators of their performance and more responsive to social praise. For instance, while narcissistic CEOs tend to aggressively adopt technological discontinuities, they are especially likely to do so when such behavior is expected to garner attention and admiration from external audiences.

Galvin et al. (2015: 163) found that some CEOs suffer from narcissistic identification with the organization:

> It is not uncommon to learn of individuals in positions of power and responsibility, especially CEOs, who exploit and undermine their organizations for personal gain. A circumstance not well explained in the literature, however, is that some of those individuals may highly identify with their organizations, meaning that they see little difference between their identity and the organization's identity – between their interests and the organization's interest. This presents a paradox, because organizational identification typically is not noted for its adverse consequences on the organization.

The CEO is the only person at that top hierarchical level in the organization. Below the CEO, there are a number of executives at the same hierarchical level. Above the CEO, there are a number of board members at the same hierarchical level. However, the CEO is alone at his or her level. The CEO is supposed to face control by the board, but the board only meets occasionally to discuss business cases. Executives below the CEO are typically appointed by the CEO and typically loyal to the CEO (Bendiktsson, 2010; Bigley and Wiersma, 2002; Chatterjee and Pollock, 2017; Chen and Nadkarni, 2017; Davidson et al., 2019; Gamache and McNamara, 2019; Gangloff et al., 2016; Khanna et al., 2015; König et al., 2020; McClelland et al., 2010; Schnatterly et al., 2018; Shen, 2003; Zhu and Chen, 2015).

The board of directors is typically incapable of controlling chief executive activities (Ghannam et al., 2019). Examples of former CEOs as white-collar crime convicts include Thomas Middelhoff at Alcantor in Germany, Boris Benulic at Kraft & Kultur in Sweden, Hisao Tanaka at Toshiba Corporation in Japan, Are Blomhoff at Betanien Foundation in Norway, and Trond Kristoffersen at Finance Credit in Norway – in addition to all the well-known names from the United States.

Control of executives is necessary to ensure the legitimate success and survival of organizations. As argued by Gill (2019), there are two important conceptual dimensions that draw together insights from studies of control and resistance in the workplace. The dimension of compatibility considers executives' subjective experiences of the fit between their personhood and modes of control, where alignment can inspire fulfillment and misalignment can prompt suffering and deviant behavior. The dimension of coherence considers executives' perception of the consistency between modes, which can be fragmented or unified to reinforce organizationally prescribed compliance and ethics, where "ethics is not equivalent to laws" (Dion, 2019: 836).

At its core, top-down control refers to the manner in which "an organization's managers can use different types of control mechanisms – such as financial incentives, performance management, or culture – to monitor, measure, and evaluate workers' behaviors and influence them toward achieving the organization's goals in efficient and effective ways" (Chown et al., 2021: 713). Similarly at its core, bottom-up control refers to the manner in which organizational members can use different types of control mechanisms – such as whistleblowing, transparency, resource access, or culture – to monitor, measure, and evaluate executives' avoidance of deviant behaviors and influence them toward achieving the organization's goals in efficient and effective ways. While the hierarchical structure remains with executives at the top of the organization in charge of the business, bottom-up control is a matter of stakeholder involvement in compliance. While top-down control is often a formal and rigid system, bottom-up control can be an informal and flexible system based on social influence (Haines et al., 2022: 185):

> Criminalization, foundational analytical territory for criminology, forms part of a 'bottom up' strategy where it becomes 'social property', untethered from law and formal criminal justice. Criminalization as social property comprises a central element of 'social control influence' over corporate harm. This is justice in the vernacular with media, social movements and citizen watchdogs exerting pressure, demanding change and bringing business to account.

When noticing wrongdoing at the top of the organization, improvisation might be a key capability for organizational members and citizen watchdogs. Capability refers to the ability to perform (Paruchuri et al., 2021), while improvisation refers to the spontaneous process by which planning and execution happen at the same time (Mannucci et al., 2021). Rather than following formal reporting lines to people who are not trustworthy, improvisation is a matter of spontaneous action in response to unanticipated occurrences, in which individuals find a way to manage the unexpected problem.

This book starts in Chapter 1 by introducing white-collar crime convenience. Executive convenience in financial crime is discussed in terms of organizational opportunity, where opportunity exists both to commit and to conceal white-collar crime. The convenience of committing white-collar crime depends on corporate executive status (Chapter 2) and access to corporate resources (Chapter 3). The convenience of concealing white-collar crime depends on corporate organizational decay (Chapter 4), lack of oversight and guardianship (Chapter 5), and criminal markets and networks (Chapter 6). Chapter 7 presents four case studies where the bottom-up approach led to detection and later conviction of white-collar offenders.

Chapter 8 supplements the main perspective of bottom-up by the outside-in perspective on white-collar misconduct and crime. Outside organizations, there are various professionals who can either help white-collar offenders commit and conceal crime, or they can help prevent and detect white-collar individuals in organizations. Lawyers can report suspicious transactions on client accounts, certified accountants as well as auditors can blow the whistle on suspected value assessments, bank officials can react to attempts to use tax havens for corruption payments, and employees in health care can detect wrongdoing in pharmaceutical firms.

Chapter 9 presents case studies where detection of white-collar crime resulted from bottom-up and outside-in notification. The case studies cover wrongdoing by an Icelandic company involved in corruption in Namibia, a Swedish company involved in corruption in Uzbekistan, a Swedish company involved in civil war in Sudan, a U.S. bank involved in customer fraud, a Japanese company involved in pharmaceutical fraud in Europe, and global auditing firms involved in the global financial crisis.

Chapter 10 extends white-collar crime from the individual level and the organizational level to the state level in terms of state-corporate crime. State-corporate crime is illegal actions that result from a mutually reinforcing interaction between institutions of political governance and institutions of economic production. State-corporate crime can be either initiated or facilitated by the state. State-initiated crime results from alignment of mutual interests, while state-facilitated crime results from the regime of public permissions. The chapter presents a number of cases that were detected by bottom-up notification and outside-in notification. While the chapter covers the topic of state-corporate crime extensively that can be quickly skimmed by the reader, a final section in the chapter returns to the core issue of bottom-up approaches to prevention and detection.

The final Chapter 11 reviews attribution of responsibility and punitiveness for financial crime. Schmidt et al. (2022) found that the greater the offender is deemed to have been directly involved (causality), aware of the consequences (knowledge), acted intentionally, and deemed morally wrong, the more responsibility attributed to the actor. Further, if the offender was deemed to have been influenced by others (coercion) in committing financial crime, the offender was deemed less responsible as evidenced by a negative coefficient. Attribution of responsibility was statistically significant in predicting recommended fine. The greater the attribution of responsibility, the greater was the recommended fine.

Also in chapter 11, attribution of responsibility and punitiveness is studied based on a number of investigation reports by fraud examiners. When multiple regression analysis is applied to knowledge, intention, and seriousness as predictors of responsibility, then the set of three predictors explain more than half of the variation in responsibility attribution with an R square of .542 and an adjusted R square of .512. Among the three predictor variables, only intention is statistically significant with a p-value of .007, while knowledge and seriousness have not sufficient significance with p-values of .055 and .406 respectively. Intentionality, that is, was the action intentional, the actor intended to commit wrongdoing, the action was no accident, and the actor planned the action in advance. Based on this sample, it is possible to conclude that the attribution of responsibility increases significantly when fraud examiners found that the offender committed the act intentionally.

This book has a multidisciplinary approach by combination of management and law that give an insight into how white-collar crime is committed and how it can be stopped. The book talks about different aspects of crime, position, corporate structure, role of employees, and responsibility of employers. The role of whistleblowers is emphasized in an ethical perspective. The book represents a rare combination for a majority of readers ranging from management, law, sociology, criminology, and sociology. The notion of bottom-up controls for addressing white-collar crime is novel and needed since control traditionally is considered from a top-down perspective. The discussion of controls themselves should serve as a valuable contribution to business, white-collar crime, and criminology literature.

# 1 White-Collar Crime Convenience

White-collar crime is financial crime based on the social and occupational position of the offender committed by a person of respectability and high social influence in the course of the offender's occupation (Sutherland, 1939, 1983). This offender-based definition emphasizes some combination of the actor's high social status, power, and respectability as the key features of white-collar crime (Benson et al., 2021) as well as the violation of stakeholder trust (Sohoni and Rorie, 2021).

The deviant behavior by white-collar offenders can be explained by the theory of convenience that suggests a triangle of financial motive, organizational opportunity, and personal willingness (Asting and Gottschalk, 2022; Braaten and Vaughn, 2019; Dearden and Gottschalk, 2020; Desmond et al., 2022; Stadler and Gottschalk, 2021; Qu, 2021). Convenience is savings in time and effort, reduced pain and strain, and other factors that make a certain path or choice attractive. Convenience is the state of being able to proceed with something with little effort or difficulty, avoiding pain and strain (Collier and Kimes, 2012; Mai and Olsen, 2016; Sundström and Radon, 2015).

## White-Collar Crime Offenders

This book is mainly concerned with offenders rather than offenses. To offend is to cause displeasure, anger, resentment, or wounded feelings. It is to be displeasing or disagreeable. It can also be to violate a moral, a guideline, a rule or a law. The offender-based perspective emphasizes characteristics of actors such as social and occupational status, respectability and power (Benson, 2021; Dodge, 2009; Friedrichs et al., 2018; Piquero and Schoepfer, 2010; Pontell et al., 2014; Stadler et al., 2013; Sutherland, 1983).

Benson and Simpson (2018: 145) found that white-collar criminals seldom think of injury or victims:

> Many white-collar offenses fail to match this common-sense stereotype because the offenders do not set out intentionally to harm any specific individual. Rather, the consequences of their illegal acts fall upon impersonal organizations or a diffuse and unseen mass of people.

Offender-focused theories explain crime in terms of personality characteristics (Koppen et al., 2010). Self-control theory is a typical theory related to deviant behavior (Gottfredson and Hirschi, 1990). Individuals with low self-control tend to be impulsive, self-centered, out for adventure, and out for immediate pleasure. Immediate pleasure may be achieved more conveniently by white-collar crime than by legal activities.

https://doi.org/10.1515/9783110986686-002

The typical profile of a white-collar criminal includes the following attributes:

- The person has high social status and considerable influence, enjoying respect and trust, and belongs to the elite.
- The elite have generally more knowledge, money and prestige, and occupy higher positions than others in the population.
- Privileges and authority by the elite are often not visible or transparent, but nevertheless known to everybody.
- The elite can be found in business, public administration, politics, congregations and many other sectors in society.
- Elite is a minority that behaves as an authority towards others.
- The person is often wealthy and does not really need crime income to live a good life.
- The person is typically well educated and connects to important networks of partners and friends.
- The person exploits his or her position to commit financial crime either for personal benefit or for organizational benefit that might help person career.
- The person does not look at himself or herself as a criminal, but rather as a community builder who applies personal rules for own behavior.
- The person may be in a position that makes the police reluctant to initiate a crime investigation.
- The person has access to resources that enable involvement of top defense attorneys and can behave in court in a manner that creates sympathy among the general public, partly because the defendant belongs to the upper class similar to the judge, the prosecutor and the attorney.

White-collar criminals are mostly men. The low female fraction can be explained by a number of factors, such as relative need for material wealth, relative opportunity to commit crime, and relative risk aversion. In addition, the detection rate for female white-collar criminals may be lower than for male criminals, for example because women are more seldom suspected of crime. Most famous United States cases are men such as Ebbers, Madoff, Raparatman and Schilling. In Germany, Blickle et al. (2006) studied a sample of 76 convicted white-collar criminals where 6 offenders were women while 70 offenders were men. The U.S. sample studied by Langton and Piquero (2007) consisted of 16 percent women and 84 percent men. A study in the Netherlands of 644 prosecuted white-collar criminals between 2008 and 2012 showed 15 percent women and 85 percent men in the sample (Onna et al., 2014).

In a Norwegian sample of 405 white-collar offenders who were convicted to prison from 2009 to 2015, there were 7 percent females and 93 percent males. The longest prison sentence of nine years was given to CEO Trond Kristoffersen at Finance Credit. Among the convicts, 42 percent were convicted of fraud, 35 percent of manipulation, 19 percent of corruption, and 4 percent of theft. The average age when committing crime was 43 years, and the average age at incarceration was 48 years. Since the detection rate in the country is estimated at one out of eleven (Gottschalk and Gunnesdal, 2018), it is not obvious that the remaining ten have the same profile as the one detected.

## Executive Convenience Orientation

How privileged individuals in the elite think and feel about time and effort varies. Chen and Nadkarni (2017: 34) found that many CEOs can be characterized by time urgency where they have the feeling of being chronically hurried:

> Time urgency is a relatively stable trait. Time-urgent people are acutely aware of the passage of time and feel chronically hurried. They often create aggressive internal deadlines and use them as markers of the timely completion of team tasks. They regularly check work progress, increase others' awareness of the remaining time, and motivate others to accomplish commitments within the allotted time.

Convenience is a concept that was theoretically mainly associated with efficiency in time savings. Today, convenience is associated with a number of other characteristics, such as reduced effort and reduced pain. Convenience is linked to terms such as fast, easy, and safe. Convenience says something about attractiveness and accessibility. A convenient individual is not necessarily neither bad nor lazy. On the contrary, the person can be seen as smart and rational (Sundström and Radon, 2015).

Convenience orientation is conceptualized as the value that individuals and organizations place on actions with inherent characteristics of saving time and effort as well as avoiding strain and pain. Convenience orientation can be considered a value-like construct that influences behavior and decision-making. Mai and Olsen (2016) measured convenience orientation in terms of a desire to spend as little time as possible on the task, in terms of an attitude that the less effort needed the better, as well as in terms of a consideration that it is a waste of time to spend long hours on the task. Convenience orientation toward illegal actions increases as negative attitudes towards legal actions increase. The basic elements in convenience orientation are the individual attitudes toward the saving of time, effort and discomfort in the planning, action and achievement of goals. Generally, convenience orientation is the degree to which an individual or a group of individuals are inclined to save time and effort to reach goals.

Convenience orientation refers to a person's or persons' general preference for convenient maneuvers. A convenience-oriented person is one who seeks to accomplish a task in the shortest time with the least expenditure of human energy (Berry et al., 2002; Farquhar and Rowley, 2009).

Convenience in the decision-making process is not only concerned with one alternative being more convenient than another alternative. Convenience is also concerned with the extent to which an individual collects information about more alternatives and collects more information about each alternative. Market research indicates that consumers tend to make buying decisions based on little information about few alternatives (Sundström and Radon, 2015). A similar process can be explored for white-collar crime where the individual avoids the effort of collecting more information about more alternatives that might have led to a non-criminal rather than a criminal solution to a challenge or problem.

It is not the actual convenience that is important in convenience theory. Rather it is the perceived, expected and assumed convenience that influences choice of action. Berry et al. (2002) make this distinction explicit by conceptualizing convenience as individuals time and effort perceptions related to an action. White-collar criminals probably vary in their perceived convenience of their actions. Low expected convenience can be one of the reasons why not more members of the elite commit white-collar offenses.

Convenience is of value because time and effort are associated with value. Time is a limited and scarce resource. Saving time means reallocating time across activities to achieve greater efficiency. Similarly, effort can be reallocated to create value elsewhere. The more effort is exerted, the more outcomes can be expected in return (Berry et al., 2002).

Convenience in white-collar crime relates to savings in time and effort by privileged and trusted individuals to reach a goal. Convenience is here an attribute of an illegal action. Convenience comes at a potential cost to the offender in terms of the likelihood of detection and future punishment. In other words, reducing time and effort now entails a greater potential for future cost. 'Paying for convenience' is a way of phrasing this proposition (Farquhar and Rowley, 2009).

Convenience is the perceived savings in time and effort required to find and to facilitate the use of a solution to a problem or to exploit favorable circumstances. Convenience directly relates to the amount of time and effort that is required to accomplish a task. Convenience addresses the time and effort exerted before, during, and after an activity. Convenience represents a time and effort component related to the complete illegal transaction process or processes (Collier and Kimes, 2012).

As Agnew (2014: 2) formulates it: "crime is often the most expedient way to get what you want" and "fraud is often easier, simpler, faster, more exciting, and more certain than other means of securing one's ends".

There are costs associated with convenience (Locke and Blomquist, 2016). Convenience stores have typically higher prices than other stores. In our perspective of crime, offenders risk detection, blame, prosecution, and conviction. In the marketing literature, distinctions are made between decision convenience, access convenience, benefit convenience, transaction convenience, and post benefit convenience (Seiders et al., 2007). In the current convenience theory for white-collar crime, we make distinctions between economical convenience, organizational convenience, and behavioral convenience.

## Executive Convenience Themes

A combination of motive, opportunity and willingness determine the extent of white-collar crime convenience as illustrated in the structural model in Figure 1.1. There are a total of fourteen convenience themes on the right-hand side in the figure. Corporate white-collar crime control is concerned with the five organizational opportunity themes of status, access, decay, chaos, and collapse. These themes are discussed in the following chapters.

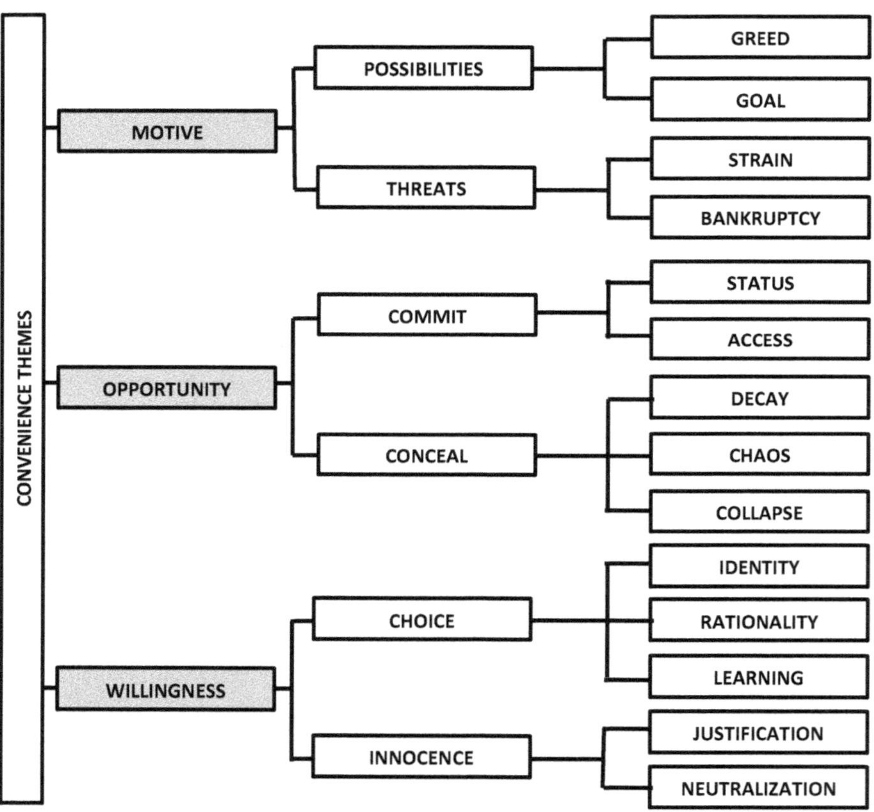


**Figure 1.1:** Structural model of convenience theory.

In the financial motive dimension, profit might be a goal in itself or an enabler to exploit possibilities and to avoid threats. Possibilities and threats exist both for individual members of the organization as well as for the organization as a whole. It is convenient to exploit possibilities and to avoid threats by financial means.

In the organizational opportunity dimension, convenience can exist both to commit white-collar crime and to conceal white-collar crime. Offenders have high social status in privileged positions, and they have legitimate access to crime resources. Disorganized institutional deterioration causes decay, lack of oversight and guardianship cause chaos, while criminal market structures cause collapse.

The personal willingness for deviant behavior focuses on offender choice and perceived innocence. The choice of crime can be caused by deviant identity, rational consideration, or learning from others. Justification and neutralization cause the perceived innocence at crime. Identity, rationality, learning, justification, and neutralization all contribute to making white-collar crime action a convenient behavior for offenders.

## Financial Possibilities and Threats

The economical dimension of convenience theory focuses on financial motives that the offender has to exploit and explore possibilities, and to reduce and avoid threats. Possibilities and threats are motives both for individuals and for the organization, as illustrated in Figure 1.1. Corporate possibilities and threats are discussed here.

Possibilities for the corporation include reaching business objectives by ignoring whether or not means are legitimate or illegitimate (Campbell and Göritz, 2014; Jonnergård et al., 2010; Kang and Thosuwanchot, 2017). Ends simply justify means that might represent crime. It may be so important to have a bottom line in accounting that satisfies investors and others that crime emerges as potentially acceptable. Dodge (2009: 15) suggests that tough rivalry among executives make them commit crime to attain goals: "The competitive environment generates pressures on the organization to violate the law in order to attain goals".

Goalsetting is often perceived in a positive light, meaning that ambitious goals increase performance (Locke and Latham, 2013). However, there is also evidence suggesting that setting high performance goals can be followed by unethical behavior (Simmons, 2018) by effective leaders (Zyglidopoulos, 2021). Welsh et al. (2020) argue that this is not only because of rewards associated with goal attainment, but also because of changing morale reasoning processes related to the goal. As such, high goal commitment facilitates unethical behavior by increasing not only the motivation to achieve the goal but also the motivation to justify doing so by any means necessary (Locatelli et al., 2017). This is known as state morale disagreement, a process through which individuals justify unethical behavior (Moore, 2015). It is part of the dark side of ambitious goals. Escalation of commitment to ambitious goals increases the likelihood of misconduct and crime (Sleesman et al., 2012, 2018).

Corporate greed implies that the organization is never satisfied, as it always wants more profit (Goldstraw-White, 2012). Greed reflects needs and desires that are socially constructed, and the needs and desires can never be completely covered or contended. There is a strong preference to maximize wealth for the corporation, possibly at the expense of violating the laws, rules, and guidelines. Economic greed is a strong motive for financial crime (Bucy et al., 2008; Hamilton and Micklethwait, 2006).

Corporations enter into exchange relationships with suppliers, customers, banks, consultants, and others. Exchanges can be thought of as discrete events nested within continuous relationships that are developing and changing over the course of time. Reciprocity such as kickbacks might be natural according to expectations in an exchange relationship to secure future business possibilities (Huang and Knight, 2017).

Finally, in the motive of possibilities for corporations, making as much profits as possible might be the ultimate goal (Naylor, 2003). Rather than viewing profits as an enabler to invest and expand, profits as such might be the final goal in itself. Financial crime can be an attractive strategic decision (Lopez-Rodriguez, 2009; Menon and Siew, 2012).

Moving down in Figure 1.1 to threats, the threat of corporate collapse and bankruptcy might cause exploration and exploitation of illegal avenues to survive, where moral panic can occur (Kang and Thosuwanchot, 2017). The survival of the corporation can become so important that no means come across as unacceptable in the current situation. Sometimes, fraud and corruption are considered temporary measures to recover from a crisis (Geest et al., 2017), where the measures will be terminated when the crisis is over. A crisis is a fundamental threat to the organization, which is often characterized by ambiguity of cause, effect, and means of resolution (König et al., 2020).

Financial balance is a strong motive for corporate economic crime (Brightman, 2009). In some markets, the only way to survive is to implement financial practices similar to the ones applied by competitors. If corruption is the name of the game, every participant on the market has to provide bribes to stay in business (Berghoff, 2018; Bradshaw, 2015). Furthermore, threats from monopolies are a strong motive for financial crime (Chang et al., 2005). Similarly, if a cartel is the name of the game, the only way to survive might be to join the cartel, where cartel members divide markets among themselves (Freiberg, 2020; Goncharov and Peter, 2019).

Threats are often noticed very late, both by individuals and by organizations. Handling threats thus becomes a matter of urgency. Individuals and firms "fail to detect threats and prevent calamities not because of an absence of signals or insufficient knowledge (or faulty awareness), but because attention bandwidth and information-processing fidelity are inherently limited" (Downing et al., 2019: 1890).

## Opportunity to Commit and Conceal

High social status in privileged positions creates power inequality compared to those without any status in their positions. The perspective of power inequality suggests that, for example, family members in family firms wield significant influence in their firms (Patel and Cooper, 2014). Family members often have legitimate access to firm resources that nonfamily executives in the firm cannot question.

Individuals with high social status in privileged positions can cooperate to create a business climate of "organized irresponsibility" (Berghoff, 2018: 425):

> The term implies that management had conspired to prevent efficient controls and therefore facilitated and promoted corruption.

Leaders reinforce a culture of financial crime by ignoring criminal actions and otherwise facilitate unethical behavior. At the same time, they try to distance and disassociate themselves from criminal actions (Pontell et al., 2021: 9):

> High status corporate criminals often go to great lengths to distance themselves from the crimes committed by their subordinates and to hide any incriminating evidence of their role in the decisions that authorized those criminal acts.

For many white-collar offenders, there is not much challenge in committing financial crime. They typically have high status and access to relevant resources. The main challenge is often to conceal committed crime, where relevant issues are decay, chaos, and collapse as illustrated in Figure 1.1. Decay in the form of institutional deterioration improves conditions of convenience for crime concealment (Barton, 2004; Donk and Molloy, 2008). Institutional deterioration can occur conveniently, resulting from external legitimacy where deviance is the norm (Kostova et al., 2008; Pinto et al., 2008; Rodriguez et al., 2005). An offender's actions have a superficial appearance of legitimacy also internally, since both legal and illegal actions in the company occur in a manner characterized by disorganization (Benson and Simpson, 2018). Conventional mechanisms of social control are weak and unable to regulate the behavior within the organization (Pratt and Cullen, 2005). Concealment of crime occurs conveniently by simply disappearing among other seemingly legitimate transactions.

Social disorganization is the inability of an organization to realize common values of its members and maintain effective social control. Social disorganization implies that the ability of social bonds to reduce delinquent behavior is absent (Forti and Visconti, 2020; Hoffmann, 2002; Onna and Denkers, 2019). Differential reinforcement of crime convenience develops over time as individuals become vulnerable to various associations and definitions conducive to delinquency.

Social disorganization occurs because the human nature is selfish, and people are unwilling to share a common culture. Culture refers to the values, beliefs, preferences, and assumptions that provides the basis for interaction and shared understandings among group members, and which differentiate one group of people from another (Malmi et al., 2020). In the perspective of life-courses with age-graded determinants of crime, it is interesting to notice that white-collar crime represents adult-onset offending. White-collar offenders are people who live more or less conventional law-abiding lives until they are adults and who then commit crime. Moving into the elite as an adult reduces social controls through social bonds (Benson and Chio, 2020).

Misconduct and crime can be hard to detect because signals of deviant behavior drown or disappear in noise (Gomulya and Mishina, 2017). Karim and Siegel (1998) define four possible outcomes in the decision matrix of an observer. First, the observer notices a noise signal when it is a crime signal (called a miss). Second, the observer notices a crime signal when it is a crime signal (called a hit). Third, the observer notices a noise signal when it is a noise signal (called a correct identification). Finally, the observer notices a crime signal when it is a noise signal (called a false alarm). The more frequent false alarms and misses occur, the greater the opportunity is successfully to conceal white-collar crime. Szalma and Hancock (2013) found that control functions typically have low signal alertness, and that such functions lack the ability to recognize and interpret patterns in signals. One reason might be that control functions have dysfunctional cognitive style and achievement motivation (Martinsen et al., 2016).

Misreporting in accounting is often a convenient way of concealing illegal transactions (Qiu and Slezak, 2019). Lack of transparency makes concealment in accounting convenient (Davidson et al., 2019; Goncharov and Peter, 2019). Managers can withhold bad news by accounting misrepresentation (Bao et al., 2019), since financial statements are a substantive component of a firm's communications with its stakeholders (Gupta et al., 2020). Balakrishnan et al. (2019) found that reduced corporate transparency in accounting is associated with increased corporate tax aggressiveness. Accounting fraud in terms of account manipulation is lacking transparency (Toolami et al., 2019).

Since accounting is no machine that can provide correct answers regarding the financial health of a company, since accounting information has limited representational properties, and since accounting cannot fully inform decision-makers (O'Leary and Smith, 2020), determination of final accounting figures are often left to the discretion of financial managers.

Shadnam and Lawrence (2011) found that morale collapse increases the tendency to financial crime. In fact, repetition of criminal actions might institutionalize such actions (Hatch, 1997). Dion (2008) found that the larger the corporation, the less deterrence effect from laws on financial crime, which may have to do with increased convenience in concealing crime.

Lack of oversight and guardianship causes chaos. The agency perspective suggests that a principal is often unable to control an agent who does work for the principal. The agency perspective assumes narrow self-interest among both principals and agents. The interests of principal and agent tend to diverge, they may have different risk willingness or risk aversion, there is knowledge asymmetry between the two parties, and the principal has imperfect information about the agent's contribution (Bosse and Phillips, 2016; Chrisman et al., 2007; Pillay and Kluvers, 2014;

Williams, 2008). According to principal-agent analysis, exchanges can encourage illegal gain for both principal and agent.

Concealing crime is convenient also because others than the offender is incapable of making sense of actions that have occurred (Weick, 1995). People tend to trust what an elite member does, based on the authority position occupied by the offender. Sense making links to crime signal detection by the challenge of perceiving and understanding a crime signal versus a noise signal, as discussed above. People without experience are unable to make sense of weak signals from white-collar offenders. They are not able to frame or categorize through words what the signal is about (Holt and Cornelissen, 2014). Even when crime signals are reported to the criminal justice system, police detectives are often unable to successfully investigate financial crime (Gilmour, 2020).

## Personal Willingness for Deviant Behavior

Personal willingness for deviant behavior increases as the gap between two antagonistic forces increases: the push of desires and the pull of self-regulation. Self-control failure arises because an executive experiences a potent and overwhelming desire that drives impulsive behaviors, while higher-level executive mental functioning is temporarily or permanently compromised and unable to override behaviors impelled by the desire. Self-control failure is a result of a desire that is too strong to stifle. Generally, self-control reflects an individual's capacity and motivation to override desires and urges in order to act in accordance with one's long-range goals (Liang et al., 2016):

> Effective human functioning requires the capacity to transcend primal desires and habitual behaviors in order to behave in a socially appropriate manner. When self-control fails, individuals disregard the long-term implications of their behaviors and succumb to their desires, such as eating fatty foods, cheating on a partner, or engaging in unethical behaviors. Ultimately, self-control failure contributes to poor physical and mental health, crime, and low-quality interpersonal relationships.

As illustrated in Figure 1.1, the willingness for deviant behavior derives from choice and innocence in convenience theory. White-collar crime can be the result of a choice based on identity, rationality, and learning, and white-collar crime can be the result of innocence based on justification and neutralization. Personal willingness for deviant behavior implies a positive attitude towards violating social norms, in addition to violating formally enacted laws, rules, and regulations (Aguilera et al., 2018). Social norms refer to standards that are understood by members of a group and that guide and constrain social behavior without the force of law (Gorecki and Letki, 2021).

The personality trait of narcissism expects preferential treatment. A pervasive pattern of grandiosity, a need for admiration, and an empathy deficit characterize narcissism. Narcissistic identification is a special type of narcissism, where the offender sees little or no difference between self and the corporation. The company money is personal money that can be spent whatever way the narcissist prefers (Galvin et al., 2015). While grandiosity and admiration belong to the motivational dimension of convenience theory, empathy deficit belongs to the willingness dimension of convenience theory where the offender possesses a sense of entitlement (Nichol, 2019). The offender shows unreasonable expectations to receive and obtain preferential treatments (Zvi and Elaad, 2018).

The choice of crime might derive from sensation seeking. Craig and Piquero (2017) suggest that the willingness to commit financial crime by some white-collar offenders has to do with their inclination for adventure and excitement. Offenders are not only seeking new, intense, and complicated experiences and sensations, as well as exciting adventures, they are also accepting the legal, physical, financial, and social risks associated with these adventures.

Learning from others by differential association was introduced by Sutherland (1983), who coined the term white-collar crime several decades earlier. The differential association perspective suggests that offenders associate with those who agree with them, and distance and disassociate themselves from those who disagree. The choice of crime is thus caused by social learning from others with whom offenders associate (Akers, 1985).

Innocent justification can occur as the offender feels entitled to financial crime after negative life events (Engdahl, 2015). The perspective of negative life events suggests that events such as divorce, accident, lack of promotion, and cash problems can cause potential offenders to consider white-collar crime a convenient solution.

By application of neutralization techniques (Sykes and Matza, 1957), they deny responsibility, injury, and victim. They condemn the condemners. They claim appeal to higher loyalties and normality of action. They claim entitlement, and they argue the case of legal mistake. They find their own mistakes acceptable. They argue a dilemma arose, whereby they made a reasonable tradeoff before committing the act (Jordanoska, 2018; Kaptein and Helvoort, 2019). Such claims enable offenders to find crime convenient, since they do not consider it crime, and they do not feel guilty of wrongdoing. These are the most frequently cited neutralization techniques in the research literature for white-collar offenders:

1. *Disclaim responsibility for crime: Not responsible for what happened.* The offender here claims that one or more of the conditions of responsible agency did not occur. The person committing a deviant act defines himself or herself as lacking responsibility for his or her actions. In this technique, the person rationalizes that the action in question is beyond his or her control. The offender

views himself as a billiard ball, helplessly propelled through different situations. He denies responsibility for the event or sequence of events.
2. *Refuse damage from crime: There is no visible harm from the action.* The offender seeks to minimize or deny the harm done. Denial of injury involves justifying an action by minimizing the harm it causes. The misbehavior is not very serious because no party suffers directly or visibly because of it.
3. *Refuse victim from crime: There is nobody suffering from the action.* The offender may acknowledge the injury but deny any existence of victims or claims that the victim(s) are unworthy of concern. Any blame for illegal actions are unjustified because the violated party deserves whatever injury they receive.
4. *Condemn those who criticize: Outsiders do not understand relevant behavior.* The offender tries to accuse his or her critics of questionable motives for criticizing him or her. According to this technique of condemning the condemners, one neutralizes own actions by blaming those who were the target of the misconduct. The offender deflects moral condemnation onto those ridiculing the misbehavior by pointing out that they engage in similar disapproved behavior. In addition, the offender condemns procedures of the criminal justice system, especially police investigation with interrogation, as well as media coverage of the case.
5. *Justify crime by higher loyalties: It was according to expectations.* The offender denies the act was motivated by self-interest, claiming that it was instead done out of obedience to some moral obligation. The offender appeals to higher loyalties. Those who feel they are in a dilemma employ this technique to indicate that the dilemma must be resolved at the cost of violating a law or policy. In the context of an organization, an employee may appeal to organizational values or hierarchies. For example, an executive could argue that he or she has to violate a policy in order to get things done and achieve strategic objectives for the enterprise.
6. *Claim blunder quota: It was a necessary shortcut to get things done.* The offender argues that what he or she did is acceptable given the situation and given his or her position. The person feels that after having done so much good for so many for so long time, others should excuse him or her for more wrongdoings than other people deserve forgiveness. Others should understand that the alleged crime was an acceptable mistake. This is in line with the metaphor of the ledger, which uses the idea of compensating bad acts by good acts. That is, the individual believes that he or she has previously performed a number of good acts and has accrued a surplus of good will, and, because of this, can afford to commit some bad actions. Executives in corporate environments neutralize their actions through the metaphor of the ledger by rationalizing that their overall past good behavior justifies occasional rule breaking.
7. *Claim legal mistake: This should never pop up as illegal in the first place.* The offender argues that the law is wrong, and what the person did should indeed

not pop up as illegal. One may therefore break the law since the law is unreasonable, unfair, and unjustified. The offender may argue that lawmakers sometimes criminalize behaviors and sometimes decriminalize more or less randomly over time. For example, money involved in bribing people were treated as legal expenses in accounting some decades ago, while corruption today is considered a misconduct and therefore criminalized.

8. *Claim normality of action: Everyone else does and would do the same.* The offender argues that it is so common to commit the offense, so that it one can hardly define it as an offense at all. The offense is no deviant behavior since most people do it or would do it in the same situation. The offender might even suggest that what may constitute deviant behavior is when people in the same situation obey the law.
9. *Claim entitlement to action: It is sometimes a required behavior in this position.* The offender claims to be in his right to do what he did, perhaps because of a very stressful situation or because of some misdeed perpetrated by the victim. This is defense of necessity, which is a kind of justification that if the rule breaking seems necessary in the mind of the offender, one should feel no guilt when carrying out the action.
10. *Claim solution to dilemma: The benefits of action outweigh costs.* The offender argues a dilemma arose whereby he or she made a reasonable tradeoff before committing the act. Tradeoff between many interests therefore resulted in the offense. A dilemma represents a state of mind in which it is not obvious for an offender what is right and what is wrong to do. For example, the criminal carries out the offense to prevent what seems to be a more serious offense from happening.
11. *Justify necessity of crime: It was necessary to carry out the offense.* The offender claims that the offense belongs into a larger picture in a comprehensive context, where the crime is an illegal element among many legal elements to ensure an important result. The offense was a required and necessary means to achieve an important goal. For example, a bribe represents nothing in dollar value compared to the potential income from a large contract abroad. Alternatively, a temporary misrepresentation of accounts could help save the company and thousands of jobs.
12. *Claim role in society: It is a natural maneuver among elite members.* The offender argues that being a minister in the government or a chief executive officer in a global company is so time-consuming that little time is available for issues that seem trivial. Shortcuts are part of the game. Some shortcuts may be illegal, but they are nevertheless necessary for the elite member to ensure progress. If someone is to blame, then subordinates are supposed to provide advice and control what the elite member is doing.
13. *Perceive being victim of incident: Others have ruined my life.* The incident leads to police investigation, prosecution, and possible jail sentence. Media is printing

pictures of the offender on the front page, and gains from crime disappear as public authorities conduct asset recovery without considering the harm caused to the offender. Previous colleagues and friends have left, and so has the family. The offender perceives being a loser and made victim of those who reacted to his crime after disclosure.

14. *Gather support: Nobody thinks it is wrong*. Most colleagues, friends, and others in the upper echelon of society think what the offender did, is quite acceptable. The supporters communicate to the public, the media, and others that it is ridiculous that the offender becomes subject to police investigation and eventually subject to prosecution and conviction. The supporters argue that it is completely misleading to portrait the white-collar offender as a criminal. The supporters may suggest that the offender was unlucky and made an unintentional mistake. They may argue that in the eyes of the public, the offense can emerge as misconduct, but certainly not crime. The offender potentially made a shortcut for very good reasons, which is tolerable and not objectionable. Given such massive support from those who condemn the criminal justice system, the offender gathers support that cause a fundamental reduction in his or her potentially guilty mind. The guilty mind may further deteriorate as the offender hires top defense attorneys who tell the offender that it is the state or someone else who, without any acceptable or plausible reason, is out there to catch him or her for an act that certainly was no crime.
15. *Claim rule complexity*: It is impossible to understand what is right and what is wrong. Some laws, rules and regulations are so complex that compliance is random. The regulatory legal environment is supposed to define the boundaries of appropriate organizational conduct. However, legal complexity is often so extreme that even specialist compliance officers struggle to understand what to recommend to business executives in the organization.

Lehman et al. (2020: 6) defined rule complexity in terms of components and connections:

> First, a rule is more complex to the extent that it comprises more components that together describe the actions and outcomes necessary for compliance. A rule with a high number of components contains more detail and requires more actions to constitute compliance. Second, a rule is more complex to the extent that it has more connections to or functional dependencies upon other rules in the same system. A rule with a high number of connections refers to actions or outcomes that may be affected by activities pertaining to another rule or set of rules.

Neutralizations are not merely after-the-fact rationalizations where offenders can live with and accept what they have done. Neutralizations imply a deterministic or causal relationship available before the offense takes place. The use of neutralization techniques function as a means of making it possible to commit violations while at the same time reducing a guilt feeling (Cohen, 2001). When potential offenders apply neutralization techniques in advance of potential criminal actions, then their willingness for criminal behaviors might increase. A simple example is speeding on the highway, where the offender can drive to fast because of neutralizations such as everyone else does it, there is something wrong with the speed limit, or nobody will get hurt anyway. Neutralizations ahead of a criminal act protect the offender from harm to his or her self-image.

## Structural Model of Opportunity

The integrated deductive theory of convenience results from a synthesis of perspectives in three dimensions as illustrated in Figure 1.1 and detailed in Figures 1.2 and 1.3:

- *Convenience in motive*. It is convenient to use illegitimate financial gain to explore possibilities and avoid threats. Climb the hierarchy of needs for status and success (Maslow, 1943), realize the American dream of prosperity (Schoepfer and Piquero, 2006), satisfy the need for acclaim as a narcissist (Chatterjee and Pollock, 2017), and restore the perception of equity and equality (Leigh et al., 2010) are some of the perspectives integrated in the motive dimension of convenience theory. In addition, goal setting is a common practice in the field of organizational behavior, where high performance goals tend to encourage unethical behavior (Welsh et al., 2019). The extra profit from financial crime enables the offender to handle desired possibilities and potential threats. It is mainly the convenience of extra profit, rather than the convenience of illegal profit, that is important in the motive dimension of convenience theory. However, under certain circumstances, there might be some extra benefits from illegal extra profit rather than extra profit in general, since illegal funds avoid the attention of external and internal control mechanisms, including compliance functions (Kawasaki, 2020). Illegitimate financial gain can thus find its ways into exploring possibilities and avoiding threats that recorded funds cannot.
- *Convenience in opportunity*. There is convenient access to resources to commit and conceal financial crime. Legitimate access to premises and systems (Benson and Simpson, 2018), specialized access in routine activity (Cohen and Felson, 1979), blame game by misleading attribution to others (Eberly et al., 2011), and institutional deterioration (Rodriguez et al., 2005) are some of the perspectives integrated in the opportunity dimension of convenience theory. A typical white-collar offender does not go into hiding as many street criminals do. Rather, the offender conceals financial crime among legal transactions to make illegal transactions seem legitimate, or the offender conceals financial crime by removing certain activities from the books. A typical white-collar offender who has convenient legitimate access to commit crime might spend most of the energy on concealing crime in the professional context.
- *Convenience in behavior*. Offenders can conveniently justify crime and neutralize guilt feelings. By neutralizing guilt feelings, offenders do not feel accountable,

ashamed or responsible (Chen and Moosmayer, 2020). Application of neutralization techniques (Sykes and Matza, 1957), sliding on the slippery slope (Welsh et al., 2014), lack of self-control (Gottfredson and Hirschi, 1990), narcissistic identification with the organization (Galvin et al., 2015), learning from others by differential association (Sutherland, 1983), and professional deviant identity (Obodaru, 2017) are some of the perspectives integrated in the willingness dimension of convenience theory. When a white-collar offender justifies crime, then it is obvious to him and her that wrongdoing occurred. However, the offender can claim that the act of wrongdoing is morally justifiable (Schnatterly et al., 2018), and that a negative life event has occurred (Engdahl, 2015). When a white-collar offender denies a guilty mind, then the offender applies neutralization techniques. When a white-collar offender makes crime as a choice, it is convenient based on identity (Galvin et al., 2015), rationality (Pratt and Cullen, 2005), and learning from others (Sutherland, 1983).

The integrated deductive theory of convenience results from synthesis within each of these three dimensions as well as among these three dimensions. According to Liska et al. (1989), theoretical synthesis requires that the postulation of abstract or general principles that will allow at least fractions of merging theories to be subsumed and interrelated. Effective synthesis can generate additional predictive power not made by the merging theories individually.

Themes identified in convenience theory derive from discourse analysis of the research literature (Chan and Gibbs, 2020; Garcia-Rosell, 2019). Chan and Gibbs (2020) argue that criminological theorizing is typically discursive in nature. Discourse can describe a group of statements that provides a language for talking and producing a particular type of knowledge about a topic (Garcia-Rosell, 2019: 1019):

> Thus, discourses provide the frames for forming and articulating ideas concerning our relationships to nature and other members of society in a particular space at a particular time.

While the theory of convenience is an integrated deductive theory, there are other kinds of integrated theories such as cross-level sequential theory and cross-level parallel theory of white-collar crime. Cross-level sequential theory is sequential end-to-end integration that specifies the propositions of one theory as sequentially following the propositions of another. As such, end-to-end integration implies a temporal ordering among the causal variables in which the first set of variables influences the next set (Krohn and Eassey, 2014), the next set influences the following set, and so on, and in turn leading to the predicted outcome (Liska et al., 1989: 5):

> End-to-end (sequential) integration refers to specifying the temporal order between causal variables, so that the dependent variables of some theories constitute the independent variables of others.

Cross-level integration is combination of micro and macro perspectives. For example, convenience theory has micro elements such as neutralization techniques applied by individuals and macro elements such as criminal market structures in society. Cross-level integration is perhaps the most difficult type of integration and perhaps the most necessary type.

An example of cross-level theory of white-collar crime is Rorie's (2015) integrated theory of corporate environmental compliance and over compliance. She integrates the license framework's emphasis on corporate-level factors with a rational choice framework that models how individual perceptions and attitudes mediate or moderate corporate-level concerns.

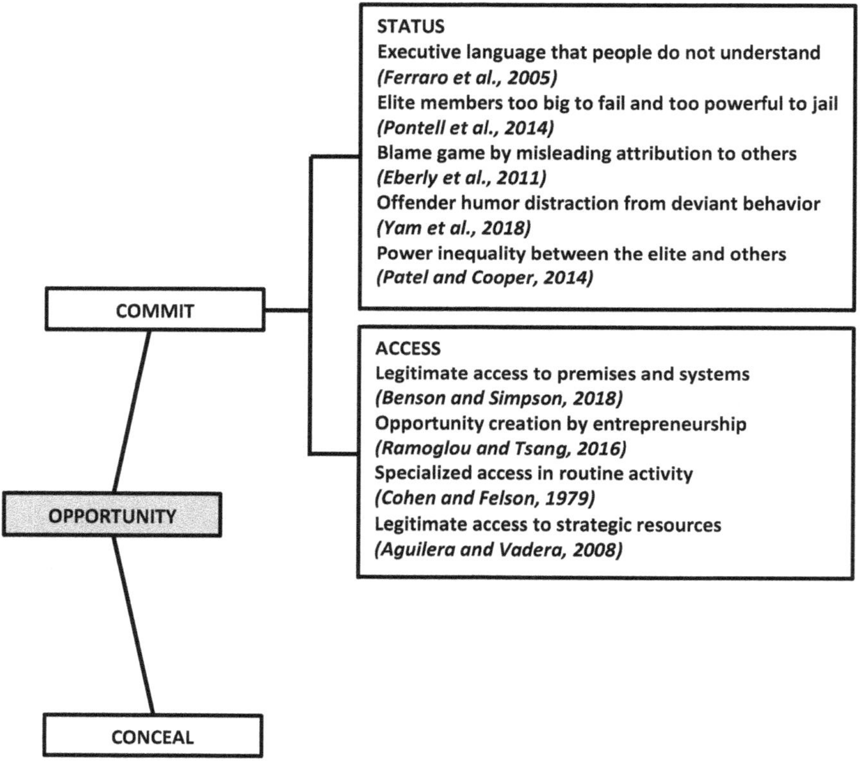


**Figure 1.2:** Structural model of opportunity in convenience theory (part 1:2).

Cross-level parallel theory is parallel side-by-side integration by partitioning the subject matter of interest into distinct categories and using different theories to explain each (Liska et al., 1989: 5):

> Side-by-side (horizontal) integration refers to the partitioning of the subject matter of crime and deviance into cases that are explained by different theories.

As a result, much attention in side-by-side integration focuses on the criteria used to partition the subject matter, and only then focuses on the theories, which can best explain each category (Krohn and Eassey, 2014). The theory of convenience does partition the subject matter of interest into distinct categories of motive, opportunity, and willingness. However, the main form of integration in convenience theory is up-and-down, rather than side-by-side or end-to-end.

One way of partitioning the subject matter is into occupational and corporate crime (Kennedy, 2020). Self-interested individuals commit occupational crime in their profession against their employers (e.g., embezzlement or receipt of bribes) and other victims (Baird and Zelin, 2009; Benson and Chio, 2020; Shepherd and Button, 2019). Occupational crime is an offense committed by an individual using the skills, knowledge and access granted to him or her by the legitimate occupation, to obtain some financial gain (Kennedy, 2020). Organizational officials commit corporate crime in the larger interest of an organization (Shichor and Heeren, 2021), such as bribing potential customers, avoiding taxes by evasion, and misrepresenting accounting to get unjustified government subsidies (Craig and Piquero, 2016, 2017; Dodge, 2020). Corporate crime may ultimately provide an individual with some tangible benefit, such as a promotion, bonus pay, or gifts for exceptional performance (Kennedy, 2020: 178):

> Yet, the primary purpose of committing a corporate crime is to provide a benefit to the corporation. Accordingly, corporate crimes have a distinctly organizational focus irrespective of whether they are committed by one person or 100 persons.

Another way of partitioning the subject matter is into different genders. Steffensmeier et al. (2013) studied how gendered focal concerns can inhibit criminal behaviors in females in the corporate context. Generally, the fraction of females who might exploit opportunity structures for white-collar crime is increasing, and it is thus an interesting kind of partitioning to study whether female offending is changing in response to changes in opportunities.

The integrated deductive theory of convenience is parsimonious, where the principle of parsimony dictates that a theory should provide the simplest possible (viable) explanation for a phenomenon. Parsimonious means the simplest theory with the least assumptions and variables but with greatest explanatory power. The parsimony principle is basic to all science and tells us to choose the simplest scientific explanation that fits the evidence. The opposite would be that the more assumptions you have to make, the more unlikely an explanation for the phenomenon being studied.

Chan and Gibbs (2020) suggest that convenience theory unifies concepts from macro-economic, meso-organizational, and micro-behavioral theories under the construct of convenience. Meso-level analysis means detailed examination of a specific group, a community, an organization, or parts of society, where outcomes may focus on phenomena between levels of individual, organization, and society. While both the motive dimension and the willingness dimension are mainly at the individual level of

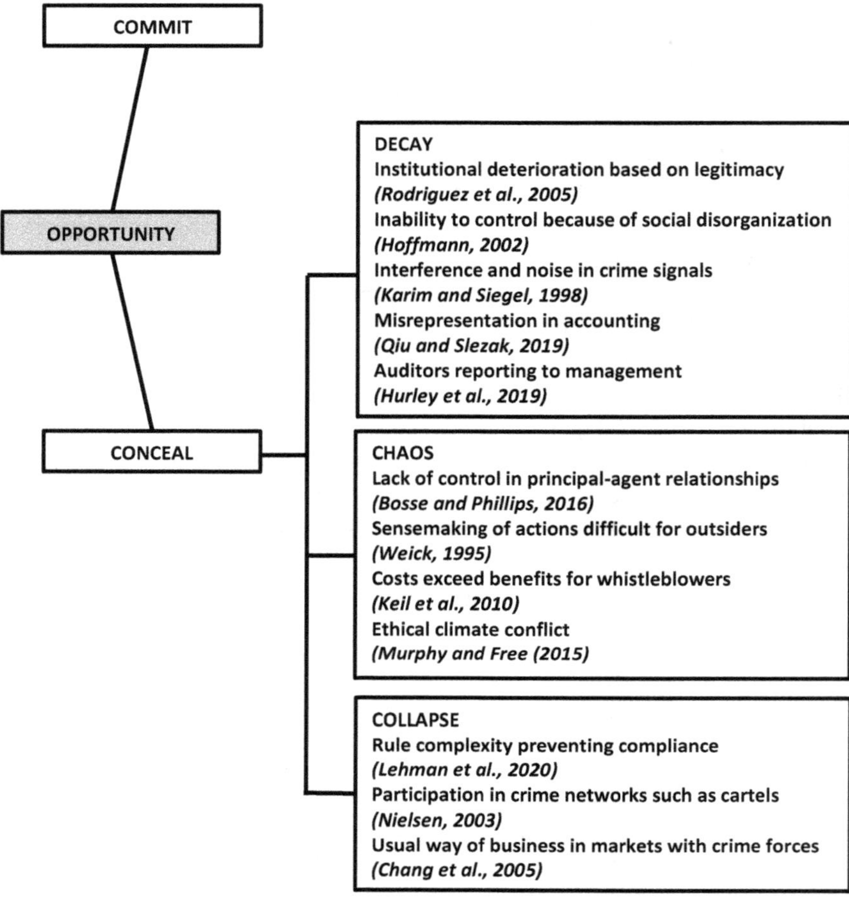


**Figure 1.3:** Structural model of opportunity in convenience theory (part 2:2).

an offender or at the group level of offenders, the opportunity dimension is mainly at the organizational and society level. The opportunity can derive from lack of controls and guardianship in the organization; and it can derive from criminal market structures in society as well. Meso-level analysis is sometimes labelled network analysis, where the researcher examines the patterns of social ties among people in a group and how those patterns affect the overall group. While not obvious and visible in convenience theory, the opportunity structure can reflect a pattern of social ties among people in the organization.

Some perspectives in the theory of convenience are not necessarily compatible because of their diverging assumptions about human nature. For example, a reviewer of this manuscript has suggested that this book brings together multiple (and sometimes rival) theoretical traditions, including strain/anomie, differential association/

learning, control/bonding/rational choice/techniques of rationalization, and even conflict. However, as long as the integration is mainly concerned with accumulation and synthesis of perspectives that influence the extent of convenience, then perspectives do not need to be compatible. If perspectives are competing, then theoretical synthesis is possible by changing the polarity of causality. For example, Hirschi (1989) argues that social control theory was developed in explicit opposition to strain theory. While social control can prevent crime, strain theory can cause crime. When integrating social control and strain into convenience, the polarity of social control is negative while the polarity of strain is positive: Less social control increases criminogenity; that is the tendency to commit crime, while more stress increases criminogenity. Stress is a psychological state that arises from a mismatch between perceived demands and one's ability to meet those demands given available resources (Linder et al., 2021).

While the theory of convenience is an integrated and at the same time general theory of white-collar crime occurrence, there might be cases of white-collar crime where the theory does not apply. State-corporate crime might be an example (Bernat and Whyte, 2020; Rothe, 2020; Rothe and Medley, 2020; Tombs and Whyte, 2020; Zysman-Quirós, 2020)

# 2 Corporate Executive Status

Corporate executive status is the first convenience theme in Figure 1.1 for organizational opportunity along the axis of committing white-collar crime. The perspective here is to discuss how a bottom-up approach to executive compliance can reduce the extent of white-collar crime convenience from executive status. Status convenience themes listed in Figure 1.2 are discussed in this chapter.

Dewan and Jensen (2020) studied high social status individuals in times of scandals that can change the role of status from being an asset to being a liability. They defined scandal as the disruptive publicity of misconduct, that is, a situation after detection and disclosure to the public. While the importance of status in convenience theory is related to prevention of blame before disclosure, Dewan and Jensen's (2020: 1657) research was concerned with status after disclosure:

> Because scandal diminishes the effectiveness of factors that make status an asset, status offers less protection during a scandal. At the same time that scandal decreases the protective benefits of status; the factors that make status a liability remain or are augmented.

Status can thus be a liability in the context of blaming, shaming, and labeling of misconduct and crime. High status creates high expectations that are seriously violated in a scandal. The disappointment causes an expectation of consequence for the person responsible for the disappointment.

Status is an individual's social rank within a formal or informal hierarchy, or the person's relative standing along a valued social dimension. Status is the extent to which an individual is respected and admired by others, and status is the outcome of a subjective assessment process (McClean et al., 2018). High-status individuals enjoy greater respect and deference from, as well as power and influence over, those who are positioned lower in the social hierarchy (Kakkar et al., 2020).

Especially individuals with high status based on prestige rather than dominance tend to be excused for whatever wrongdoing they commit. Individuals who attain and maintain high rank by behaving in ways that are assertive, controlling, and intimidating are characterized as dominant. Individuals who attain and maintain high rank by their set of skills, knowledge, expertise, and their willingness to share these with others are characterized as prestigious (Kakkar et al., 2020).

## Disclosure of Executive Language

Executive status can allow executive language that nobody understands. For example, one might suggest that elite members are considered too big to fail and too powerful to jail (Pontell et al., 2014), and there is power inequality between the elite and others (Patel and Cooper, 2014). Therefore, subordinates tend to accept executive

https://doi.org/10.1515/9783110986686-003

language that they do not really understand (Ferraro et al., 2005), and they get distracted from observing deviant behavior by offender humor (Yam et al., 2018). A consequence of strange language and offender humor might be an acceptance of blame game by misleading attribution to others (Eberly et al., 2011).

Executives and others in the elite may use language that followers do not necessarily understand. Followers nevertheless tend to trust executive messages. Language shapes what people notice and ignore (Ferraro et al., 2005), and language is a window into organizational culture (Holt and Cornelissen, 2014; Srivastava and Goldberg, 2017; Weick, 1995). Offender language can cause obedience among followers (Mawritz et al., 2017).

Individuals with high social status in privileged positions thus sometimes use language that people simply do not understand. Executives and others in the elite may use language that followers not necessarily understand – however nevertheless they trust executive messages (Ferraro et al., 2015). Cryptology is concerned with techniques for secure communication in the presence of third parties called adversaries. Cryptology is about constructing and analyzing protocols that prevent third parties or the public from understanding messages. Similarly, in an organizational context, executive communication applies a management language that few others understand.

According to Ferraro et al. (2005), language affects what people see or not see; how they see it; and the social categories and descriptors that they use to interpret their reality. Language shapes what people notice and ignore, and what they believe is and is not important. Reality is socially constructed, and language plays an important role in such constructions. Srivastava and Goldberg (2017) argue that language is a window into culture. Subcultures develop in the organization, where the language is different from other parts of the organization. The language through which people in the elite communicate with colleagues on the job illustrates how people fit into an organization's culture or subculture. Language use can predict an individual's influence and adaption on the job and can reveal distinct linguistic patterns for executives involved in misconduct and crime.

## Removal of Powerful People

Hostile and abusive supervision by powerful executives is detrimental to the well-being of the corporation. Mawritz et al. (2017) argue that abusive supervision, defined as subordinates' perceptions of the extent to which supervisors engage in the sustained display of hostile verbal and non-verbal behaviors, can create substantial costs to organizations and their employees. One recommendation for curbing such behavior is the non-acceptance of a primitive impulsive system found among some executives (Liang et al., 2016). Sometimes, failing self-control among executives is caused by poor-performing subordinates (Liang et al., 2016; Mawritz et al., 2017).

Then a recommendation might imply that poor performance is corrected or compensated in joint efforts by empowered employees.

Executives need to have an internal locus of control, where locus of control refers to individuals' perceptions about whether the consequences of their behaviors are within (internal) or beyond (external) their own personal control. They have a need to influence their own outcomes, rather than their circumstances (Valentine et al., 2019).

Hostile and abusive supervision by powerful executives can reduce the status of those executives since status is a property that rests in the eyes of others (Kakkar et al., 2020: 532):

> Status is a property that rests in the eyes of others and is conferred to individuals who are deemed to have a higher rank or social standing in a pecking order based on a mutually valued set of social attributes. Higher social status or rank grants its holder a host of tangible benefits in both professional and personal domains. For instance, high-status actors are sought by groups for advice, are paid higher, receive unsolicited help, and are credited disproportionately in joint tasks. In innumerable ways, our social ecosystem consistently rewards those with high status.

Harvin and Killey (2021: 509) studied whether a firm's CEO who has an extraordinary personal reputation or superstar status can have an adverse impact on the independence of an auditor who is engaged in the audit of the firm's financial statement:

> As indicated in the experiment that was conducted in the study, the superstar status of a CEO of a firm being audited appears to hanve the potential to have a negative impact of the strategic risk assessment of an auditor's overall risk assessment of an audit during the planning stage of an audit. It would be very troublesome if an auditor unwittingly or consciously lowered the strategic risk assessment as a result of the CEO's superstar status. The strategic risk assessment of an audit determines the level of substantive audit tests that are performed as well as the amount of audit time that is devoted to the completion of the audit.

Declining status in a hostile environment can cause executive falling of powerful people from the privileged elite (Kakkar et al., 2020). Then white-collar offenders no longer are too powerful to fail or too powerful to jail (Pontell et al., 2014). Friends in key positions and elite networks may abandon them since they are no asset anymore to the relationships, but rather potential liabilities (Dewan and Jensen, 2020).

Dewan and Jensen (2020) studied high social status individuals in times of scandals that can change the role of status from being an asset to being a liability. They defined scandal as the disruptive publicity of misconduct, that is, a situation after detection and disclosure to the public. While the importance of status in convenience theory is related to prevention of blame before disclosure, Dewan and Jensen's (2020: 1657) research was concerned with status after disclosure:

> Because scandal diminishes the effectiveness of factors that make status an asset, status offers less protection during a scandal. At the same time that scandal decreases the protective benefits of status; the factors that make status a liability remain or are augmented.

Status can thus be a liability in the context of blaming, shaming, and labeling of misconduct and crime. High status creates high expectations that are seriously violated in a scandal. The disappointment causes an expectation of consequence for the person responsible for the disappointment.

Removal of powerful people might include prosecution for corporate wrongdoing (Henning, 2017: 503):

> The Department of Justice has made it a priority in corporate criminal investigations to require that companies single out those within the organization responsible for any wrongdoing.

Attempts to emphasize individual culpability can cause an upsurge of prosecutions of corporate executives who oversee companies that engage in misconduct. When executives push hard for profits and the personal gain that comes from corporate success, Henning (2017) argued that there should be no blurred line into fraud and corruption.

## Detection of Misleading Attribution

Executives may reinforce a culture of financial crime by ignoring criminal actions and otherwise facilitate unethical behavior. At the same time, they try to distance and disassociate themselves from criminal actions (Pontell et al., 2021: 9):

> High status corporate criminals often go to great lengths to distance themselves from the crimes committed by their subordinates and to hide any incriminating evidence of their role in the decisions that authorized those criminal acts.

Misleading attribution of blame to subordinates by executives is both a matter of detection and reaction (Eberly et al., 2011). Generally, attribution is concerned with how individuals make judgments about responsibility (Piening et al., 2020: 335):

> Attributions of responsibility involve a series of yes-no judgments in which individuals first determine whether a negative event has been caused by internal or external factors. If the event is attributed to internal causes, the process continues to determine whether the cause was controllable or not, whereas in case of external causality, the organization cannot be held responsible, so the process stops.

Linked to the blame game is shaming, where suspected elite members express social disapproval of innocent individuals in the organization, thereby attempting to gain social control on perceptions of criminality. Shaming implies stigmatization and disapproval (Amry and Meliala, 2021). Social control is based on attachment, commitment, involvement, and belief, where a control mechanism is informal punishment in the appearance of shaming.

The attribution perspective implies that white-collar offenders attempt to attribute causes of crime to everyone else but themselves in the organization. Attribution theory is about identifying causality predicated on internal and external circumstances (Eberly et al., 2011). External attributions place the cause of a negative event on external factors, absolving the account giver and the privileged individual from personal responsibility. Innocent subordinates receive blame for crime committed by elite members (Lee and Robinson, 2000). According to Sonnier et al. (2015: 10), affective reactions influence blame attribution directly and indirectly by altering structural linkage assessments:

> For example, a negative affective reaction can influence the assessment of causation by reducing the evidential standards required to attribute blame or by increasing the standards of care by which an act is judged.

When the Siemens corruption scandal emerged in the public, top management attempted to blame lower-level managers (Berghoff, 2018: 423):

> At first the company defended itself with set phrases like 'mishaps of individuals' and isolated offenses committed by a 'gang' of criminals, or 'This is not Siemens'.

Status-related factors such as influential positions, upper-class family ties, and community roles often preclude perceptions of blameworthiness (Slyke and Bales, 2012). According to the attribution perspective, parties involved in a personal conflict or crime suspicion will naturally wonder 'Why is this happening?' in the hope that if they understand the negative event, they might be able to predict its cause. The cause can be either individual behavior (personal attribution) or organizational behavior (system attribution). The attribution perspective suggests that, all else being equal, the odds are in favor of making a personal attribution (Keaveney, 2008). If a white-collar offender fails to attribute crime to another individual, then there is the alternative of blaming the system.

However, bottom-up detection of misleading attribution can cause self-conscious emotions of guilt and shame among potential and actual white-collar offenders, making deviance less convenient (Zhong and Robinson, 2021: 1439):

> These are painful emotions that individuals experience when they perceive their actions have violated a standard, prompting a negative evaluaton of their behavior in the case of guilt or a negative evaluation of their global self in the case of shame. Prior studies have revealed that many forms of wrongdoing can beget guilt and/or shame, including transgressions, cheating, psychological aggression, ostracism, lying and deception, and unethical behavior.

Katz (1979) found that financial crime higher up in the organization will be ignored to a larger extent than lower down in the organization, or blame is allocated elsewhere (Keaveney, 2008; Lee and Robinson, 2000; Sonnier et al., 2015). For example, the blame for the ignition switch failure at General Motors was moved away from the chief executive officer and far down the hierarchy to some middle managers in the organization (Jenner Block, 2014).

Attribution theory explains individuals' attribute responsibility for both own and others' behavior. The central premise is that attributions of responsibility depend on whether individuals view the causes of behavior as a result of internal or external factors. If individuals determine that a behavior results from internal factors in terms actor personality characteristics and actor disposition, then they typically will attribute the behavior to the actor. Alternatively, individuals can attribute the behavior to other people or the situation such as social structure or organizational context. The strength of attribution in terms of responsibility can depend on a number of factors such as causality, knowledge, intentions, and seriousness (Gailey and Lee, 2005).). Blameworthiness is the extent to which it is clear that an individual engaged in a questionable act (Dewan and Jensen, 2020).

## Disregard of Offender Humor

White-collar offenders attempt to use humor to distract attention from their crime. Offender humor distraction as suggested by Yam et al. (2018) implies that potential white-collar offenders can influence the organizational opportunity structure by aggressive humor. Aggressive humor is a negatively directed style of humor that an individual carries out at the expense and detriment of one's relationships with others.

It can be teasing with a humorous undertone, or it can be victimization of the receiver. It can be the opposite of self-irony, where the offender makes jokes about others and make them look ridiculous. The more aggressive an offender's style, the more a sense of humor will signal acceptability of norm violations for the offender. Aggressive humor is a form of hostile behavior.

Aggressive leader humor expands the organizational opportunity for white-collar crime, and it influences the willingness of victims of such humor (Yam et al., 2018: 349):

> The more aggressive a leader's style, the more a sense of humor will signal acceptability of norm violations, which will be positively associated with deviance.

Aggressive humor refers to a specific style of humor aimed at teasing or ridiculing. It may include sarcasm humorously to convey disapproving information to followers. Aggressive humor may signal to followers that the accepted social norm of being respectful towards others is not important. It signals that violating norms of human decency is acceptable.

The leader humor perspective suggests that leader sense of humor is positively associated with followers' perceived acceptability of norm violations. When leaders display humor and, as a result, violate norms, followers will likely perceive that it is socially acceptable to violate norms in the organization for two reasons (Yam et al., 2018: 352):

> First, leaders' formal position makes them strong sources of normative expectations. Leaders, as role models, are more likely to be observed by followers who are scanning the environment for information on how to behave in the work context. In other words, leaders who make light of norm violations in order to produce humor are likely to imply to followers that mild norm violations in the organizations are generally acceptable. Second, when a leader acts in a humorous manner, others will likely react with laughter and amusement, an implicit signal of approval. Followers will be likely to interpret this social information as signaling the acceptability of norm violations. When a norm violation is enacted – and interpreted by others – in a playful, humorous way, it also signals to followers that violations need not be taken seriously or scrutinized.

Therefore, a bottom-up approach to executive deviance is to avoid acceptance of executive language that they do not really understand (Ferraro et al., 2005) and avoid distraction from observing deviant behavior by offender humor (Yam et al., 2018). A consequence of ignorance of strange language and offender humor might be detection of the blame game by misleading attribution to others (Eberly et al., 2011). Furthermore, leaders with an aggressive humor might practice morally ambiguous leadership (Dion, 2020), where their ambiguity can become vulnerable to bottom-up criticism.

## Correction of Power Inequality

Marxist criminology views the competitive nature of the capitalist system as a major cause of financial crime (Siegel, 2011). It focuses on what creates stability and continuity in society, and it adopts a predefined political philosophy. Marxist criminology focuses on why things change by identifying the disruptive forces in capitalist societies, and describing how power, wealth, prestige, and perceptions of the world divide every society. The economic struggle is the central venue for the Marxists. Marx divided society into two unequal classes and demonstrated the inequality in the historical transition from patrician and slave to capitalist and wage worker. It is the rulers versus the ruled. Marx also underlined that all societies have a certain hierarchy wherein the higher class has more privileges than the lower one. In a capitalist society, where economic resources equate to power, it is in the interest of the ascendant class to maintain economic stratification in order to dictate the legal order (Petrocelli et al., 2003).

Conflict theory provides an explanation of crime, since it is concerned with social inequality, class and racial differences, and the power used by the ruling class through its criminal justice apparatus. Conflict theorists see inequality based on differences in wealth, status, ideas, and religious beliefs. Not only do capitalist societies generate vast inequalities of wealth, but also those who own the wealth, who control large corporations and financial and commercial institutions, influence those who have political power to get the laws they want (Lanier and Henry, 2009b).

Conflict theory is a perspective in criminology that emphasizes the social, political, or material inequality of a social group, and that draws attention to power differentials, such as class conflict. Crime stems from conflict between different segments of society fueled by a system of domination based on inequality, alienation, and justice. Crime is harm that comes from differences in power (Lanier and Henry, 2009a).

While there is power inequality between executives and employees (Patel and Cooper, 2014), corporate white-collar control mechanisms have to be perceived as fair to be successful. Fairness issues play a key role in determining how willing executives are to work toward the performance standards the organization seeks to enforce (Long et al., 2011).

High social status in privileged positions creates power inequality compared to those without any status in their positions. The perspective of power inequality suggests that, for example, family members in family firms wield significant influence in their firms. Family members often have legitimate access to firm resources that non-family executives in the firm cannot question (Patel and Cooper, 2014). Kempa (2010) found that white-collar offenders have unlimited authority to get it the way they want.

Power inequality is reduced when white-collar crime by executives and others in the elite are punished. One of the peculiar aspects of white-collar crime is that the privileged and powerful punish their own: Why does the ruling class punish their own?

*Reason 1: Reduce Conflict.* Since white-collar crime is crime by the wealthy and powerful, it seems to contradict social conflict theory. There are no reasons why the wealthy and powerful would like to see laws that turn their own actions into regular criminal offences. When Sutherland (1939) first coined the term “white-collar crime”, there were indeed reactions in the audience of upper-class people. They asked why one should define actions by privileged individuals of the influential classes as crime at the level of street crime by ordinary criminals. According to Brightman (2009), Sutherland’s theory of white-collar crime first presented in 1939 was controversial, particularly since many of the academics in the audience perceived themselves to be members of the upper echelon in American society. The audience was the American Sociological Association where Sutherland gave his address and first presented his theory of white-collar crime. What Podgor (2007) found to be the most interesting aspect of Sutherland’s work is that a scholar needed to proclaim that crime of the upper socio-economic class is in fact crime that should be prosecuted. It is apparent that prior to the coining of the term “white-collar crime”, wealth, and power allowed many persons to escape criminal liability.

Veblen’s (1899) sociological study of the “leisured classes” and their rapacious conspicuous consumption had an influence on Sutherland’s (1939) research. Josephson (1962) who coined the term “robber barons” in the 1930ties was also an influential scholar at that time. Therefore, Sutherland’s work on white-collar crime seems to fit with conflict theory, where he might have seen a need to reduce the level of conflict in society by defining obvious unjustified misconduct by privileged individuals as regular crime. This is in line with Arrigo and Bernard (1997), who apply conflict theory to explain initiatives for more prosecution of white-collar criminals. Seron and Munger (1996: 187) quoted that "The plain fact is that in a new stage of capitalism, class divides as ruthlessly as it did in the age of the Robber Barons."

*Reason 2: Government Influence.* Another reason for starting to define capitalists and other persons of respectability and high social status as regular criminals when they abuse their powers for personal or organizational profit is the need of governments to gain some kind of control over the business sector and the market economy. Business and professional elites had achieved political influence beyond what most democratic governments found acceptable. Even worse, some enterprises were so powerful that they became almost untouchable for government interventions. They were too powerful to fail, and too powerful to jail (Pontell et al., 2014).

Criminological attention on the activities of business enterprises and other organizations, their creativity and power, remains in a conflict with political influence of business executives, capitalists, and members of the professional elites. Haines (2014: 20) discusses corporate fraud as an example, where she argues that:

> Criminalization of corporate fraud deflects attention to one of these actors, the business and its directors, without clear recognition of the role played by government itself.

Haines (2014) argues that governments critically, in close consultation with the professions, enact legal and regulatory reforms that engender confidence in both the accuracy of accounts and materiality of money while also further institutionalizing their underlying ambiguities. Hence, even as governments are excited to sanction corporate criminals with more vigor, they are at the same time implicated in the creation of corporate criminals. Corporate fraud implies that there has been a criminal misrepresentation of a financial or business state of affairs by one or more individuals for financial gain, where banks, shareholders, and tax authorities are among the victims. Yet, misrepresentation is a matter of opinion rather than accuracy. For example, estimating values of products in stock is no exact science. If nobody wants to buy products in stock, they have no value. While governments work at arm's length through external auditors, law enforcement is reluctant to prosecute unless misrepresentation of the value of a business is completely out of range.

*Reason 3: "Our" Laws.* A third reason for the prosecution of the wealthy and powerful individuals and corporations is that their own laws did not intend to target members of their own class. The lawmakers had others in society in mind. Caught by surprise, that members of their own class violate their own laws, leads the ruling class to turn laws against their own allies. When those allies demonstrate non-conforming and deviant behavior, others in the ruling class take on the task of prosecuting deviating members of the elite. "As we are reminded today, those who make the laws don't have the right to break the laws", Richard Frankel, the specialist agent in charge of the Criminal Division of the New York office of the Federal Bureau of Investigation, said at a news conference.

FBI held its news conference as Sheldon Silver, the speaker of the State Assembly in New York, faced prosecution for corruption. State prosecutors charged Silver with having exploited his position as one of the most powerful politicians in the state of New York to obtain millions of dollars in bribes and kickbacks. Prosecutors accused Silver's law practice of being a fiction where the sources of large payments of bribes were hiding (Rashbaum and Kaplan, 2015: A24). Silver was arrested on Manhattan on a five-count indictment in January 2015. US attorney Preet Bharara alleged that the Manhattan democrat used New York's ethics laws to hide his scheme – allowing him to become wealthy off his position in power (Spector, 2015).

Silver resigned a few weeks later as speaker (McKinley, 2015). At the same time, Malcolm A. Smith, a former majority leader of the New York State Senate, was convicted of federal corruption charges including bribery, wire fraud, and extortion (Vega, 2015).

*Reason 4: Deviant Behavior.* A fourth reason might be disappointment within the ruling class. The ruling class in society faces decisions over which values to enforce. When individuals in their own upper-level class violate some of these values, then the majority defines it as a crime. Those who violate values of fair competition among capitalists and market access, for example, are potential criminals, even if they belong to the same class as those condemning them.

President George W. Bush's connections to Enron and CEO Kenneth Lay were well documented in major American newspapers. However, when Enron emerged as a deviant organization with a bad apple CEO, Lay and other top executives were prosecuted. Lay died of a heart attack before his conviction (Bendiktsson, 2010).

*Reason 5: Crime Victims.* A fifth and final reason might be the victim of crime. If the victim of white-collar crime were another person in the upper class, then the ruling class would like to protect that person. Victimization of upper-class members by other upper-class members can be considered a crime. Upper-class members need protection against deviant individuals in their own class. It is an inter-group conflict in the dominant class (Wheelock et al., 2011). Maybe Madoff can serve as an example. Rich Jews placed their money in Madoff's investment fund with the promise and expectation that the rate of return would be extraordinarily good. Instead, they lost their money. Wealthy people were victims of Madoff's Ponzi scheme. The government had to sanction such behavior by Madoff, and he received a record prison sentence of 150 years (Ragothaman, 2014).

# 3 Access to Corporate Resources

Corporate executive access to resources is the second convenience theme in Figure 1.1 for organizational opportunity along the axis of committing white-collar crime. The perspective here is to discuss how a bottom-up approach to executive compliance can reduce the extent of white-collar crime convenience from executive access to resources. Access convenience themes listed in Figure 1.2 are discussed in this chapter.

A white-collar offender has typically legitimate and convenient access to resources to commit crime (Füss and Hecker, 2008; Huisman and Erp, 2013; Lange, 2008; Pinto et al., 2008; Reyns, 2013). A resource is an enabler applied and used to satisfy human and organizational needs. A resource has utility and limited availability. According to Petrocelli et al. (2003), access to resources equates access to power. Other organizational members are losers in the competition for resources (Wheelock et al., 2011). In the conflict perspective suggested by Petrocelli et al. (2003), the upper class in society exercises its power and controls the resources. Valuable resources are typically scarce, unique, not imitable, not transferrable, combinable, exploitable, and not substitutable (Davis and DeWitt, 2021).

## Restrictions on Access to Systems

White-collar crime can be distinguished from ordinary crime ("street crime") based on the status of offenders, their access to legitimate professions, the common presence of an organizational form, and the extent of the costs and harmfulness of such crime (Cullen et al., 2020). While street criminals hide themselves after an offense, white-collar criminals hide the offense while staying in the same positions (Michel, 2016). This is because they have legitimate access to premises and systems to commit financial crime (Benson and Simpson, 2018).

While executive access to premises and systems has to be monitored, customization and transmutation is needed to ensure that control mechanisms achieve the intended control outcomes based on executives' own assessment of their management challenges (Chown, 2021). Transmutation captures the idea that organizational units including management implement control regimes that are different from the mandated and general control mechanism of the organization. While there is no more need for trust regarding executive work versus others' work in an organization, control mechanisms implemented in management need to ensure intended control outcomes.

Berghoff and Spiekermann (2018: 291) argued that all economic transactions depend on a certain degree of trust, without which transaction costs would simply be too high for economic activity:

https://doi.org/10.1515/9783110986686-004

> White-collar criminals abuse the good faith of various stakeholders, from customers to the general public, from shareholders to the authorities. Therefore, white-collar crime often coincides with the breach of trust.

Offenders take advantage of their positions of power with almost unlimited authority in the opportunity structure (Kempa, 2010), because they have legitimate and often privileged access to physical and virtual locations in which crime is committed, are totally in charge of resource allocations and transactions, and are successful in concealment based on key resources used to hide their crime. Offenders have an economic motivation and opportunity (Huisman and Erp, 2013); linked to an organizational platform and availability, and in a setting of people who do not know, do not care or do not reveal the individual(s) with behavioral traits who commit crime. Opportunity includes people who are loyal to the criminal either as a follower or as a silent partner, for example, when the follower perceives ambitious goals as invariable.

In the rare case of detection of possible crime, the potential offender has access not only to better defense as a strategic resource, but also often access to an alternative avenue of private investigation. When suspicion of misconduct and crime emerges, then the organization may hire a fraud examiner to conduct a private investigation into the matter. The enterprise takes control of suspicions by implementing an internal investigation. An external law firm or auditing firm is engaged to reconstruct past events and sequence of events. Typically, the resulting investigation report points to misconduct, while at the same time concluding that there have been no criminal offenses. The police will monitor the internal investigation and await its conclusion. When the conclusion states that there may be misconduct, but no crime, then the police and prosecution tend to settle down with it (King, 2020b).

However, the threat of dismissal following corporate scandals limits corporate involvement in executive destiny. Even when the executive is not necessarily to blame, the executive is a potential scapegoat that the organization deprives of access to resources. Dismissal occurs instantly, where the former privileged individual has no access anymore to defense attorneys, documents, or colleagues. The corporation has to survive at the expense of an executive (Ghannam et al., 2019).

Legitimate access to crime resources can be illustrated by the case of a chairman of the board who published his autobiography (Olav, 2014, 2015). The chairman used a tax haven where he had an account when he ran business through another company there (Bjørklund, 2018; Oslo tingrett, 2015a). A tax haven is a country or place with very low or no rates of taxation for foreign investors, where foreigners enjoy complete secrecy about their investments. Money laundering of proceeds from criminal activity is an attractive opportunity in tax havens. On the legitimate side, the use of tax havens enables transfer-pricing strategies to lower overall tax burdens for multinational corporations. Subsidiaries located in tax havens serve multinationals to avoid taxes by shifting income from high-tax countries to low-tax countries. Firms also use tax havens in strategies that involve intercompany debt or leasing arrangements to shift income across jurisdictions. Tax authorities in various countries attempt to challenge this kind of tax evasion (Dyreng et al., 2019; Guenther et al., 2019). Chairman Olav was sentenced to five years in prison.

## Disclosure of Entrepreneurialism

High social status in privileged positions is sometimes associated with entrepreneurship, where an entrepreneurial individual can create opportunities for deviant behavior (Ramoglou and Tsang, 2016). The entrepreneurship perspective emphasizes that entrepreneurs discover and create innovative and entrepreneurial opportunities (Smith, 2009; Tonoyan et al., 2010; Welter et al., 2017). Criminal entrepreneurs actualize illegal opportunities in the shadow economy (Mc Elwee and Smith, 2015). Scheaf and Wood (2021: 2) found that entrepreneurial fraud has stimulated a wide array of research related to white-collar crime, where they provided the following definition of entrepreneurial fraud:

> Enterprising individuals (alone or in groups) deceiving stakeholders by sharing statements about their identity, individual capabilities, elements of new market offerings, and/or new venture activities that they know to be false in order to obtain something of value.

While the common understanding of entrepreneurship is focused on the positive and productive aspects, entrepreneurial fraud focuses on the dark aspects. It is all about deception used to obtain valuable resources from stakeholders (Scheaf and Wood, 2021).

Ramoglou and Tsang (2016: 738) argued that opportunities are not the result of innovation, discovery or creation: "They are objectively existing propensities to be creatively actualized". Criminal entrepreneurs thus actualize illegal opportunities in the shadow economy (McElwee and Smith, 2015). Criminal entrepreneurship represents the dark side of entrepreneurialism. To understand entrepreneurial behavior by white-collar criminals, important behavioral areas include "modus essendi", "modus operandi", and "modus vivendi". Modus essendi is a philosophical term relating to modes of being. Modus operandi is method of operating, which is an accepted criminological concept for classifying generic human actions from their visible and consequential manifestations. Modus vivendi represents the shared symbiotic relationship between different entrepreneurial directions (Smith, 2009). Entrepreneurs are often important economic agents, driving forward employment, opportunities, and economic development. Entrepreneurship is associated with innovation, adaptation, change and dynamism, hard work, willpower, and overcoming challenges and struggles. According to Welter et al. (2017), entrepreneurship is a broadly available social technology for creating organizations that may pursue a myriad of goals. Tonoyan et al. (2010) found that viewing illegal business activities as a widespread business practice provides the rationale for entrepreneurs to justify their own corrupt activities.

## Review of Specialized Access

White-collar offenders have legitimate access to premises (Benson and Simpson, 2018; Williams et al., 2019), and they have specialized access in routine activities (Cohen and Felson, 1979). The routine activity perspective suggests three conditions for crime to occur: a motivated offender, an opportunity in terms of a suitable target, and the absence of a capable or moral guardian. The existence or absence of a likely guardian represents an inhibitor or facilitator for crime. The premise of the routine activity perspective is that crime is to a minor extent affected by social causes such as poverty, inequality, and unemployment. Motivated offenders are individuals who are not only capable of committing criminal activity but are willing to do so. Suitable targets are financial sources that offenders consider particularly attractive. Lack of guardians is not only lack of protective rules and regulations, audits and controls, but also lack of mental models in the minds of potential offenders that reduce self-control against attraction from criminal acts. Reyns (2013) expanded the routine activity perspective into online routines where insider business cybercrime occurs without direct manual contact.

Corruption is a typical crime category among white-collar offenses. Lange (2008) defines organizational corruption as the pursuit of individual interests by one or more organizational actors through the intentional misdirection of organizational resources or perversion of organizational routines. Pinto et al. (2008) makes a distinction between corrupt organizations and organizations of corrupt individuals. A corrupt organization is usually a top-down phenomenon in which a group of organizational members – typically, the dominant coalition, organizational elites, or top management team – undertakes corrupt actions. An organization of corrupt individuals is an emergent, bottom-up phenomenon in which informal processes facilitate personally corrupt behaviors that cross a critical threshold such that the organization deserves the characteristic of being corrupt.

## Limits to Strategic Resources

A white-collar offender has usually access to resources that are valuable (application of the resource provides desired outcome), unique (very few have access to the resource), not imitable (resource cannot be copied), not transferrable (resource cannot be released from context), combinable with other resources (results in better outcome), exploitable (possible to apply in criminal activities), and not substitutable (cannot be replaced by a different resource). According to Petrocelli et al. (2003), access to resources equates access to power. Others are losers in the competition for resources (Wheelock et al., 2011). In the conflict perspective suggested by Petrocelli et al. (2003), the upper class in society exercises its power and controls the resources.

Opportunity is dependent on social capital available to the criminal. The structure and quality of social ties in hierarchical and transactional relationships shape opportunity structures. Social capital is the sum of actual or potential resources accruing to the criminal by virtue of his or her position in a hierarchy and in a network. Social capital accumulated by the individual in terms of actual and potential resources, which are accessible because of profession and position, creates a larger space for individual behavior and actions that others can hardly observe. Many initiatives by trusted persons in the elite are unknown and unfamiliar to others in the organization. Therefore, white-collar criminals do not expect consequences for themselves.

Allocation of control rights to strategic resources might vary with governance structures (Rashid et al., 2022). In addition, residual rights of control occur because of incomplete organizing of exchanges. Alvarez and Parker (2009) argued that incomplete contract theory suggests that the relevant party to an exchange should receive these residual rights in order to maximize its overall value for the organization. That is the party that expects to create the most value from the exchange.

The resource-based perspective postulates that differences in individuals' opportunities find explanation in the extent of resource access and the ability to combine and exploit those resources. Executives and other members of the elite are potential offenders that are able to commit financial crime to the extent that they have convenient access to resources suitable for illegal actions. Access to resources in the organizational dimension makes it more relevant and attractive to explore possibilities and avoid threats using financial crime. The willingness to exploit a resource for fraud and corruption increases when a potential offender has a perception of relative convenience. Criminal acts disappear from easy detection in a multitude of legal transactions in different contexts and different locations performed by different people. The organizational affiliation makes crime look like ordinary business. Offenders conceal economic crime among apparently legal activity. Offenders leverage resources that make it convenient to conceal crime among regular business transactions. In particular, businesses that practice secrecy rather than transparency enable convenient concealment of financial crime (Transparency, 2018). Chasing profits leaves people more creative in finding ways to make more legal as well as illegal profits for themselves and the organization, and people become more creative in concealing crime in various ways (Füss and Hecker, 2008). Offenders attempt to carry out crime in such a way that the risk of detection is minimal and even microscopic (Pratt and Cullen, 2005).

Strategic resources are normally used by executives in legitimate actions to achieve business objectives. Executives typically develop strategic plans, then mobilize strategic resources, and finally apply the resources in a process of strategic plan implantation. This is the typical top-down approach by the board and management in most organizations when conducting legitimate business activities.

In a bottom-up approach to prevent deviance by executives, strategic planning is not relevant. Rather, the opposite of planning is most effective. The opposite of planning followed by implementation at a later point in time is improvisation. Improvisation is defined as the spontaneous process by which, planning and execution happen at the same time. It is the convergence of planning and execution such as the more proximate the design and solving in time, the more that activity is improvisational. Improvisation is a reactive, spontaneous action in response to unanticipated occurrences, in which law-abiding individuals find a way to manage the unexpected problem, and thus sometimes create something novel in response to the unknown (Mannucci et al., 2021: 614):

> Drawing on these shared definitional elements, we developed a working definition of improvisation that we used as our compass as we navigated between theory and the field: improvisation is a spontaneous action in response to unanticipated occurrences that is characterized by the convergence of planning and execution.

Situated improvising is localized attempts to cope practically with novel complexities and accomplish specific tasks. It is distributed rather than focused and experimental rather than planned. The locus of change is practice, and a practitioner is the entrepreneur at work. Practitioners act as entrepreneurial change agents only to the extent their situated improvising break with the dominant logic in their field, but not in the sense that they deliberately intend to discard existing legal and institutional arrangements. It is the urgency of the work at hand that calls for improvising own handling of unknown complexity. Improvising thus generates institutional change that accidentally happens. It is propelled by the urgency of the challenge that directs the improvisation so that the improvisation itself is not random (Smets et al., 2012).

Mannucci et al. (2021) suggested stages of improvisation for knowledge workers such as attorneys in law firms discussed by Smets et al. (2012). Stages of growth models for maturity levels help to assess and evaluate a variety of phenomena (e.g., Masood et al., 2020; Röglinger et al., 2012; Solli-Sæther and Gottschalk, 2015). Stage models predict the development or evolution of improvisaton maturity from basic performance to superior results (Iannacci et al., 2019: 310):

> They also suggest that this development is progressive (i.e., each successive stage is better than the previous one), stepwise (i.e., each step is a necessary prerequisite for the following step in the sequence), and prescriptive (i.e., each step must occur in a prescribed order in accordance with a pre-existing plan or vision), thus emphasizing the chain of successful events rather than the mechanisms by which subsequent stages come about.

Mannucci et al. (2021: 630) described their three-stage model from imitative improvisation via reactive improvisation to generative improvisation:

> In the initial stage of improvisation development, players' sensemaking process is limited by their basic understanding of structures. As they do not fully grasp how to initiate improvisational action in response to unexpected events, they develop imitative improvisation skills by observing and taking inspiration from others' improvisational actions (. . .) Over time, players complement imitative improvisation with the more reactive improvisation skills that extant literature typically describes. Reactive improvisation focuses on 'what is happening' and 'how to react'. When improvising reactively, players engage in a sensemaking process to interpret unfolding events and develop and appropriate and original response (. . .) Some players further broaden their improvisation skillset by becoming the originators of unexpected events.

At the third level of generative improvisation, knowledge workers like elite law firm lawyers initiate improvisational actions without the need for an external trigger. They focus less on 'what is happening' and 'how to react' by directing their attention to 'what could happen' and 'how can I change what happens'. The lawyer has a desire to co-create rather than just modify what will happen. Personal initiative is a core feature at generative improvisation (Mannucci et al., 2021).

# 4 Corporate Organizational Decay

An institution is a system of interrelated formal and informal elements – rules, guidelines, norms, traditions, beliefs – governing relationships between institutional members within which members pursue their mutual interests (Győry, 2020). Institutional deterioration can occur conveniently as a result of external legitimacy where deviance is the norm (Rodriguez et al., 2005). Executive deviance enacted at institutional deterioration is dependent on a number of factors. For example, in the case of government corruption for multinational enterprises in host countries, both pervasiveness and arbitrariness are important factors. Pervasiveness is the average firm's likelihood of encountering bribery, while arbitrariness is the inherent degree of ambiguity associated with corrupt transactions in a given nation or state (Rodriguez et al., 2005). Pinto et al. (2008: 686) define the beneficiary of corruption as the actor deriving direct and primary benefit from the action: "For example, even if individuals can benefit financially from corruption on behalf of the organization (e.g., through bonuses or high prices for their stocks), the organization is still the primary and direct financial beneficiary".

## Transparency in Deterioration

Transparency is understood as conditions that make it relatively easy for observers to accurately evaluate phenomena of interest (Haack et al., 2021) since the phenomena occur in a setting with elaborate reporting procedures (Sorour et al., 2021). Internal transparency refers to the possibility for and ability of organizational members to know what is going on in the organization (Maas and Yin, 2021: 4):

> Organizations can manage the level of transparency through policies to actively distribute information among managers and employees, or alternatively, policies to deliberately suppress information flows. Examples of the former type include intranet webpages, newsletters, meetings, and publicly accessible databases. To illustrate, some organizations actively disseminate information about managers by making the managers' work calendar visible to everyone in the firm (. . .) Examples of policies to prevent transparency include physical and organizational barriers that restrict access to reports and databases, and the aggregation of data, such that it cannot be traced back to individuals or departments. Notably, internal transparency is not necessarily the result of a deliberate transparency policy. It is also affected by other organizational design choices and can be an unintended consequence of the implementation of an unrelated policy or technology. For example, organizations become more transparent if units share a physical location, if they move to an open office space, implement knowledge sharing systems, or frequently organize social events where people from different units come together.

It becomes more convenient to commit financial crime by white-collar offenders in organizations characterized by moral deterioration and collapse. The institutional perspective of moral deterioration suggests that opportunities improve for white-

https://doi.org/10.1515/9783110986686-005

collar criminals. For example, Bradshaw (2015) found criminogenic industry structures in the offshore oil industry.

The institutional perspective contributes an understanding of organizational behavior that experiences influence from individuals, groups, other organizations, as well as the larger society of which they are a part. The perspective emphasizes how organizational structure and organizational culture derive from norms, attitudes and rules, which are common to most organizations in society. While organizational structure is characterized by design of positions in terms of job specialization, behavioral formalization, unit grouping and unit size (Donk and Molloy, 2008), organizational culture is characterized by accepted practices, rules, and principles of conduct that are applied to a variety of situations and that define appropriate attitudes and behaviors for organizational members, as well as generalized rationales and beliefs (Barton, 2004). Guiso et al. (2015) found that organizational cultures which promote low levels of integrity are associated with negative business outcomes such as low employee productivity and corporate profitability. Integrity is the quality of acting in accordance with the moral values, norms, and rules that are considered valid and relevant within the context in which the actor operates (Loyens et al., 2021) as well as adherence to accepted ethical, regulatory, and normative principles (Paruchuri et al., 2021).

Berghoff and Spiekermann (2018: 291) found that white-collar crime is often systemic and part of a culture, either of a corporate culture inside the firm or of a culture in the firm's environment:

> In the first case, the corporation's control mechanisms are typically weak, intentionally or unintentionally, which is an obstacle to the prevention and the investigation of economic crimes. Individual responsibility is therefore hard to ascertain. Defendants routinely deny responsibility and point to their superiors who made them commit crimes, or to their inferiors who engaged in shady practices without their knowledge or authorization.

The institutional perspective applied to white-collar crime means that white-collar offenders find opportunity for and acceptance of illegal behaviors because of moral collapse generally in their organizations. The institutional perspective argues that business enterprises are much more than simple tools and instruments to achieve financial goals and ambitions. The perspective says that organizations are adaptable systems that recognize and learn from the environment by mirroring values in society. This reasoning is relevant to explain why business organizations tend to be similar in the same industry and the same nation and region (Kostova et al., 2008).

Moral collapse happens when organizations are unable to see that bright line between right and wrong. Seven signs of ethical collapse can become visible: (i) pressure to maintain those numbers; (ii) fear and silence antidotes to openness; (iii) young ones and a bigger-than-life CEO; (iv) a weak board; (v) conflicts; (vi) innovation like no other; and (vii) goodness in some areas atones for evil in others.

Shadnam and Lawrence (2011: 379) apply the institutional perspective to explain moral decline and potential crime in organizations:

> Our theory of moral collapse has two main elements. First, we argue that morality in organizations is embedded in nested systems of individuals, organizations and moral communities in which ideology and regulation flow "down" from moral communities through organizations to individuals, and moral ideas and influence flow "upward" from individuals through organizations to moral communities. Second, we argue that moral collapse is associated with breakdowns in these flows and explore conditions under which such breakdowns are likely to occur.

Shadman and Lawrence (2011: 393) formulated several research hypotheses, which imply that the likelihood of moral decline will vary depending on a number of circumstances:

- Moral collapse is more likely to happen in organizations that operate in moral communities in which flows of corporate ideology and culture disappear. Either it can happen through a lack of commitment to formal communication mechanisms by community leaders, or it can happen through the disruption of informal communication networks by high rates of membership turnover.
- Moral collapse is more likely to happen in organizations in which structures and practices diminish the organization's capacity to absorb and incorporate morally charged institutions from the organization's moral community, because the organization monopolizes the attention of its members and/or because the organization delegitimizes the morally charged institutions rooted in the moral community.
- Moral collapse is more likely to happen in organizations in which accusing individuals of misconduct creates significant social and economic costs for the organization or the moral community within which it operates.
- Moral collapse is more likely to occur in organizations to the degree that employment conditions undermine disclosure and/or work arrangements diminish the effectiveness of surveillance.

The institutional perspective is mainly a sociological and public policy perspective on organizational studies. The perspective sheds light on normative structures and activities. The institutional perspective in public policy emphasizes the formal and legal aspects of government structures. Signs from organizations represent observations as indications of values in organizational members. When activities occur repetitively in the same way and within the same structure, then those activities become part of the institution itself, as the sum of activities based on shared perceptions of reality are an institution.

## Replacement of Disorganization

The institutional perspective considers the processes by which structures, including schemes; rules; norms; and routines become established as authoritative guidelines for social behavior. Triggers of institutional adaption include political, cultural and social influences. Behavioral patterns supported by norms, values and expectations lead to cultural influence. A desire to equal others implies social influence. Normative institutional pressure is concerned with conformity, where deviance and nonconformity is disliked, disapproved or even dismissed (Witt et al., 2021).

The institutional perspective is in line with the dysfunctional network perspective, in that organizations tend to mirror the basic elements of their environments. The largest business corporations can more easily absorb the negative impact of legal sanctions that certain governmental or regulatory agencies might impose on them. The largest business enterprises might have better lawyers and other resources, so that they are able to contend with legal pursuits in more effective and efficient ways. Microsoft versus the United States and Microsoft versus the European Union are typical examples. Therefore, laws and regulations tend to have less deterrent effect in the case of large business organizations (Dion, 2008).

Institutional deterioration often occurs at the same time as social disorganization, which further improves the opportunity structure for white-collar crime. The disorganization perspective argues that structural conditions lead to higher levels of social disorganization – especially of weak social controls – in organizations and between organizations, which in turn results in higher rates of crime (Pratt and Cullen, 2005). Of course, rates of financial crime vary across time and space in private and public sector with different motivational bases (Kjeldsen and Jacobsen, 2013; Miceli and Near, 2013; Perry et al., 2010; Wright, 2007).

Social disorganization increases offenders' opportunities to commit financial crime without any likelihood of detection. Offenders have unrestricted and legitimate access to the location in which the crime is committed without any kinds of controls (Williams et al., 2019). Offenders' actions have a superficial appearance of legitimacy also internally, since both legal and illegal actions in the organization occur in a manner characterized by disorganization (Benson and Simpson, 2018).

The social disorganization perspective argues that crime is a function of people dynamics in the organization and between organizations, and not necessarily a function of each individual within such organizations. Business enterprises experiencing rapid changes in their social and economic structures that are in a zone of transition will experience higher crime rates. Management mobility is another structural factor or antecedent that can produce organizations that develop into socially disorganized entities. Conventional mechanisms of social control are weak and unable to regulate the behavior within organizations (Pratt and Cullen, 2005).

Especially in knowledge organizations where the hierarchical structure tends to be weak, social controls among colleagues are of importance to prevent financial crime. An unstable and disorganized unit will suffer from lack of knowledge exchange and collaboration to prevent and detect white-collar crime (Swart and Kinnie, 2003).

Structural antecedents include not only management instability and rapid organizational changes, but also external factors such as family disruptions and no intelligence about life outside work. Social disorganization may well occur at the very top of organizations, where chief executives have created large business space for themselves without access for others. The board of directors is incapable of controlling chief executive activities (Ghannam et al., 2019).

Rivalry among members of the top management group, sometimes incorrectly labeled a team, can create silos of allies and enemies in the organization that hardly communicate honestly with each other. There are no ties allowing others to act collectively to fight problems (Pratt and Cullen, 2005). Corporate disorganization weakens the ability of social bonds to circumscribe delinquent behavior. In enterprises characterized by instability and heterogeneity, there is reduced likelihood of effective socialization and supervision. The impact of social bonds varies by type of organization, and disorganized units negatively affect the ability of social bonds to reduce delinquent behavior (Hoffmann, 2002; Onna and Denkers, 2019).

## Detection of Crime Signals

Concerted ignorance can occur in deteriorated organizations, where the normalization of deviant thinking and behavior in organizations develops. Employees slowly adapt to organizations' deviant norms and values that become dominant due to the higher authority of deviating individuals (Katz, 1979). For example, Shichor and Heeren (2021: 99) described concerted ignorance at Wells Fargo:

> Management expectations of making profits through lower level employees, without being interested in how the results are achieved can be characterized as "concerted ignorance" which is a general way of covering up when open discussion of certain practices or policies would threaten the solidarity and cohesion in an organization.

Shichor and Heeren (2021) found that concerted ignorance was created by an organizational emphasis on decentralization. Concerted ignorance was promoted by the common interest of limiting the knowledge each member of the organization obtains about other members of the organization.

The essence of a deteriorated institution is that its norms, behaviors, and ways of thinking are rooted in its deviant culture. For example, Campbell and Göritz (2014) identified corrupt organizations as enterprises that systematically receive bribes or provide bribes that lead to advantages in competitions. Executives who facilitate corruption either on the bribed or bribing side harm other companies for the advantage of their own organizations. In corrupt organizations, executives perceive corrupt behavior as appropriate.

Disorganized institutional deterioration can cause potential whistleblowers to become reluctant to blow the whistle on observed wrongdoings. Potential whistleblowers can fear organizational death and job loss, in addition to reprisals and retaliation. They may feel strongly for their organization, and they may be dependent on the income from their jobs. As argued by Crosina and Pratt (2019), organizations can foster deep bonds among their members, whether in the form of person-organization fit, organizational commitment, organizational identification, or some other type of attachment. A potential scandal from exposure of white-collar crime suspicion can threaten members' bonds to the organization. Organizational failure and closure can lead to organizational mourning, which Crosina and Pratt (2019: 67) define as "the thoughts, feelings, and actions that individual members undergo when processing and responding to the loss of their organization". The threat of organizational collapse is a stressor that can prevent attention to possible crime, which can create a scandal. Job loss because of a corporate scandal is detrimental to individuals' needs, desires, and goals. Job loss in conjunction to organizational death results in a large number of people entering the stage of organizational mourning that they all would like to avoid.

Making sense of executive language, attorney language, and other professionals' languages is difficult for outsiders (Weick, 1995). People tend to trust what they do not understand based on the authority positions occupied by senders of messages. Sense making links to crime signal detection by the challenge of perceiving and understanding a crime signal, as discussed below. The sense-making perspective consists of both the interpretation of information and generating results from interpretations (Huff and Bodner, 2013). People give meaning to experiences by the sense-making process. Since most people have little or no experience with fraud and corruption, they will not understand crime signals related to financial crime. People without experience are not able to make sense of weak crime signals from white-collar offenders. They are unable to frame or categorize through words what the signal is about (Holt and Cornelissen, 2014). Thus, even if a signal of fraud or corruption is present, colleagues and subordinates are unable to make sense of it since they lack experience. Only experience can help to give meaning. Without experience in the organization, a white-collar offender can feel quite safe, as nobody will be able to make sense of crime signals. It is a matter of detecting a given signal against a background of noise that represents a situation of uncertainty (Manning and Kowalska, 2021).

Uncertainty about a signal is caused by information asymmetry between actors (Paruchuri et al., 2021: 564):

> When lacking adequate information to assess the true value of an object, actors attend to observable attributes or actions of the object to alleviate uncertainty.

Training in crime signal detection is a matter of separating real signals from noise signals. The perspective of crime signal detection suggests that there is often too much interference and noise for white-collar crime to reach the attention of observers. There are four possibilities in the decision matrix of the observer of potential misconduct and crime (Karim and Siegel, 1998: 368):
- The observer notices a noise when it is a signal (called a miss)
- The observer notices a signal when it is a signal (called a hit)

- The observer notices a noise when it is a noise (called a correct identification)
- The observer notices a signal when it is a noise (called a false alarm)

The observer needs to decide concerning the event and classify it as either a signal or a noise. In an organizational context, where less powerful individuals may suspect powerful individuals, the less powerful will conveniently prefer to think of the event as a noise signal rather than as a crime signal. The perspective of crime signal detection holds that the observation of a stimulus depends on both the intensity of the stimulus and the physical and psychological state of the observer. An observer's ability or likelihood to detect some stimulus depends on the intensity of the stimulus as well as the extent of alertness of the observer. Perceptual sensitivity depends upon the perceptual ability of the observer to detect a signal or target or to discriminate signal from non-signal events (Szalma and Hancock, 2013). Furthermore, detecting persons may have varying ability to discern between information-bearing recognition (called pattern) and random patterns that distracts from information (called noise), as illustrated by the four possibilities in the decision alternatives above.

There is a need for content analysis of executive language (Duriau et al., 2007; Patrucco et al., 2017; Saunders et al., 2007). Content analysis assumes that language reflects both how people understand their surroundings and their cognitive processes (Hsieh and Shannon, 2005). Cognition refers to what people think and how they think, and cognitive processes affect the way in which people interpret and make sense of what is around them.

## Transparency in Accounting

An element of disorganized institutional deterioration is the opportunity of fraudulent misreporting in accounting (Qiu and Slezak, 2019). Lack of transparency makes concealment in accounting convenient (Goncharov and Peter, 2019). Elite members can withhold bad news by accounting misrepresentation (Bao et al., 2019). Balakrishnan et al. (2019) found that reduced corporate transparency is associated with increased corporate tax aggressiveness.

Disorganized institutional deterioration in combination with lack of corporate social responsibility cause both internal and external collapse. Executives in the organization do not care about the community, the environment, or product safety (Davidson et al., 2019).

Lack of government and governance is another enabler of disorganized institutional deterioration. The last decades have seen a shift of regulatory authority of business conduct from governments to the private sector. Self-regulation and self-policing has become the norm rather than the exception when it comes to white-collar crime suspicions (Kourula et al., 2019).

Kourula et al. (2019: 1103) define government as those public actors, who have exclusive authority over legitimate force in a specific territory:

> In our contemporary world, governments defined in this way are generally coextensive with nation-states. By virtue of this unique mode of authority, the "sine qua non" of state power, governments have the capacity, within their jurisdictions, to impose legally binding constraints and sanctions over non-governmental actors, whether in politics, society, or markets.

When there is suspicion of corporate white-collar crime, the government branch typically involved is the national criminal justice system. The police have the task of investigating suspicions by reconstructing past events and sequences of events. If the police find sufficient evidence of law violation, then the case moves to the prosecution. The defendant faces the prosecutor in court, where a jury or a judge decides whether the suspected criminal is guilty of law violation.

A bottom-up approach to prevention and detection of white-collar crime is increased transparency in accounting. The discourse and rituals of transparency, account-giving, and verification are central to corporate governance (Mehrpouya and Salles-Djelic, 2019: 13):

> Transparency has been a normative shell through which financial accounting and audit standards have been pushed around the world. Under the contemporary governance paradigm, financial disclosure regimes are an important dimension of what it means to make organisations, states and individuals transparent and accountable. Champions of transparency, such as the former head of the IMF, Michel Candessus, describe transparency as the "golden rule" of the new international financial system, "absolutely central to the task of civilizing globalization". (. . .) Transparency implies unhindered access to information for the public. However, the definition of the public, targets and beneficiaries of transparency, along with associated programs and technologies, has been contested and has evolved through time.

Mehrpouya and Salles-Djelic (2019) found that a range of organizations mobilized transparency to champion public accountability. Transparency was also championed to fight corruption and protect customers.

## Corporate Social Responsibility

As stated above, disorganized institutional deterioration in combination with lack of corporate social responsibility cause both internal and external collapse. The introduction and improvement in corporate social responsibility might represent a bottom-up approach by employees who are concerned with the legitimacy of current business practices. If the reputation and the legitimacy of the business practice deterioriates, then key personnel with an ethical orientation might leave the organization and cause decline in business performance as a consequence of employee turnover. Legitimacy relates to the perception that the organization is operating in a desirable and appropriate way that is consistent with a broader system of norms, values, and beliefs (Sorour et al., 2021).

The bottom-up approach might focus on the signaling effect of corporate social responsibility (CSR), where signals are observable actions that a firm takes to provide information to stakeholders about its unobservable intentions and capabilities (Jardine et al., 2020: 851):

> Specifically, the activities that serve as CSR signals indicate that a firm is willing and able to act with a long-term vision and to take into account the interests of different stakeholders. For example, by hiring a female board member (an observable action), a firm can signal to job seekers that it is both willing and able (its unobservable intentions and capabilities) to support women in their careers. Similarly, by engaging in CSR activities (an observable action), a firm can signal to governments that it would be a trustworthy partner (an unobservable intention) for a government procurement contract.

CSR refers to both policies and practices where policies signal unobservable intentions, while practices signal unobservable capabilities. For example, a policy of zero tolerance against corruption wherever the company operates signals an intention, while the practice of detecting and punishing an offender within the organization signals a capability. While instrumental CSR by CSR signals can enhance the ethical standard within the organization, the firm might also suffer from external attacks if the signals are not trustworthy (Jardine et al., 2020).

Traditionally, CSR has referred to business participation in social problem solving, disaster and fraud avoidance, business involvement in public policy, efforts to provide guiding principles for corporate behavior, and a shift from responsibility to responsiveness (Mitnick et al., 2021). Furthermore, CSR reflects a firm's understanding and acknowledgement of its role in society and the environment (Zhang et al., 2021: 160):

> Accurate CSR disclosure requires firms to report items clearly, using specific language and quantitative measures to achieve a comparable and verifiable description of nonfinancial performance.

Beji et al. (2021: 133) argued that CSR is a management concept whereby companies not only fully meet the applicable legal obligations, but also go beyond by extending their efforts to promote more socially responsible projects:

> Specifically, companies become more concerned about the protection of human rights, employees' conditions, environmental issues, and communities' expectations. They manage their business according to specific ethical standards.

Rather than appealing to the good will of potential offenders to commit themselves to CSR and avoid offenses, an alternative route is to draw out the negative consequences of lack of compliance as described by the concept of falling from grace (Kakkar et al., 2020) and never returning to their former self (Hunter, 2022: 37):

> For white-collar offenders, the experience of punishment often stands in stark contrast to the lives they led prior to entering the criminal justice system, which challenges self-perception through forced association with criminal others, perhaps best exemplified by the experience of prison. Potentially more difficult however is their experience of community reactions to their offending. Upon contact with the community – whether during or after punishment – white-collar offenders find their perceptions of self challenged.

According to Piquero (2012), many top executives and other members of the elite in society have a fear of falling from their positions. Drawing out the negative consequences of offending by the concept of falling from grace (Kakkar et al., 2020) might lead to the outcome of suicide. For example, Kang and Thosuwanchot (2017) applied Durkheim's four categories of suicide to organizational crime. A recent example from Norway might illustrate such an outcome as an anecdotal evidence of falling from grace. A bank executive had helped a friend with loans and in exchange received favors. It was a matter of fraud against the bank as well as corruption. The board at the bank first suspended and then dismissed the executive on February 7, 2022. The local and national media coverage of the case was extensive (e.g., Kværnes, 2022). He killed himself a few weeks after the exposure of his wrongdoing in the media. On Monday, March 21, 2022, he drove his car in high speed into the front of an oncoming truck and died. The priest reported in the memorial service in the local church about the deceased (Hellerud, 2022: 5):

> The priest then told how difficult the last four or five months had been for Rune Hvidsten. He was suspended from his job as bank manager on November 24 last year after media reports about serious matters. On February 7 this year, he was dismissed by the board of Askim and Spydeberg Savings Bank.
>
> –He has not been himself and felt inaction and sometimes also alone. There are many who have stood up and helped him. Many conversations out in the barn with family and with especially close friends. But it was impossible not to let the pressure around affect the mood. Rune was scared. He has been hospitalized and felt powerless in an inhuman situation and in a vulnerable role. The very last time Rune lived he still showed a lot of courage and was a bit on edge. But then . . .

It is completely quiet in the church while Bård Haugstvedt continues:

> –On Monday, March 21, what was not supposed to happen happened. Rune, who is sitting in a car, collides with a truck on Enebakk road in Siggerud. Life could not be saved. Rune died suddenly in traffic. A 58-year-old man died far too quickly. Many have felt injustice and anger. A difficult time for everyone and it is extremely difficult to accept that Rune should die in this way.

The former bank executive left behind three sons, a stepson, his mother and his cohabitant for the last twenty years (Hellerud, 2022). His death represents a form of anecdotal evidence of the potentially dramatic consequence of falling from grace after facing allegations of white-collar crime.

Employee concern with the legitimacy of current business practices is often linked to negative organizational identity that refers to how the business relates to stakeholders and why it relates to them as it does. A negative organizational identity implies that there is a lack of mediation between external pressures and internal demands for continuity. As such, a CSR activity may be introduced as a result of a cognitive process in accordance with a shared perception constitutive of the organization's desired identity. In line with this reasoning, Sorour et al. (2021) conceived of the CSR engagement process as one that allows for the communication and orientation of organizational identity through an informal co-creation involving organizational actors and stakeholders.

Bottom-up approaches to both transparency and CSR can foster a mutual reinforcing effect between the two approaches. Transparency can foster the substantive adoption of CSR, while CSR to be trustworthy requires transparency. The bottom-up call for a condition under which it is relatively easy for external observers to accurately determine the degree to which a practice is implemented forces and enables an organization to explore, embrace, and eventually enact the behavioral prescriptions enshrined in CSR policies and principles (Haack et al., 2021).

Not only is CSR problematic in view of transparency if there is reluctance to implement efficient and effective policies and actions. CSR is also problematic given the widely used definition of CSR in accounting research as sacrificing profits in the social interest (Martin, 2021). Of course, a concept such as CSR does not only have benefits. There will also be costs such as potentially sacrificing profits. This accounting research definition explicitly recognizes that an organization may often need to make tradeoffs between maximizing shareholder value and engaging in CSR.

The role of CSR can be strengthened further by the accumulation of social capital within the firm. Social capital refers to personal relationships, social norms, and civic participation. The concept of personal relationships measures the strength of social capital in the form of network and community. It reflect the perceived level of opportunity ot make friends, the ability to count on colleagues for help, the frequency of helping others, and the frequency of giving informal help including emotional support (Papadimitri et al., 2021). The expectation that other members of the organization will provide help in various ways when there is suspicion of white-collar wrongdoing is a form of intangible asset that can result in lower crime convenience for offenders. Social norms refer to standards that are understood by members of a group and that guide and constrain social behavior without the force of law (Gorecki and Letki, 2021). Civic participation refers to the extent of organizational citizenry where loyalty rests with the organization in the long run and not with the current executives. The concept of civic participation measures the frequency of volunteering for the organization, the frequenc of voicing opinion within the organization, and the general altruistic willingness among organizational members (Papadimitri et al., 2021).

Research reviewed by Kundro and Nurmohamed (2021) indicated that peer reporting of unethical behavior demonstrated that in-group parties are unlikely to show leniency to their peers' cover-up behavior when the misconduct threatens the interest of group members. A strong social capital within the firm, transparency of the firm, and substance CSR will all contribute to the reduction in white-collar crime convenience. A cover-up refers to actions to conceal unethical behavior and crime. A cover-up emerges in direct follow-up response to a prior unethical or criminal action. It is an intentional form of further unethical behavior or crime.

An example of executive cover-up is the Wirecard scandal in Germany (Chazan and Storbeck, 2020a, 2020b; McCrum, 2019, 2020). Wirecard had hired audit firm KPMG (2020) to conduct a fraud examination into alleged increase in revenue through fictious customer relationships and other forms of accounting manipulation. Wirecard's motive to hire KPMG was, according to Storbeck (2020), to get a clean bill of health from fraud examiners at KPMG:

> With the KPMG investigation in full flow, the Wirecard executives behind the fraud saw Project Panther and a deal with Deutsche, which was first reported by Bloomberg, as one possible way to fend off discover, says an adviser to the payments group who was involved in the discussions. But they also worked on a separate plan: a vast cover-up operation in Asia.

Since cover-ups allow problematic behavior to continue and often escalate causing additional damage, it is important for insiders to create a punishment regime in the best interest of the organization. An element of such a punishment regime might be to leak stories to the police and to the press. Application of negative consequences for involved individual executives might easily make the organization distance and disassociate itself from the offenders and thereby avoid harming organizational reputation. This bottom-up approach represents a reversal of the common top-down approach where leaders reinforce a culture of financial crime by ignoring criminal actions and otherwise facilitate unethical behavior. At the same time, they try to distance and disassociate themselves from criminal actions (Pontell et al., 2021: 9):

> High status corporate criminals often go to great lengths to distance themselves from the crimes committed by their subordinates and to hide any incriminating evidence of their role in the decisions that authorized those criminal acts.

As illustrated by the above perspectives, corporate social responsibility requires substance to be trustworthy in terms of transparency and social capital when an executive scandal hits the organization. Furthermore, a bottom-up approach to CSR has to replace window dressing by documented actions against actual misconduct events. Window dressing is the discrepancy between the outside positive presentation of an enterprise and the real negative situation within the enterprise. One of the examples throughout this book is the Nordic bank Nordea where Vienola (2021: 19) found extensive CSR activities:

> In Nordea, responsibility plays a big role and they have a wide range of CSR activities. Nordea's website has an extensive sustainability section. They use the Environmental, Social, and Corporate Governance (ESG) model and have explained it on the site as well. Nordea takes ESG principles into account when assessing business risks and opportunities related to investments and financing. They publish a detailed sustainability report annually. The report for the year 2019 starts with the CEO's statement followed by a summary of 2019 and its key data. Sustainability targets for 2020 and main focus areas described in short articles, including embedding human rights, responsible supply chain, people performance, diversity and inclusion, community engagement and embracing new technologies.

However, investigative journalists, critical researchers, and other knowledgeable people and institutions regularly detect Nordea involved in misconduct and wrongdoing. Mannheimer Swartling (2016) described how the bank had its subsidiary in Luxembourg illegally backdating contracts and help clients facilitate tax evasion and money laundering in tax havens. This information was leaked from the Panama Papers by investigative journalists. The bank first denied its link to the Panamian law firm Mossack Fonseca, which specializes in establishing corporate mailbox companies in tax havens (Associated Press, 2016). Gunn Wærsted resigned from her group executive position at Nordea and chair at Nordea Luxembourg (Trumpy, 2016). Nordea is a bank with money laundering issues as described by Wingerde and Merz (2021).

The bottom-up perspective of sustainable finance might help prevent bank involvement in financial crime such as tax evasion (Mannheimer Swartling, 2016), corruption (Kleinfeld, 2019, 2020a; Seljan et al., 2019), and money laundering (Bruun Hjejle, 2018; Clifford Chance, 2020). Reduction in crime convenience contributes to sustainable finance, where sustainable finance represents "the assimilation of sustainability aspects into standard risk and return calculus associated with investment decision making" (Ionescu, 2021: 95), while "sustainability as a way to improve environmental and social conditions is neither an easy task nor a subject to debate on" (Paun and Pinzaru, 2021: 280). While "research on sustainable finance is traditionally considered to be the domain of economists" (Kuhn, 2020: 1), the focus of this book is on the domain of criminologists with the organization rather than the individual or the society as the main unit of analysis.

Sacrificing profits in the social interest (Martin, 2021) is a statement in contrast to the statements that good ethics pay and that what is good for business is good for society (Lynn, 2021: 513):

> The exploration of linkages between business interests and social welfare is a relatively new phenomenon in the business and society literature. While sentiments such as "what is good for business is good for society" have permeated popular discourse surrounding business for at least the past century, efforts to scientifically prove ties between ethical behavior and financial benefit only gained a real foothold in managerial research in the 1970s. Prior to this, the forms of socially conscious business behavior gained prominence in the 1960s – when corporations first felt pressures from environmental and humanitarian groups to divest or curb

> harmful behaviors – drew upon frameworks of "doing good to do good" rather than "doing good to do well". However, in the mid-1970s questions of responsibility to society gave way to strategies of responsiveness to environmental expectations.

Lynn (2021) very much questioned the positive link between ethical behavior and economic performance since inquiries into the link have been "plagued with flaws, inconsistencies, and sloppy application, leaving much of it simply unconclusive". A different perspective was introduced by Dion (2021: 687) who suggested that in itself it important to overcome "the blind and egoistic quest for wealth".

## Sharing of Audit Reports

Concealing illegal transactions may result from the failure of auditors to do their job. Alon et al. (2019) argue that accounting and auditing functions have undergone a legitimacy crisis in recent years. Auditors are supposed to serve as gatekeepers to protect shareholders and other stakeholders, but deviant corporate management tend to hire and control auditors instead of letting auditors report to the board of directors or the supervisory board (Hurley et al., 2019). Skeptical auditors tend to be replaced by less skeptical auditors. Reporting fraud to public authorities will also harm auditors (Mohliver, 2019: 316):

> As organizations, audit firms are often severely penalized for client malfeasance. Yet the individual auditors working for these firms are susceptible to "motivated blindness" stemming from conflicts of interest that bias their moral judgment toward choices that help their clients.

The lack of detection by auditors can also be explained by standardization. Herron and Cornell (2021) found that audit work is standardized which harms auditors creativity, thereby preventing recognition of and responses to fraud cues. Standardization harms an improvisational style of thinking, tolerance for unpredictability, and uncertainty, and open-mindedness that is associated with responses to perceived fraud risk cues.

Mohliver (2019: 310) found that some auditors prioritize their clients' interests over their legal obligation by recommending client malfeasance, for example in terms of illegal stock option backdating:

> The findings suggest that professional experts' involvement in the diffusion of liminal practices is highly responsive to the institutional environment.

Similarly, Chan and Gibbs (2022) found that guardians can become offenders where a convergence occurs of motivated offenders, suitable targets, and absent guardianship. The convergence triggers two crime-conducive outcomes. First, it provides motivated offenders access to the target of interest. Second, it reduces offenders' perceived likelihood of being detected.

Mohliver (2019) found that auditor bias towards accepting deviant financial reports increased when there is ambiguity about the appropriateness of a course of action. Financial misreporting that is viewed favorably by the client organization can be recommended by external auditors on the grounds that such reporting is already adopted among companies served by the same auditing firm.

There is a need for governance. Kourula et al. (2019: 1104) define governance as those private actors, who direct behaviors in business conduct by rulemaking, enforcement and sanctioning:

> By "governance" we refer not to corporate governance, but to the wider concept of societal governance, that of the collective means to give "direction to society" which we take to include direction to society's politics and markets.

This wide definition of governance is supported by Davies and Malik (2022), who emphasized regulatory regimes and criminal justice interventions in support of political priorities that give direction to corporate governance. Similarly, Johnson (2022: 23) reviewed a hybrid regulatory approach toward the enforcement of corporate financial crime in the UK and USA, where an element of the approach is deferred prosecution agreements that "impose a financial penalty and behavioral commitments on a corporate entity for a defined period of time in exchange for the deferral of a criminal prosecution".

When there is suspicion of corporate white-collar crime, the governance branch typically involved should be the compliance function, potentially cooperating with internal and external auditors as well as various controllers. Internal or external fraud examiners have the task of investigating suspicions by reconstructing past events and sequences of events. If fraud examiners find sufficient evidence of law violation, then the case stops, moves internally or moves externally to the national criminal justice system. If secrecy to protect corporate reputation is the main concern, then the case typically stops and remains internal. However, organizations with inefficient or non-existing compliance functions or governance branch generally, contribute to disorganized institutional deterioration.

## Community Social Pressure

Haines et al. (2022: 184) examined "how social control in the form of community pressure might be used to control corporate harm and shape business conduct in a more socially responsible direction". They suggested a social license to civilize, control, or repel corporate activity. They defined a social license as acceptance of a business or business activity within a particular community. The social license adds to the legal license to operate business activities. The social license forms part of a bottom-up strategy where criminalization becomes social property independent of the criminal justice system. The social license is predominantly centered on social permission for business activity where the media, social movements, and citizen watchdogs exert pressure, demand change, and bring enterprises to account. Similarly, Sale (2021) defined social license as the acceptance of business or organization by the relevant communities and stakeholders.

Haines et al. (2022) studied community pressure against unconventional gas exploration by a large resources company in New South Wales (NSW) in Australia. While the bottom-up approaches by various stakeholders were successful in reducing corporate harm, a number of issues emerged related to athority, meaning, and value. For example, an issue was to identify who were entitled to represent the community. Those chosen and accepted to represent the community might be those considered mature enough for the role, while critical and excentric voices can be deemed unsuitable.

In the case study, the social license went far beyond the legal license (Haines et al., 2022: 191):

> Company representatives felt that an a priori assertion of their legal right to access land would be met by anger and defiance. Relying on their legal rights would be seen as arrogant and likely to lead to lengthy court disputes, one argued 'we never tested it' (their legal rights). Unlike coal mines where land to be mined is acquired by coal companies, gas companies did not need to acquire land (as subsurface resources in NSW are owned by the state), but they did need access to land in order to access those resources.

Sale (2021: 785) studied Wells Fargo and Uber as cases of "how the failure to account for the public nature of corporate actions, regardless of whether a 'legal' license exists, can result in the loss of 'social' license. This loss occurs through publicness, which is the interplay between inside corporate governance players and outside actors who report on, recapitulate, reframe and, in some cases, control the company's information and public perception".

Most of Wells Fargo's profits and growth were coming from the Community Bank. Executives as well as other employees in the community banking division at Wells Fargo had their motives for financial wrongdoing. Both pressures and possibilities were their motives. Sanger et al. (2017: 2) found that there was an explicit and strong "pressure on employees to sell unwanted or unneeded products to customers". The banking division was a sales-driven organization. Hired people got instructions in these sales practices and would lose their job otherwise.

The threat of job loss became a reality after disclosure of the account fraud scandal: "Approximately 5,300 employees had been terminated for sales practices violations through the September 2016 settlements with the Los Angeles City Attorney" (Sanger et al., 2017: 2).

Before the termination of all those employees, "poor performance in many instances led to shaming or worse" (Sanger et al., 2017: 30). Investigators found that employees below the branch manager level – lower level in-branch managers and non-managers – frequently cited branch managers as actively directing misconduct or offering inappropriate guidance to subordinates on what constituted acceptable conduct. "Everyone was aware of what was implied when the manager would state 'it's late in the day and we need a certain number of accounts by the end of the day'" (Sanger et al., 2017:37).

An important possibility was compensation, as ambitious sales goals linked directly to incentive compensation (Sanger et al., 2017: 20):

> Employees were measured on how they performed relative to these goals. They were ranked against one another on their performance relative to these goals, and their incentive compensation and promotional opportunities were determined relative to those goals. The system created intense pressure to perform, and, in certain areas, local and regional managers imposed excessive pressure on their subordinates.

Because of such deviant practices, Wells Fargo lost its social license as the process of publicness exposed additional frauds (Sale, 2021: 833):

> Take for example, the car loan repossession scandal. Between 20,000 and 570,000 customers of the bank were enrolled in and charged for car insurance without their knowledge, and when some of them failed to make payments on the unknown insurance, they had their cars repossessed. Even though Wells Fargo said it was "extremely sorry" and promised to refund customers and work with credit bureaus, its response lacked credibility.

The idea here is that the legal license was not necessarily violated, while the social license was certainly violated. Therefore, board members and executives could probably not be prosecuted in court, while the business suffered from social disapproval (Sale, 2021: 837):

> Although it is unclear what information the Wells Fargo board received, ex post investigations reveal that the company's decentralized nature and, perhaps, management evasion resulted in fragmented reporting, which in turn contributed to the sustained nature of the fraud. Yet, if the board had pressed with questions about management strategy and its downside risks, the board would have ensured dialogue about the types of underlying facts necessary to develop legitimacy, credibility, and trust and thus helped to protect the company's social license.

The typical outcome of social licence violations seems to be the dismissal of executives at various levels in an attempt to regain trust:

- CEO Carrie Tolstedt at Community Bank in the United States had to leave her position despite her attempts to blame individual employees (Sanger et al., 2017: 103): "Tolstedt emphasized that a large organization could not be perfect, and that the sales practice problem was a result of improper action on the part of individual employees".
- CEO Birgitte Bonnesen at Swedbank in Sweden had to leave her position after the money laundering scandal investigated by Clifford Chance (2020).
- CEO Thomas Borgen at Danske Bank in Denmark had to leave his position after a similar money laundering scandal investigated by Bruun Hjejle (2018).
- CEO Martin Winterkorn at Volkswagen in Germany had to resign because of the emission manipulation scandal (Jung and Sharon, 2019).

Many more examples of dismissed chief executives come to mind. However, more interesting to mention are situations where blame is attributed downwards in a corporate hierarchy. An example is General Motors after the Cobalt ignition switch failure. Rather than blaming CEO Mary Barra, several others had to leave. Bill Kemp, a senior lawyer in the automobile company, was one out of several who received blame for the lack of reaction to the ignition switch failure (Shepardson and Burden, 2014).

From the perspective of social license, bottom-up as well as inside-out concerns should occupy board members' and top executives' attention. Negative statements by politicians, activists, employees, journalists, and others can indeed harm the business as well as harm the career of people in trusted elite positions. While some companies initially attempt to respond by secrecy, the eventual publicness of wrongdoing, although not illegal, will cause damage. Therefore, as argued by Sale (2021) and Haines et al. (2022), the bottom-up approach of securing corporate social license contributes to corporate control of white-collar crime.

# 5 Oversight and Guardianship

Guardianship is supervision that may prevent crime by the presence of individuals who are capable and willing to detect and react to wrongdoing. However, as argued by Chan and Gibbs (2022), the presence of guardians does not necessarily equate to capability in crime prevention, especially when studied in a dynamic prespective. For example, potential offenders may over time learn how guardians operate and thus how to avoid the attention of guardianship functions.

Lack of oversight and guardianship causes chaos. As argued by Long et al. (2011), different types of controls that convey performance standards to executives increase the perceived relevance of particular aspects of fairness in organizations. They introduced the concept of fairness monitoring to characterized controlled individuals' efforts to gather and process fairness information to make sense of their organizational roles.

Chan and Gibbs (2022: 5) argued that "a guardian's willingness to intervene is shaped by that guardians' perception of their own responsibility, potential risk of harm, prior emergency training, and social ties". Therefore, in our bottom-up perspective, guardians have to be influenced by increasing their perception of personal responsibility, by removing potential sources of harm from them, by professional emergency training, and by strengthened social ties to ethical employees and managers.

## Coordination of Principals and Agents

The agency perspective suggests that a principal is often unable to control an agent who does work for the principal. The agency perspective assumes narrow self-interest among both principals and agents. The interests of principal and agent tend to diverge, they may have different risk willingness or risk aversion, there is knowledge asymmetry between the two parties, and the principal has imperfect information about the agent's contribution (Bosse and Phillips, 2016; Chrisman et al., 2007; Pillay and Kluvers, 2014; Williams, 2008). According to principal-agent analysis, exchanges can encourage illegal gain for both principal and agent.

The perspective of principal and agent suggests that when a principal delegates tasks to an agent, the principal is often unable to control what the agent is doing. Agency problems occur when principal and agent have different risk willingness and different preferences, and knowledge asymmetry regarding tasks exists (Eisenhardt, 1989). The principal-agent perspective (or simply agency perspective) can illuminate fraud and corruption in an organizational context. The principal may be a board of a company that leaves the corporate management to the chief executive officer (CEO). The CEO is then the agent in the relationship. The CEO in turn may

https://doi.org/10.1515/9783110986686-006

entrust tasks to other executives, where the CEO becomes the principal, while people in positions such as chief financial officer (CFO), chief operating officer (COO), and chief technology officer (CTO) are agents. Agents perform tasks on behalf of principals. A CEO may cheat and defraud owners (Khanna et al., 2015; Zahra et al., 2005; Williams, 2008), and a purchasing manager can fool the CEO when selecting vendors (Chrisman et al., 2007) by taking bribes that can cause the company to pay more for inferior quality, for instance. The agency perspective assumes narrow self-interest among both principals and agents. The interests of principal and agent tend to diverge, and the principal has imperfect information about the agent's contribution (Bosse and Phillips, 2016). According to principal-agent analysis, exchanges can encourage illegal private gain for both principal and agent (Pillay and Kluvers, 2014). Managers are viewed as opportunistic agents motivated by individual utility maximization. Taking an economic model of man that treats human beings as rational actors seeking to maximize individual utility – when given the opportunity – then executives and other members of the elite will maximize their own utilities at the expense of shareholders and others.

In our perspective of control, Malmi et al. (2020) applied agency theory to study culture and management control interdependence. They found support for their three research hypothesis: (1) Delegation of authority and incentive contracting operate as complements for firms in the Anglo cultural region but are independent in the Germanic and Nordic cultural regions; (2) Delegation of authority and subordinate participation in planning operate as complements for firms in the Germanic and Nordic cultural regions but are independent in the Anglo cultural region, and (3) Delegation of authority and value-based input controls (i.e. selection based on values and socialization) operate as complements for firms in the Nordic cultural region but are independent in the Anglo and Germanic cultural regions.

## Sensemaking of Executive Actions

As evidenced by many internal investigation reports by fraud examiners after white-collar crime scandals, internal auditors, external auditors, compliance committees and other internal and external control units do not function properly (e.g., Bruun Hjejle, 2018; Clifford Chance, 2020; Deloitte, 2015, 2017; Mannheimer Swartling, 2016; Shearman Sterling, 2017). Oversight and control functions tend to be formal units without any insights into the substance of business activities. They tend to review procedures rather than transactions within procedures. Therefore, ineffective control functions are often an important part of the opportunity structure for white-collar crime. For example, at Toshiba Corporation, lack of controls was an important element of the opportunity structure (Deloitte, 2015; Demetriades and Owusu-Agyei, 2021). Fraud examiners emphasized lack of internal controls by accounting and auditing functions, as well as lack of finance control in each corporate division. At Wells Fargo, corporate control functions were constrained by the decentralized organizational structure (Shearman Sterling, 2017; Shichor and Heeren, 2021). Fraud examiners excused corporate control functions since they suffered from harm by the decentralized organizational structure and a culture of substantial independence for business units. At Fuji Xerox, CEO Whittaker had gained control over reporting lines to manipulate accounting (Deloitte, 2017). At Danske Bank where money laundering occurred in their Estonian branch, corporate control functions did not work because the branch operated computer systems different from computer systems at the headquarter (Bruun Hjejle, 2018). Telenor executives ignored corruption rumors at VimpelCom since the chief compliance officer and chief legal officer did not know how to handle whistleblowing (Deloitte, 2016).

Lack of oversight and guardianship becomes even worse when auditors slide over on the wrong side of the law (Mohliver, 2019).

## Protection of Whistleblowers

Lack of whistleblowing is an important part of the opportunity structure for white-collar crime. When people notice wrongdoing in the organization, they are reluctant to report it because of perceived retaliation threats. As argued by Keil et al. (2010), costs tend to exceed benefits for individual whistleblowers. In addition, as argued by Bussmann et al. (2018), employees in societies characterized by collectivist values are reluctant to blow the whistle on others. Therefore, as argued by Rashid et al. (2022), higher awareness of whistleblower laws and whistleblowing procedures among employees is an important bottom-up prevention approach.

Whistleblowing is the disclosure by an individual in an organization or in society of deviant practices to someone who can do something about it (Bjørkelo et al., 2011). Whistleblowing is an action by employees who believe that their business or colleague(s) are involved in activities of misconduct or crime, cause unnecessary harm, violate human rights, or contribute to otherwise immoral offenses (Mpho, 2017). Whistleblowing is the disclosure by an organizational member of deviant practices to someone who can do something about it.

Anderson (2022: 1) defined government whistleblowers as “those who disclose classified government documents in violation of the law but do so to bring to light serious government wrongdoing”. In his research article, whistleblowers Edward Snowden and Julian Assange are studied by radical theory related to assumptions about audience, professionalism, and ultimate aims.

Whistleblowers stand out as a group of reporters who have made observations and who are willing to disclose what they have observed. However, executives may try to withhold bad news (Bao et al., 2019) and punish whistleblowers by reprisals and retaliation.

A potential whistleblower might thus be afraid of retaliation. Retaliation makes informants reluctant to blow the whistle. Reprisal and retaliation against a whistleblower represent an outcome between an organization and its employee, in which members of the organization attempt to control the employee by threatening to take, or actually taking, an action that is detrimental to the well-being of the employee (Mesmer-Magnus and Viswesvaran, 2005; Rehg et al., 2009).

The lack of whistleblowing is an organizational inhibitor in relation to addressing white-collar crime and thus an enabler of wrongdoing. Shepherd and Button (2019) suggest that a range of avoidant rationalizations constructed by observers justify not noticing, reporting or tackling white-collar crime. These rationalizations and justifications for disregard of observed wrongdoing can be similar to those rationalizations applied by offenders when committing crime, such as denial of victim and denial of damage (Kaptein and Helvoort, 2019).

There is a strong interaction between crime signal detection and whistleblowing intentions among potential whistleblowers. A low uncertainty that there is a crime signal will relate positively to whistleblowing intentions. If the signal is weak and confused by noise, whistleblowing intentions are likely to deteriorate as the potential whistleblower considers risk for him or her (Brown et al., 2016). It is convenient for an offender to know that even though others in the organization may develop suspicions, they will not notify others about what they have observed. They are not sure if something wrong has occurred, they are not sure who to notify, and they are not sure if any whistleblowing may have consequences for themselves in the form of reprisals. That is why many people are reluctant to report suspicion of misconduct and crime, even when they feel quite certain that something wrong has happened. Many who have cast light on critical conditions have experienced unwillingness, and they have been isolated and considered less attractive in the labor market afterwards (Rehg et al., 2009). According to Shawver and Clements (2019), potential whistleblowers often decide not to report ethical wrongdoing because of the likelihood of retaliation.

Interactions between crime enablers occur in the organizational opportunity dimension of convenience theory. Interactions can also occur across dimensions, which we return to in the description of the crime convenience triangle later in this book.

In the bottom-up approach of whistleblowing to address suspicions of white-collar crime, it is important for whistleblowers and their allies to avoid conspiracy theories. Sometimes executives, board members, and shareholders might seem to enter into a conspiracy without doing so. The thought of conspiracy can emerge as whistleblowers receive no feedback regarding their notices, and when whistleblowers experience reluctance to talk to them about perceived wrongdoing. Whistleblowers can then easily fall into the trap of considering management and others involved in a conspiracy to conceal wrongdoing and make whistleblowers subject to retaliation, reprisal, and refuting.

Conspiracist beliefs and theories are defined as essentially false narratives where multiple agents are believed to be working together toward malevolent ends. The theories are essentially attempts to explain the ultimate causes of significant social and political events by claims of secret plots concerning two or more powerful actors. Conspiracy theories help make sense of events that are confusing, difficult to comprehend, or poorly explained by mainstream sources of information (Furnham and Grover, 2021). Conspiracy theories are lay theories that attribute the cause or concealment of an event to secret, unlawful, and malevolent processes controlled by multiple actors working together (Furnham, 2021). When conspiracy theories dominate the thinking of bottom-up controllers, then the thinking resembles tunnel vision that is defined not as seeing the light in the end of the tunnel, but rather as seeing nothing else but the light in the end of the tunnel.

It has been suggested that conspiracy theories are held by people with four particular characteristics: patternicity (the tendency to find meaningful patterns in random noise), agenticity (the beliefs that the world is controlled by invisible, intentional agents), confirmation bias (the strong preference to seek and find conformational evidence for what they believe), and hindsight bias (tailoring after-the-fact explanations to what they already know happened). Furthermore, people who are convinced that everything in the world is unjust and unfair are more likely to endorse conspiracy theories (Furnham, 2021).

Furnham and Grover (2021) studied potential links between personality disorders and belief in conspiracy theories. They found that people who tend to be paranoid seem more likely to endorse conspiracy theories. Paranoia is a tendency on the part of an individual or group toward excessive or irrational suspiciousness and distrustfulness of normal others. Furthermore, believers in conspiracy theories tend to see the world as being out of line rather than seeing themselves being out of sync with the world around them. Also, less educated people tend in general to be less skeptical, more religious, and more attracted to popularist theories.

## Reduction in Ethical Climate Conflict

The ethical climate can be another element of the opportunity structure for white-collar crime. The ethical climate perspective defines five distinct climate types within organizations: instrumental, caring, independence, rules, and law and code. A work climate is the sum of perceptions that provide meaningful insights into the working environment, which people can agree characterize an organization's values, practices and procedures. The instrumental climate is the climate in which Murphy and Free (2015) believe fraud is most likely to occur. Instrumental means that executives and others in the organization tend to prioritize decisions that either provide personal benefits or serve the organization's interests with little regard for ethical considerations. There is association between instrumental climate and workplace deviance extending to fraud. Workplace deviance is voluntary behavior that violates significant organizational norms and in so doing threatens the well-being of an organization, its members, or both. However, fraud and corruption can be a consequence of following, rather than violating, an organizational norm. For example, a case against Siemens in Germany alleged that Siemens executives abroad routinely bribed foreign officials as part of an overall pattern of corporate conduct in marketing. The climate encouraged corruption and fraudulent behavior as normal and acceptable (Murphy and Dacin, 2011; Tankebe, 2019).

## Corporate Principal Agent Dynamics

The principal-agent perspective can help illustrate convenience dynamics in the organizational dimension of the theory of convenience. Principal is a term for a person or a body that leaves work to an agent. The agent carries out work for the principal. Typically, the agent provides the principal with some sort of specialized service based on the agents' expertise and availability. The principal may be a board of a company that leaves the corporate management to the CEO. The CEO is then the agent in the relationship (Shen, 2003). The CEO may in turn entrust tasks to other executives, where the CEO becomes the principal, while people in positions such as chief financial officer (CFO), chief operating officer (COO) and chief technology officer (CTO) are agents. Agents perform tasks on behalf of principals.

The agency perspective describes problems that may arise between principal and agent because of diverging preferences and different values, asymmetry in knowledge of activities and performance, and different attitudes to risk. Principals must always suspect that agents make decisions that benefit themselves at the expense of principals. For example, a CEO may cheat and defraud owners (Williams, 2008), and a purchasing manager can fool the CEO when selecting vendors (Chrisman et al., 2007); for example, by taking bribes that can cause the company to pay more for inferior quality.

Agency theory applies the assumption of narrow self-interest. The problem arises whenever one party (a principal) employs another (an agent) to carry out a task. The interests of the principal and agent diverge, and the principal has imperfect information about the agent's contribution (Bosse and Phillips, 2016). According to principal-agent analysis, exchanges encourage extraordinary gain (Pillay and Kluvers, 2014). Executives and others in trusted positions are opportunistic agents motivated by utility maximization. Taking an economic model of man that treats human beings as rational actors seeking to maximize utility, when given the opportunity, executives will maximize their utilities at the expense of their principals.

In agency theory, there are three problems: preferences (principal and agent may have conflicting values or goals), risk (principal and agent may not have the same kind of risk aversion or risk willingness), and knowledge (principal and agent may not have the same information and insights). Figure 5.1 illustrates the relevant causal relationships. Preferences, risk, and knowledge are variables on the left-hand side in the diagram. The right-hand side of the diagram is one part of Figure 5.1 that relates to organizational opportunity.

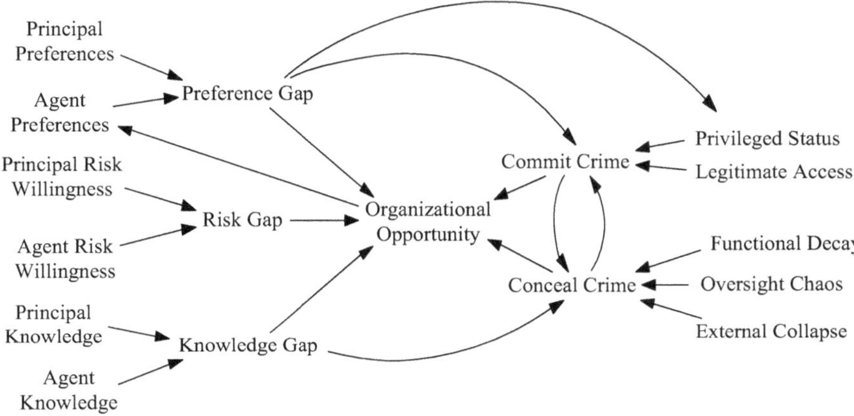


**Figure 5.1:** Dynamic model of the agency perspective in convenience theory.

In terms of preferences, the principal's and the agent's best interests may not be in line with each other. Desires and goals of principal and agent may be in conflict. Thus, there is a preference gap as illustrated in Figure 5.1. In terms of risk, the principal and the agent may have different attitudes towards risk. In terms of knowledge, it is difficult or expensive for the principal to verify what the agent is actually doing.

The model in Figure 5.1 assumes that gaps influence the extent of organizational opportunity for white-collar crime. A larger gap in preferences might restrict organizational opportunity. A larger gap in risk willingness might also restrict organizational opportunity. On the other hand, a larger gap in knowledge can expand the organizational opportunity.

The model in Figure 5.1 introduces some new causal feedback loops. For example, greater organizational opportunity for white-collar crime can influence agent preferences. Change in agent preferences can cause a larger preference gap, which in turn leads to reduced organizational opportunity. The causal loop of organizational opportunity, agent preferences, and preference gap thus represents a negative loop that stabilizes rather than reinforces organizational opportunity.

Another example of a new loop includes preference gap, privileged status, commit crime, organizational opportunity, agent preferences and back to preference gap. If the preference gap increases, the privileged position of the offender might face new limitations and restrictions. Then the convenience of committing crime drops, and organizational opportunity drops accordingly. This feeds back to agent preferences as a correction, thereby reducing the preference gap. This loop started with an increase in preference gap and ended up with a reduction in preference gap. This is thus another negative feedback loop.

Shareholders employ some agents in terms of board members. Board members recruit an agent as chief executive officer. The CEO employs a number of top executives. Top executives recruit middle managers. Thus, principals and agents work at different levels of corporate hierarchy, and some are both in the role of principal in one relationship and in the role of agent in another relationship.

Not only agents can abuse their positions. Principals can also abuse their positions. The model in Figure 5.1 might function also in the study of white-collar crime by principals, for example board members. By causing large gaps in preferences and risks, while reducing the knowledge gap, executives' organizational opportunity drops, while board members themselves can create opportunities for themselves.

Principals expect agents to make decisions in the best interest of the principals. However, due to agency problems, agents may not make decisions in the best interest of principals. On the contrary, agents may be succumbed to self-interest, opportunistic behavior and ignorance of both reasonable and unreasonable requests from principals.

Generally, corruption and other forms of economic crime are in agency theory considered the consequence of the principal's inability to control and prevent the agent from abusing his or her position for personal gain (Li and Ouyang, 2007). However, the principal may as well be the criminal. For example, the CFO may provide inside information to a board member who abuses the information for insider trading. The point here is that the principal and the agent have different roles in an organizational context, where they both have little information about each other's activities.

While occupational crime is an agency problem where the criminal abuses agency roles for personal benefit, corporate crime is a structural problem where the enterprise is to benefit. Most countries' jurisdictions make a similar distinction between a natural person (individual) and a juridical person (organization), and demand criminal liability in terms of prison versus fine.

Agency theory is a management theory often applied to crime, where normally the agent, rather than the principal, is in danger of committing crime. White-collar crime is thus illegal and unethical actions usually by agents of organizations (Vadera and Aguilera, 2015). There is an opportunity for the white-collar offender to carry out the regular job at the same time as crime is committed, because the principal is unable to monitor what the agent is doing, what knowledge the agent applies, and what risk the agent is willing to take (Chrisman et al., 2007; Li and Ouyang, 2007; Williams, 2008). Agency theory argues that the principal is unable to control the agent because of lack of insight and access to activities performed by the agent in roles such as mayor, chairperson, or CEO (Eisenhardt, 1989; Garoupa, 2007).

Dynamic models presented so far in this book derive from system dynamics modeling, where cause-and-effect relationships as well as causal loops determine the extent of financial motive, the extent of organizational opportunity, and the extent of personal willingness for deviant behavior over time. System dynamics is a methodology to frame, understand and discuss complex issues and problems. The methodology can help understand phenomena like white-collar crime occurrences by modeling causes and effects linked to such occurrences. The basis of the system dynamics approach is the recognition that the structure of any system and the many circular, interlocking, and time-delayed relationships among its components determine motives, opportunities and willingness, rather than each component itself (Randers, 2019; Sterman, 2018). Feedback loops are the recursive, repeated and iterative cycles of interactions among factors that influence motive, opportunity, and willingness for white-collar crime.

Organizational dynamics is the interplay among factors that determine organizational behavior over time. Factors create, extend, or modify organizational opportunity for white-collar crime. Organizational dynamics result from continuous changes in a number of interlocked variables (Pitelis and Wagner, 2019). As already mentioned, an organization is a system of coordinated actions among individuals and groups with boundaries and goals (Puranam, 2014). Dynamic performance models propose that opportunity evolves as people's abilities, learning, and other differences change (Christian et al., 2015).

# 6 Markets and Networks

The final topic in Figure 1.3 is collapse from rule complexity preventing compliance (Lehman et al., 2020), participation in crime networks such as cartels (Nielsen, 2003), and financial crime as the usual way of business in markets with crime forces (Chang et al., 2005). Collapse represents a convenient situation for everybody ready to commit white-collar crime. Antitrust is here an important perspective for both bottom-up and outside-in efforts to prevent collapse and restore ethical business performance. Antitrust refers to laws, regulations, guidelines, and other measures that encourage competition by limiting the power of any particular firm and by preventing deviant executives from pursuing the route of crime networks such as cartels with other businesses in the same industry. An example mentioned by Edelman (2021) is the airline industry in the United States where there is an oligopoly of four major airlines. Antitrust is not only a matter of compliance at the organizational level but also at the national and global leve as "a global consensus has emerged recognizing the central role that competition law plays in promoting a nation's prosperity" (Yoo et al., 2021: 843).

## Reduction in Rule Complexity

Rule complexity can create a situation where nobody is able to tell whether an action represented a criminal offense. It is impossible to understand what is right and what is wrong. Some laws, rules and regulations are so complex that compliance becomes random, where compliance is the action of complying with laws, rules and regulations. The regulatory legal environment is supposed to define the boundaries of appropriate organizational conduct. However, legal complexity is often so extreme that even specialist compliance officers struggle to understand what to recommend to business executives in the organizations (Lehman et al., 2020). Then regulatory inspection does not work for compliance (Braithwaite, 2020). Business executives can thus find the large grey zone in legal matters a convenient space for misconduct and crime. This is especially so when operating internationally and globally where states do not agree on what should be legal and illegal activities (Boghossian and Marques, 2019; Pontell et al., 2020). Eberlein (2019) argues that globalization opens markets for corporations but outstrip the capacity of states to regulate and enforce laws on cross-border business conduct for the public good. Similarly, Schneider and Scherer (2019: 1147) argue, "The extent to which state authorities can regulate the externalities and the behavior of multinational corporations is limited", and "Gaps in governance abound in today's globalized world". There is an erosion of state power and a shift towards private regulation. National

https://doi.org/10.1515/9783110986686-007

governments collectively are taking limited initiatives through the OECD, European Union, United Nations and other multinational organizations.

Maher et al. (2019) found that governments not just in global business, but also in local business are reluctant to intervene. They observed an ambiguity of the state to involve itself. This is in line with the observation by Pontell et al. (2014) that some companies are too big to fail, and some white-collar offenders are too powerful to jail.

When rule complexity is linked to anomie in the sense of low commitment to mainstream rules in the organization (Schoepfer and Piquero, 2006); then the organizational opportunity for financial crime is further enhanced. The organization is reluctant to follow mainstream rules that are too complicated. The reluctance becomes stronger when mainstream rules will harm business performance. Trying to follow the law may result in inefficient business practices that depress organizational results and hurt careers of organizational members. Noncompliance might allow the corporation to be more profitable than competitors who follow the rules.

## Avoidance of Crime Networks

Monopolies, cartels and crime networks do not only represent threats in the motivational dimension of convenience theory (Chang et al., 2005; Geest et al., 2017). For deviant members of the elite, monopolies, cartels and crime networks can represent attractive avenues for extra profits (Freiberg, 2020; Goncharov and Peter, 2019). Participation in criminal networks can be attractive (Nielsen, 2003), especially if criminogenic market symptoms cause markets with crime forces to be the usual way of doing business (Chang et al., 2005).

The final topic of collapse in Figure 1.3 is concerned with organizational opportunity for white-collar crime from interactions with the external environment. Rule complexity, crime networks, and deviance by other actors externally are all factors that can enhance the convenience for white-collar offenders internally. An additional perspective here is situational action suggesting that crime is a social and behavioral outcome of interactions between human beings and their environments. What the right or wrong thing to do or avoid doing in a situation depends on the interaction of internal and external factors (Kessler and Reinecke, 2021). Interaction with the external situation might enable a potential offender to perceive more deviant alternatives for action (Kroneberg and Schultz, 2018; Liu et al. 2020). The situational action perspective addresses how environments shape crime opportunities and, subsequently, how modifications in environments can increase criminal opportunities (Huisman and Erp, 2013). When the situational action perspective by Wikstrom et al. (2018) distinguishes between three stages, (1) perception of action alternatives (legal alternatives, illegal alternatives), (2) process of choice (habit, rational deliberation), and (3) action, then Kroneberg and Schultz (2018) conceptualize lack of self-control as well as lack of deterrence on the axis from (2) to (3). The latter items belong in the willingness dimension of convenience. The situational action perspective aims to integrate personal and environmental explanatory perspectives within the framework of a situation. Kleinewiese (2020: 1) expanded the situational action theory (SAT) to groups:

> Building upon previous literature on social cohesion in groups (such as team spirit / esprit de corps); the group present in the setting is presumably more likely to be identified by the individual if such group cohesiveness is high. When perceived, the moral norms of the group and deterrence should have an influence through becoming part of the setting in the causation of crime, according to SAT. This application suggests that SAT is a fruitful approach for explaining the impacts of groups on crime.

As cited above, Aguilera and Vadera (2008: 434) describe a criminal opportunity as "the presence of a favorable combination of circumstances that renders a possible course of action relevant". Coleman (1987: 409) describes an opportunity as any "potential course of action, made possible by a particular set of social conditions, which has been symbolically incorporated into an actor's repertoire of behavioral possibilities". Figures 1.2 and 1.3 illustrate circumstances and conditions such as status and access to commit crime; and decay, chaos and collapse to conceal crime.

## Combat of Criminal Market Forces

As mentioned earlier in this book, Sutherland (1983) emphasized attitudes in society where people consider white-collar crime as less serious than traditional street crime. While convenience theory so far emphasizes factors at the individual and organizational level, Sutherland (1983) emphasized hypotheses at the community level. In its earlier version, convenience theory was lacking explicit representations of community level factors such as criminal market structures including competition-avoiding cartels (Goncharov and Peter, 2019) and corruption networks (Nielsen, 2003).

In its current version, convenience theory applies three levels of analysis. In addition to the individual and the organization as units of analysis, the community is the unit of analysis mainly in an opportunity perspective. Community level factors such as corruption networks enable individuals and organizations to commit and conceal white-collar crime. At the community level, the focus is not on the isolated individual act of providing a bribe or receiving a bribe, but rather "the systematic, pervasive sub-system of bribery that can and has existed across historical periods, geographic areas, and political-economic systems" (Nielsen, 2003: 125). If the third level of criminal market structures is defined as the individual perceptions of structures rather than the actual structures, then the extent of criminal market structures can vary with white-collar offenders.

While cartels can represent painful corporate economic threats as discussed earlier in economical dimension of convenience theory, a cartel can represent an opportunity for those enterprises that have joined the cartel. In many markets, there are cartels that regulate the supply side. Cartel members agree not only on market division but also on prices to various customers (Goncharov and Peter, 2019).

The social exchange perspective aids explanations of how power structures in cartels and corruption networks develop and institutionalize through relationship building and social exchanges among participating enterprises. The perspective suggests that organizational activities are contingent on the actions of other organizations. The successful cartels and networks are dependent on generation of obligations and fulfillment of rewards. Relational efforts in an industry or in a community lead to repeated patterns of interactions that may develop into durable institutions of interdependencies in cartels and networks (Cropanzano and Mitchell, 2005; Lawler and Hipp, 2010).

Cartels and corruption networks are important to many global business enterprises. When the corruption case at Siemens became public, Murphy and Dacin (2011) found that the business climate encouraged corruption and fraudulent behavior as normal and acceptable. To cope with the scandal, Siemens replaced its management board (Berghoff, 2018: 423):

> Siemens is one of the world's leading electrical engineering corporations. In 2006, a massive corruption scandal erupted, concluded in 2008 with a record fine. For Siemens the largest risk was being barred from government contracts. As a consequence, it replaced virtually its entire managing board, an unprecedented procedure in the history of the company.

However, the criminal market structures did not change. Siemens thus "thrived in the cozy world of national monopolies and cartels, which guaranteed high margins and no worries about rivals" (Berghoff, 2018: 425). While the new management at Siemens attempted trust repair among stakeholders by introducing updates rules and guidelines, Eberl et al. (2015: 1205) found that the new rules were paradoxical in nature and thus difficult to implement in practice:

> Our findings suggest that tightening organizational rules is an appropriate signal of trustworthiness for external stakeholders to demonstrate that the organization seriously intends to prevent integrity violations in the future. However, such rule adjustments were the source of dissatisfaction among employees since the new rules were difficult to implement in practice. We argue that these different impacts of organizational rules result from their inherent paradoxical nature.

After a white-collar scandal, many companies attempt window dressing by introducing new rules for their employees. However, the new rules do not necessarily apply to those levels in the organization where you find the criminals. For example, when top executives at the Norwegian company Yara were charged with corruption, and one of them ended up in prison, the company introduced new anti-corruption rules that did not apply to the top executives. They continued to enjoy the freedom of choice in their business decisions. The chief compliance officer continued to report to an executive whose predecessor in the position ended up in jail.

## Victims of Cartel Crime Activities

Cartels are associations of independent corporations in the same industry that strive to reduce competition. When competitors join forces in controlling a market, then excluded competitors as well as customers of the cartel participants become victims (Freiberg, 2020; Goncharov and Peter, 2019; Nielsen, 2003). A bottom-up approach to executive deviance among cartel members would be to blow the whistle on white-collar crime. An alternative is the outside-in approach where outsiders notice and report wrongdoing. For example, customers may notice that the prices are extremely high, or they may notice that some vendors are reluctant to provide supplies since there are other vendors assigned to those customers by the cartel agreement.

Cartels are illegal associations of corporations who cooperate rather than compete on the same markets. Cartel members enter into agreements where they divide markets among themselves, decide on pricing, and agree on production quotas for each member. The purpose is to avoid competition to increase profits without a need for efficiency, effectiveness, and innovation. Customers of cartel members suffer by paying too much for goods and services of inferior quality (Bertrand and Lumineau, 2016; Jaspers, 2020). If cartel is the name of the game in an industry, the only way to survive might be to join the cartel, where cartel members divide markets among themselves (Freiberg, 2020; Goncharov and Peter, 2019; Nielsen, 2003).

When the Soviet Union turned partly into Russia and the iron curtain in East Europe fell down, then many west-European companies wanted to approach the Russian market. One of them was a small Norwegian ABB subsidiary that was in the business of producing signaling cables for car and computer manufacturers. In every BMW car there was one meter of cable produced in Norway, and in many Siemens computers, there was a short piece of cable produced in Norway. When approaching the Russian market, meetings in Moscow with interested parties were quite successful. However, when returning to Norway, the sales approach was stopped by the headquarters in Switzerland. Norwegians were told that they were not allowed to approach the Russian market. The Russian market belonged to the Finnish cable producer Nokia. In return, Nokia stayed away from Sweden and Norway, while ABB stayed away from Finland as well as Russia. This came as no surprise to the Norwegian subsidiary, since they already knew that the local cable market in Norway was divided between ITT (later Alcatel) and ABB, where some wholesalers were customers of ITT, while other wholesalers were customers of ABB.

It was no surprise to the Norwegians also because they had the same experience in other parts of the cable market. Just like they themselves were part of a cartel in the cable market, they knew that their customers were part of cartels as well. When they sold cables for electricity rather than for signals, large construction entrepreneurs such as Skanska (Landre, 2006), Peab (Gedde-Dahl et al., 2007), Veidekke (Landre, 2006; Lilleås, 2011), NCC (Landre, 2006; Lilleås, 2011), AF Group (Brandvol, 2016), and others did not really compete with each other. When the main airport in Norway at Gardermoen outside the capital of Oslo was expanded, the costs far exceed forecasts because of cartel activity. Similarly, when the Norwegian parliament buildings in Oslo were renovated and expanded, the costs far exceeded forecasts because of cartel activity. It was expended that the same would be the case when the new government center in Oslo should be rebuilt in the late 2020ies after the terrorist attack in 2011. The named companies had experienced some minor fines and lenience in exchange for cartel confessions to Norwegian regulatory authorities (Lilleås, 2011). One frequent cartel pricing approach is to agree among cartel members on who is next in line. That business provides a very expensive offer to the customer. The other cartel members provide offers as well, but they price their offers even higher than the business that is next in line (Goncharov and Peter, 2019).

The chief executive at ABB from 1988 to 2002 was the Swede Percy Barnevik stationed in Zürich in Switzerland. After Barnevik's resignation, he became the center of a giant pension dispute that shook Sweden in 2003. When the new ABB board made the pension payment public, Barnevik was forced to resign from other positions and return a large fraction of his pension to ABB (Shah, 2002). A few years earlier, researchers compared ABB's Percy Barnevik to Virgin's Richard Branson in terms of charisma in action by transformational abilities (Vries, 1998) as one of the new global leaders (Katz, 1999). Barnevik's fall from grace was thus very steep.

A cartel is an association of independent firms in the same industry that strive to reduce competition by agreeing on areas such as market sharing, pricing levels, and production quotas. A cartel is collective misconduct of firms (Bertrand and Lumineau, 2016: 983):

> Instead of competing with one another, cartel members rely on each other's agreed course of action. Consequently, these underhanded agreements reduce the member firms' incentives to provide new or better products and services at competitive prices. Their clients (other businesses or final consumers) ultimately pay more for lower quality. Final consumers observe a reduction in their welfare, and businesses suffer from more expensive inputs. By artificially decreasing the natural level of competition in the market, cartels decrease the overall competitiveness not only of the cartelized industry but also of other industries. The damage to customers and other businesses can thus be significant, particularly when cartels are able to last for years.

Bertrand and Lumineau (2016) studied cartels that were prosecuted between 2001 and 2011 by the Directorate General for Competition within the European Commission. The directorate is responsible for enforcing the European antitrust regime. The sample consisted of 41 cartels with 463 members. The study purpose was to understand the variety of age-based experience, the separation in uncertainty avoidance, and the power disparity in cartels. The study found evidence that the diversity of members involved in cartels is a critical factor of the longevity of such secret activity. The cartels with the longest lifetime until detected and prosecuted were characterized by a high variety of age-based experience, by cultural similarity, and by one firm being the leader in each cartel. Cartels survived for a shorter period of time when group members had similar backgrounds, did not share the same values, and did not have a leader to manage the group.

Markets with crime forces can represent painful corporate economic threats. In many markets, there are cartels that regulate the supply side. A cartel is an implicit agreement between firms in the same industry to fix prices, to divide customers and markets among themselves, to fix industry outputs, to allocate territories, or to divide profits (Goncharov and Peter, 2019: 152):

> Cartel members seek to act collectively, as if they were a single monopolist, thereby maximizing the collective profit. By doing so, cartels violate competition policy and severely reduce consumer welfare through price-fixing activities that increase the price of goods far beyond the competitive level. Recent evidence shows that the average price overcharges by cartels prosecuted by U.S. and EU cartel authorities were 48.4 and 32.2 percent, respectively.

Supply to some customers occurs only from some vendors, while supply to other customers occurs only from other vendors in the cartel. There is only symbolic competition between vendors as far as they all seem to offer their products to all potential customers. Cartel members agree not only on market division but also on prices to various customers. When a public procurement officer asks for offers from all potential vendors, they may all provide an offer. However, they have agreed who is next in line by determining the relative price offer among themselves. The vendor next in line provides an expensive offer to the public procurement officer, while the remaining vendors provide offers that are even more expensive to the public procurement officer.

In Norway, large construction projects for the government and municipalities tend to suffer from cost overruns, where responsible politicians and bureaucrats typically have to leave their positions while there is suspicion of cartel arrangements among construction firms that drive construction projects into cost overruns. When the University of Oslo was to expand its campus in 2021, the construction project became almost twice as expensive as calculated in advance (Pettrem, 2021). In the city of Oslo where a substantial cost overrun occurred when developing a reserve water source for all six hundred thousand inhabitants, the top politician Lan Marie Berg, in the position of environmental council, had to resign from her post (Lønnebotn, 2021):

–Before we talk about Lan Marie Berg and the water supply case, I would first like to say: "Why is the cost overrun so large? My hypothesis is that there is a cartel".

Petter Gottschalk, an economist and professor at BI Norwegian Business School, has followed the case of Oslo's new reserve water supply closely. This week it became known that the construction work will be NOK 5.2 billion more expensive than estimated, and city councilor Lan Marie Berg had to resign for not having informed the city council well enough.

–A cartel is not price collaboration, as many believe. Cartel activity means that you share the market and contracts among cartel members. Whose turn is it now? The cartel members agree, and the company in question submits an expensive tender. The other cartel members, the "competitors", then submit even more expensive tenders. We saw this when the airport at Gardermoen was expanded, and the budget cracked. And it was repeated in the expansion of the Norwegian parliament Stortinget. Even when one is annoyed that it will become more expensive, other contractors would put themselves even higher in price. Cartel activities are incredibly widespread in Norway, and I will not be surprised if the construction of the new government quarter becomes twice as expensive as estimated. Due to cartel activities, many construction enterprises have been fined for cartel activities over the years, but they continue like before, since the fines are so low.

–But this is a criminal offense, isn't it?

–Yes, when competitors communicate with each other and make agreements that affect the free market, then it is a criminal offense. But the Norwegian competition authority (Konkurransetilsynet) does not have the competence to investigate such matters, and the National authority for investigation and prosecution of economic and environmental crime in Norway (Økokrim) does not prioritize them, so it happens over again and again. The chief executive at the Storting had to leave after the budget gap there, and now Lan Marie Berg has to leave her position in Oslo.

Being a member of a cartel is illegal in most countries, yet they exist all over the world. Trying to operate outside a cartel in an industry can be painful and impossible to survive. To stay in the industry, businesses have to adapt to the usual way of business in markets with crime forces. In some markets, there is no other choice but to break the law. If a cartel completely dominates a market, then a new entrant may perceive no other choice but to join the cartel and cooperate with others on price fixing and other illegal activities. The market is such that the only way to survive is to implement financial practices similar to the ones applied by competitors. If corruption is the name of the game, every corporation in the industry has to provide bribes to stay in business.

Secrecy and concealment are at the center of cartel activities preventing detection (Bertrand and Lumineau, 2016). Therefore, Jaspers (2020) found that cartel confessions are an essential source for competition authorities in uncovering cartels. Confessions can be attractive to cartel members when leniency offers corporations the possibility to come clean about their involvement in cartels. A confessing cartel member can achieve immunity from competition authorities, especially if the cartel member is the first to notify authorities of that particular cartel and if authorities had no ongoing suspicion or investigation against the cartel.

# 7 Corporate Case Studies

The bottom-up approach to prevention and detection of white-collar crime in organizations by privileged individuals is exemplified by case studies in this chapter.

## Embezzlement by Chief Executive

This case of a bottom-up approach to executive convenience is concerned with a chief executive officer (CEO) who committed embezzlement in the organization. Two employees in the organization noticed deviant executive behavior and notified the chairperson on the board about the misconduct. The chairperson at first did not believe the allegations against the CEO, since the CEO was a well-respected priest and businessperson. When the two employees threatened to notify the media if the board did not react, then the chairperson confronted the chief executive with the accusations. After a while, the CEO admitted fraud.

The CEO had a convenient financial motive, a convenient organizational opportunity, and a convenient personal willingness for deviant behavior. With embezzled money, he could afford an apartment in Spain where he had parties with local prostitutes. He was alone in charge of money transfers to Spain, so there was no control. He found himself entitled to spend some company money and live a different life in Spain than he could not allow himself at home in Norway.

The CEO, Are Blomhoff, had studied religion and business administration. He quickly climbed the ranks at the foundation Betanien, which is owned by the Methodist Church. The foundation operates a number of nursing homes for elderly, kindergartens for children, and health care services in the city of Bergen in Norway. Blomhoff quickly climbed in the ranks at Betanien as he was able to obtain government funding for a number of projects and received international recognition as he collaborated on projects in Israel, Estonia, and other places. He was well known and well respected in many religious institutions (Ellingsen, 2015; Johnsen, 2013).

Blomhoff climb to the top of the organization where he had a close and trusted relationship with Christian Hysing-Dahl, the chairperson of the board at the foundation. He developed a business idea of establishing a nursing home in Spain where retired and sick Norwegians could stay in a climate more suitable for treatment and recovery, and where manpower costs and other operating expenses are far lower than at home. Blomhoff personally took on the project and arranged for money transfers from Norway to Spain to finance property purchase and construction work. He was in charge of causing money transfers from Norway, and he was the only person who had authority to withdraw money at the bank in Spain. The two employees who were involved in the project noticed that Blomhoff privately did strange things, but they had no evidence of the money that he spent originating from corporate funds.

https://doi.org/10.1515/9783110986686-008

They only suspected Blomhoff of financial wrongdoing and went with their suspicions to Hysing-Dahl.

Money for the construction project originated at Betanien's bank account in Norway and ended up in Betanien's bank account in Spain. Blomhoff was in charge at both sides, as he initiated transfers of money and confirmed receipt of money. While auditors in Norway thought auditors in Spain would review money transfers, auditors in Spain believed auditors in Norway would review accounts. Nobody else but Blomhoff was involved in financial matters regarding the Spanish project (Riis and Øverland, 2018).

Blomhoff faced an opportunity for white-collar crime in the form of embezzlement. There was an opportunity that simply invited Blomhoff to take advantage of his privileges while in Spain. He knew that it was wrong and that it was bad, but the opportunity was so attractive that violating the law became an obvious choice for him as an offender.

At first, he embezzled some money as he bought himself a private apartment in Spain, where the embezzled money helped finance his apartment. Next, he arranged parties that looked more and more like orgies, where he recruited prostitutes to participate. He developed a drinking problem, but stayed at work (Buanes, 2015).

When he returned to Norway on business trips, he was sober and behaved like a priest, executive, and family man. He developed two different kinds of lifestyle, one for Norway and another one for Spain.

Two employees at Betanien observed Blomhoff's wrongdoing and wanted to blow the whistle on him. They got in touch with the chairperson at the foundation, Christian Hysing-Dahl, but he would simply not believe them. When the whistleblowers threatened to tell investigative journalists in a major Norwegian newspaper (Gustafsson, 2015), Hysing-Dahl hired auditing firm BDO (2014) to conduct a fraud examination. At the same time, Hysing-Dahl confronted Blomhoff with the allegations, and Blomhoff confessed a minor amount that he had embezzled (Johansen, 2015; Riis and Øverland, 2018). As fraud examiners from BDO (2014) detected larger amounts, then Blomhoff confessed those as well. In 2015, Blomhoff received a sentence in a Norwegian district court of three years in prison for embezzlement (Drammen tingrett, 2015). Two months later, Hysing Dahl resigned from the chair of the board together with most of the other board members (Johansen, 2015; Nakling, 2015).

As illustrated in Figure 7.1, Blomhoff's motive was individual possibilities in the form of greed to enjoy a deviant lifestyle in Spain. He had access to resources to commit crime, and the lack of guardianship represented chaos to conceal crime. As discussed by Desmond et al. (2022), people within religious organizations are not subject to much surveillance or accountability mechanisms:

> The organizational component is particularly influential for crimes within religious organizations; religious staff is often considered by others to have specialized knowledge and to be the

epitome of trustworthy and, therefore, these individuals are not subject to much surveillance or accountability mechanisms.

It was a rational choice by Blomhoff to commit financial crime, as he believed nobody would detect or blow the whistle on his wrongdoing. If someone did, he thought the foundation board would not believe what others told them about him. He neutralized potentially guilt feelings by feeling sorry for himself.

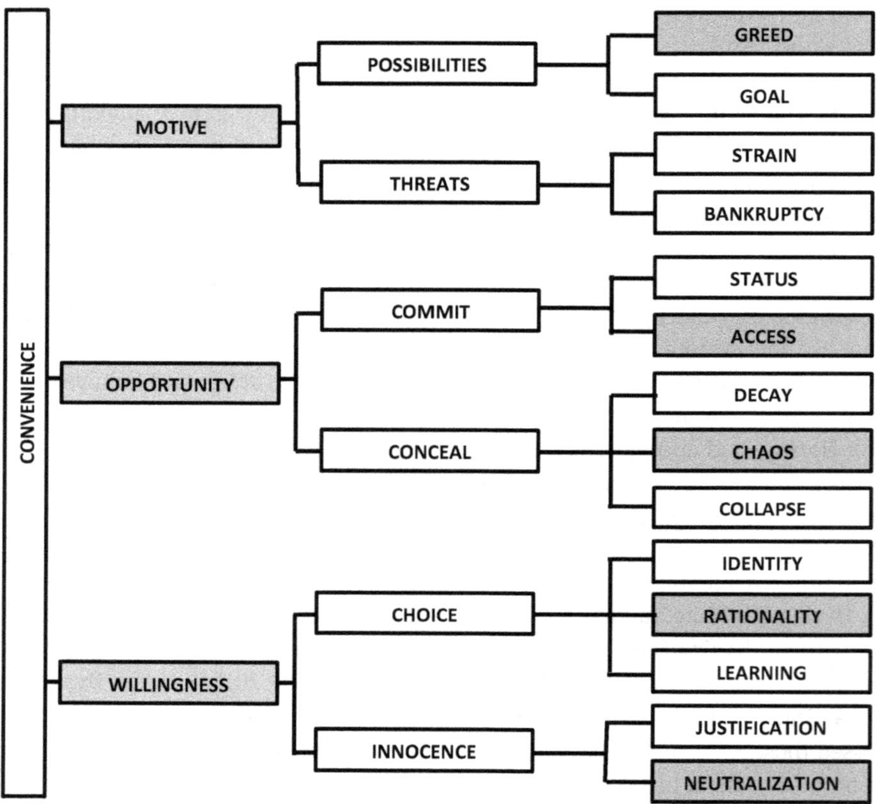


**Figure 7.1:** Convenience themes in the case of Are Blomhoff.

## Accounting Fraud by Chairperson

The Olympus Corporation's board of directors removed in 2011 the newly appointed chief executive Michael C. Woodford. He had been pointing out for some time inappropriate transactions conducted by his predecessor Tsuyoshi Kikukawa who now occupied the chair on the board. Woodford had questioned fees in excess of $1 billion that Olympus aid to obscure companies, which appeared to serve the purpose of hiding old losses, and appeared to have organized crime connections.

When the Olympus scandal became known, the corporate reputation collapsed, and the company's stock market valuation fell by 80 percent. Olympus Corporation is a manufacturer of technology products based in Japan. Kikukawa had to resign as chairperson when the scandal became public, and he was one of three Olympus defendants in court in 2013.

When Woodford confronted Kikukawa with the emerging scandal, Kikukawa disliked it strongly (Deloitte, 2011: 146):

> When Woodford pointed out the incident as an obvious scandal, and asked for the resignation of officers, such as Kikukawa, the directors did not verify the substance that was pointed out, and in siding with Kikukawa, who was the chairman, that they agreed to the dismissal of Woodford from the representative director position.

There is evidence of involvement from Kikukawa when only three people had authorization to move funds among acquired firms in 2009: Kikukawa, Yamada and Mori. The same three executives were defendants in a Japanese court four years later.

Olympus had violated the Financial Instruments and Exchange Act and the Companies Act, and soon board members had to resign. The police in Japan arrested eleven past and present Japanese directors, senior managers, auditors, and bankers for alleged criminal activities. Prosecutors said they believed the former chairperson Tsuyoshi Kikukawa – who had also been chief executive before Woodford – was the main architect of the fraud scheme (Soble and Nakamoto, 2012).

British newspaper 'The Guardian' interviewed former Olympus chief executive Michael Woodford as the man who blew the whistle on a fraud of one billion pounds (Neate, 2012):

> He first got wind of the claims just weeks after taking over as chief executive – the first foreigner, or *gaijin*, to run the company, and only the fourth at any major Japanese company – when a friend emailed him a translation of "amazingly detailed" claims published in Facta, a local magazine with a campaigning remit similar to Private Eye.
>
> "When I got to the office, I expected everyone to be talking about it. But no one mentioned it". By lunchtime he summoned two of his most trusted colleagues and asked them if they had read it. They had, but said that Tsuyoshi Kikukawa, Olympus's previous CEO and then chairman, had "told them not to tell me". Eventually Woodford demanded a meeting with Kikukawa and Hisashi Mori, then deputy president and "Kikukawa's permanent sidekick".

The purpose of the following investigation by Deloitte (2011) was to find out whether there was any fraudulent or inappropriate conduct or unreasonable business judgment on the part of Olympus. They should focus especially on acquisitions and other related transactions. Examiners searched through documents and conducted 189 interviews. Interviewees included executives and employees of Olympus, including some who had retired. Where considered necessary, examiners interviewed accounting auditors as well as persons who had been in charge of the companies that were involved in the securities investments in question. The focus of attention was deferred losses related to investment securities.

In the 185-pages report, Deloitte (2011: 185) draw the following conclusion:

> Due to the discovery of the fraudulent accounting over many years lead by top management, the credibility of Olympus has been tarnished. The extraordinariness of the misconduct in this case and course leading to its discovery delivered a blow to stakeholders such as the shareholders, good ordinary investors, and business partners, and it is extremely regrettable that it has affected in no small way the trust of many Japanese corporations that are engaged in honest management. However, Olympus was originally a sound company with earnest employees and strong technical capabilities, and the misconduct was carried out by the entire company. Olympus should remove the seat of disease centered on the old management, and literally renew itself in heart and mind.

Deloitte (2011) mentioned Tsuyoshi Kikukawa 88 times in their 185-pages report. Kikukawa became chief executive at Olympus in June 2001. Soon after, he published management policies covering five years. In the document, Kikukawa defined targets of 1 trillion yen sales and 110 billion yen operating income.

Examiners argue that Kikukawa was aware of a loss separation scheme to dispose of unrealized losses on financial assets, a scheme that he inherited from his predecessor. Examiners' evidence is a document dated September 12, 2003, prepared by the chief financial officer and addressed to four people including Kikukawa. The report includes categories of deposits, bonds, investment trusts, and disbursements. It is an interesting question whether a chief executive must read all documents received. It is imaginable that the overload of documents sent from anywhere is simply too much for a chief executive to read and understand. For a chief executive, a sender of information cannot require or expect the chief executive as a receiver to familiarize him or her with all information provided. It might be argued that a chief executive has to read whatever comes from a chief financial officer, but even that is not necessarily so. When a document ends up at three other executives, the chief executive can assume that others will read it and potentially raise issues from the document with the chief executive where appropriate. Therefore, the document as claimed by examiners is no solid evidence of Kikukawa's knowledge of the fraudulent scheme. The following conclusion regarding reports from the chief financial officer seems thus unfounded (Deloitte, 2011: 19):

> This means that Shimoyama, Kishimoto, Kikukawa and Ota were keeping a regular watch on the status of the unrealized losses and the administration of the funds that included the unrealized losses.

There is no evidence in the report that other executives briefed Kikukawa about the disposition of the unrealized losses, although Deloitte (2011) claims briefing occurred.

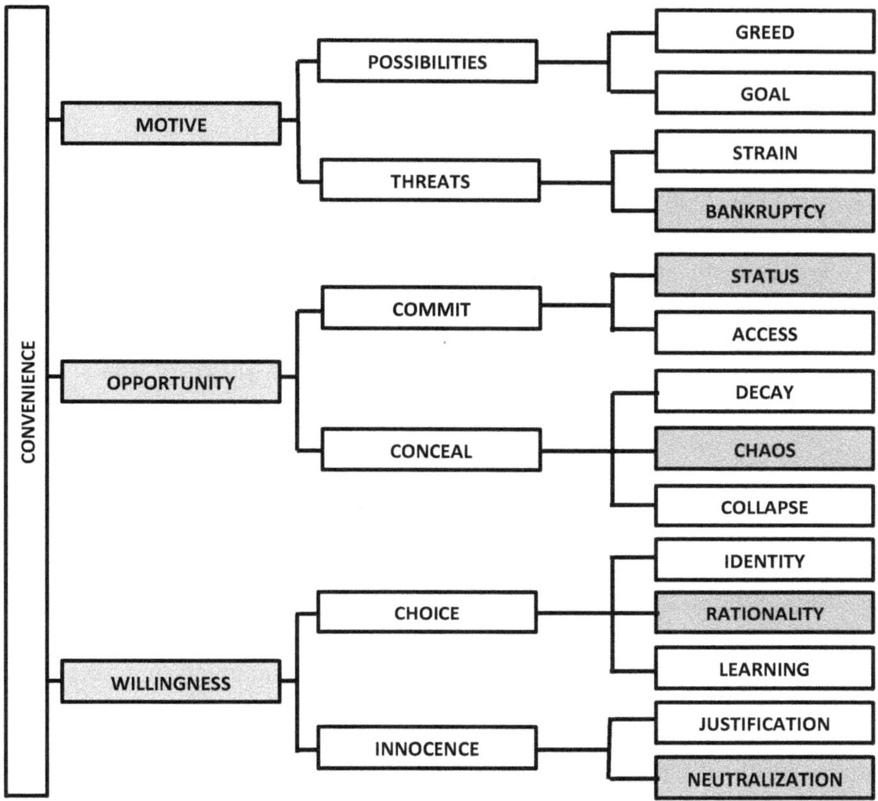


**Figure 7.2:** Convenience themes in the case of Tsuyoshi Kikukawa.

Another allegation against Kikukawa regards a fraudulent business investment fund, where examiners claim that Kikukawa was "the officer in charge of this topic". Again, there is no evidence. Examiners may claim that Kikukawa should have been in charge, but they have no evidence of him actually handling the fund. Typically, a chief executive handles few or no topic alone.

Maybe it is matter of translation from Japanese to English, but it is not convincing that "the members comprising the committee are said to have been" (Deloitte, 2011: 31). This is again an implication of Kikukawa's direct involvement if what is "said to have been" is actually facts.

More solid evidence of Kikukawa's involvement occurs in the minutes from a board of director's meeting in 2008, where Kikukawa in the meantime had become the chair. "In the end, the chairman (Kikukawa) asked, would that be all right, and since there were no opinions of absolute opposition, it was approved" (Deloitte, 2011: 45).

An interesting kind of evidence is the signature of Kikukawa. Some chief executives sign contracts and other documents that trusted colleagues present to them.

Based on trust, some chief executives sign without reading, especially if the document is a dozen or more pages long. Examiners presents Kikukawa's signature as evidence of his knowledge of the contents. "Kikukawa signed the contract as the representative of Olympus", or it "had the seals of Kikukawa" (Deloitte, 2011: 50, 54, 56, 60, 64). The role of his signature versus his knowledge is more evident in the quote stating that; "Mori immediately obtained Kikukawa's signature" (Deloitte, 2011: 65). Here Mori obtained a signature probably based on personal trust rather than review of the document.

Kikukawa's motive was corporate gain from reputation threats and investor uncertainty as illustrated in Figure 7.2. His status gave him convenient opportunity, and chaos enabled convenient concealment of crime. Crime was a rational choice, where neutralization of guilt is possible by blaming higher loyalty to the corporation.

## Corruption by University Coach

In 2019, it became public knowledge that the FBI was investigating the so-called college scandal under the code name "Operation Varsity Blues". The FBI was tipped off by a financier they questioned in another case, about a coach at Yale who asked for bribes. The financier was probably the father of a student who told about rumors of corruption. It was thus another case of a bottom-up approach to detection of white-collar convenience.

The coach at Yale, Rudolph Meredith, chose to cooperate with the FBI, and further tipped off about Rick Singer – the man who orchestrated the scam that covered large parts of the scandal. Singer himself seized the opportunity to be early in the spotlight and collaborate by gathering evidence against the families and universities he had previously helped.

The college scandal was mainly about rich parents who bought college admissions for their children at prestigious universities in the United States, with payments hidden as donations. Test results and application forms were manipulated, and holes in the admissions systems were exploited to get the children admitted. As several of the cases occurred at the State University of California, an investigation was initiated into admission routines and processes, and whether those procedures could lead to exploitation for illegal acts. The schools investigators selected were four of the university campuses: UC Berkley, UC Los Angeles, UC San Diego, and UC Santa Barbara.

The University of California was investigated by the auditor of the state of California. The California state auditor found that qualified students faced an inconsistent and unfair admissions system that had been improperly influence by relationships and monetary donations (State Auditor, 2020). Several rich and mighty people were involved in the corruption scandal.

On May 22, 2020, actress Lori Anne Loughlin in Hollywood pleaded guilty to one count of conspiracy to commit wire and mail fraud. Her husband Mossimo Giannulli, an American fashion designer, pleaded guilty to one count of conspiracy to commit wire and mail fraud and honest services wire and mail fraud. On August 21, 2020, Loughlin was sentenced to two months in prison while her husband was sentenced to five months. They had committed federal program corruption by bribing employees of the University of California to facilitate their children's admission. In exchange for the bribes, employees at the university designated the couple's children as athletic recruits with little or no regard for their athletic abilities. The bribed university officials did assess officially that their two daughters were qualified for the women's rowing team although none of them had trained in the sport of rowing nor had plans to do so. Loughlin and Giannulli paid $500,000 in bribes for the corrupt university service (Puente, 2020; Taylor, 2020).

Rudolph Meredith was Yale women's soccer coach. He pleaded guilty and helped build the case against other coaches at various universities (Schlabach, 2019). Figure 7.3 illustrates convenience themes in his case. As a coach, he was responsible for securing funding to his team. The more funding and the more successful soccer games, the more money he would make for himself. It was thus a motive of possibilities both of the individual and the corporate types. Lack of oversight and guardianship at the university enabled concealment of the crime. It was a rational choice where guilt feelings could be neutralized by the claim of higher loyalty.

In the United States, it is great prestige to be a student at a highly ranked university. Admission assessment is based on the fact that there is a minimum requirement for grades and test results, but in addition, other factors are also assessed. In other words, it is not necessarily applicants with the best academic results that are accepted. Among the top universities, the heads of sports departments or coaches can make more money than university presidents. When economic factors and deficient processes are mixed, the result can be a major scandal.

The wealthy and influential actress Loughlin said in court that she acted out of love for her daughters. This is in line with the financial crime motive of social concern. Agnew (2014) introduced the motive of social concern and crime, where there is a desire to help others, and thus moving beyond the assumption of simple self-interest. However, as argued by Paternoster et al. (2018), helping others can be a self-interested, rational action that claims social concern. Social concern belongs to the convenience theme of motive-possibilities-individual as illustrated in Figure 7.4.

Agnew (2014) believes that social concern consists of four elements, namely that 1) individuals care about the welfare of others, 2) they want close ties with others, 3) they are likely to follow moral guidelines such as innocent people should not suffer harm, and 4) they tend to seek confirmation through other people's actions and norms. That a person puts others before oneself will initially lead to less crime. However, economic crime may be committed where the welfare of others and their success is the motive.

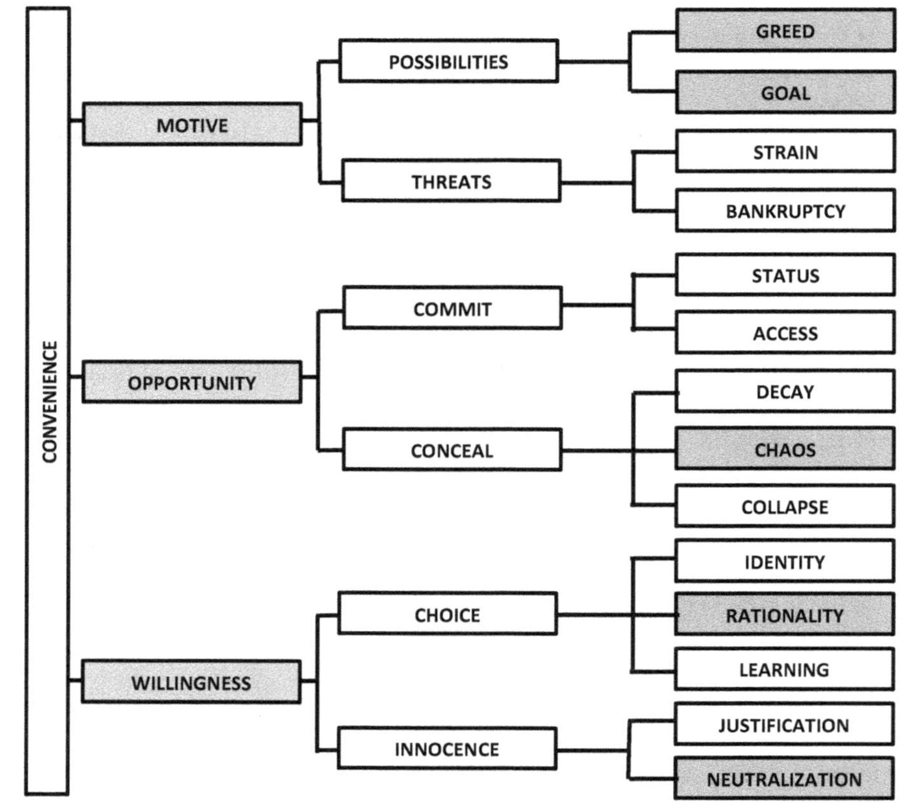


**Figure 7.3:** Convenience themes in the case of Rudolph Meredith.

In the opportunity dimension of convenience theory, actress Loughlin had high social status as indicated in Figure 7.4. Status is an individual's social rank within a formal or informal hierarchy, or the person's relative standing along a valued social dimension. Status is the extent to which an individual is respected and admired by others, and status is the outcome of a subjective assessment process (McClean et al., 2018). High-status individuals enjoy greater respect and deference from, as well as power and influence over, those who are positioned lower in the social hierarchy (Kakkar et al., 2020: 532):

> Status is a property that rests in the eyes of others and is conferred to individuals who are deemed to have a higher rank or social standing in a pecking order based on a mutually valued set of social attributes. Higher social status or rank grants its holder a host of tangible benefits in both professional and personal domains. For instance, high-status actors are sought by groups for advice, are paid higher, receive unsolicited help, and are credited disproportionately in joint tasks. In innumerable ways, our social ecosystem consistently rewards those with high status.

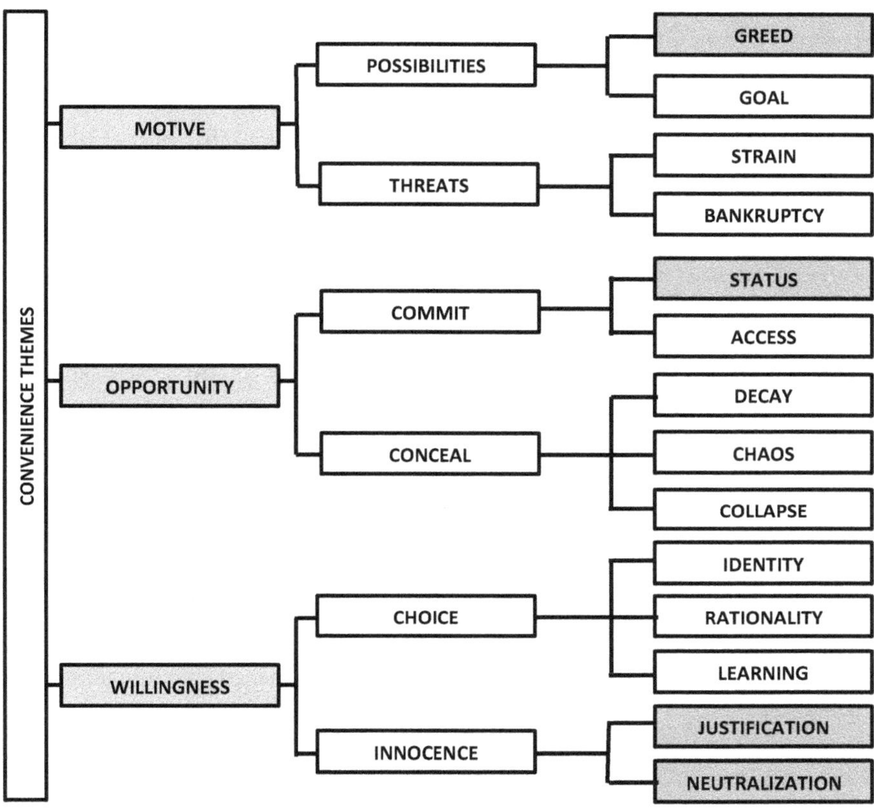


**Figure 7.4:** Convenience themes for Loughlin at the University of California.

Especially individuals with high status based on prestige rather than dominance tend to be excused for whatever wrongdoing they commit. Individuals who attain and maintain high rank by behaving in ways that are assertive, controlling, and intimidating are characterized as dominant. Individuals who attain and maintain high rank by their set of skills, knowledge, expertise, and their willingness to share these with others are characterized as prestigious (Kakkar et al., 2020).

The willingness of actress Lori Anne Loughlin to bribe university officials might derive from an innocence perspective of both justification and neutralization. She found the act of wrongdoing morally justifiable (Schnatterly et al., 2018), probably based on upper echelon information selection (Gamache and McNamara, 2019). She applied the neutralization technique number five presented earlier in this book: *Justify crime by higher loyalties: It was according to expectations*. The offender denies the act was motivated by self-interest, claiming that it was instead done out of obedience to some moral obligation (Sykes and Matza, 1957). The offender appeals to higher loyalties. Those who feel they are in a dilemma employ this technique to indicate that the dilemma must be resolved at the cost of violating a law or policy. In the context of an organization, an employee may appeal to organizational values or hierarchies. For example, an executive could argue that he or she has to violate a policy in order to get things done and achieve strategic objectives for the enterprise. Similarly, the actress felt an obligation to help her daughters into a respectable educational institution.

## Fraudulent Procurement by Executives

In the Norwegian municipality of Grimstad, a female employee left her position and started a health care services firm. Before she left, she made sure that the firm had a signed contract for delivery of services from the firm to the municipality. Her sister and brother-in-law stayed in their executive positions at the municipality (Karlsen, 2018). When procurements had risen to NOK 100 million (about USD 11 million), a manager in a different branch of the municipality noticed that no competition arrangement for alternative vendors of health care services had occurred. The newly hired municipal councilor did not want to intervene in the procurement process, and the municipal mayor said he knew nothing about it. Depending on whether politicians on the board in the municipality belonged to ruling parties or opposition parties, they were either against or in favor of an investigation into the alleged fraudulent procurement (Berg, 2016).

The manager in the branch different from the health care branch in the municipality informed opposition politicians about his findings. The newly hired municipal councilor got upset and tried to terminate the manager. Opposition politicians protected the manager and asked for an independent investigation into the allegations. As emphasized by Nesti (2014: 62), “public procurement is extremely vulnerable to instances of fraud, corruption and waste due to the amount of money circulating between the public and the private sector”.

The control committee in the municipality eventually decided to ask audit firm BDO (2016) to review the matter. Reviewers detected that relevant email accounts had been deleted or emptied shortly before the review started. Other relevant sources of information were also difficult to retrieve. Therefore, the examiners could draw no conclusions regarding the allegations of misconduct and potential crime. The police was reluctant to investigate the matter (Berg, 2017; Sved, 2018).

The election in 2019 changed the opposition parties to becoming the ruling parties. They asked the councilor to leave her position because of her reluctance to handle potential procurement fraud. In the meantime, both the sister and the brother-in-law had left their positions in the municipality (Karlsen, 2020). The whistleblowing manager was still in the municipality when the councilor was forced to leave her position and the organization in 2020 (Sved and Frigård, 2020). The following year, in 2021 at the age of 65 years old, the whistleblower decided to go for retirement, when the new mayor and the new councilor agreed to pay him financial compensation for his struggle and suffering for more than six years (Berg, 2021).

An executive convenience theme in the dimension of motive was concern for others. Family members inside the municipality wanted to help the sister start and prosper in her entrepreneurial activity of providing health care services to the municipality. Agnew (2014) argued that a financial motive for some offenders is to satisfy the desire to help others as social concern. The family members had access to resources as indicated in Figure 7.5. It was a rational choice of public procurement without inviting alternative vendors of health care services.

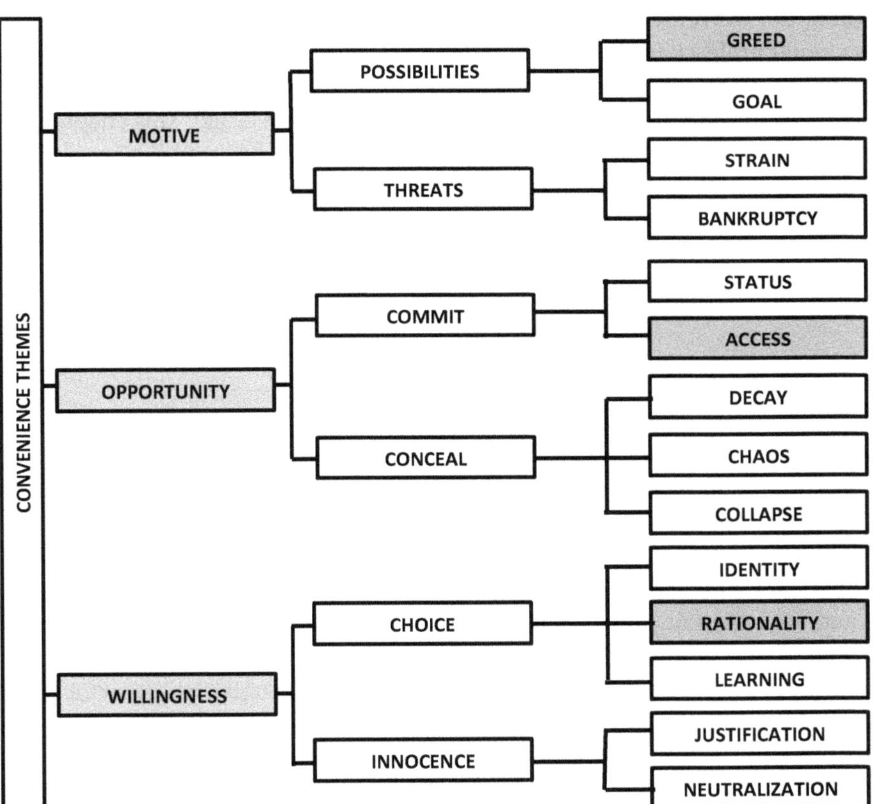


**Figure 7.5:** Convenience themes for executives in the municipality.

# 8 Crime Service Professionals

Bottom-up approaches have been discussed so far in this book. It is matter of people in the organization who prevent potential white-collar offenders from committing financial crime and who detect white-collar offenders having committed financial crime. A different approach in the same line of reasoning is the outside-in approach where outsiders rather than insiders prevent and detect white-collar wrongdoing in the organization. The outside-in approach involves professional service providers such as law firms, accounting firms, auditing firms, real estate agencies, and banks with their lawyers, accountants, auditors, real estate agents, and bank clerks.

Often, the convenience of white-collar crime is dependent on the cooperation with external professionals who may turn a blind eye to potential law violations by and together with their clients. Instead of turning a blind eye, they might indeed help their clients with compliance to avoid misconduct and crime. This chapter discusses the outside-in perspective of corporate control of white-collar offenses as it influences crime convenience such as lawyers, auditors, accountants, real estate agents, and health care workers. Many other external helpers can contribute to an outside-in effort of prevention and detection. An example is the art market where money laundering and fraud takes place (Oosterman et al., 2021).

## Law Firm Client Barriers

A law firm is in the business of applying legal knowledge to client opportunities and threats (Gottschalk, 2014). Lawyers and their clients enjoy the attorney-client privilege in many jurisdictions such as the United States and Norway. Attorney-client privilege is the name given to the common law concept of legal professional privilege (Oh, 2004). The privilege is the lawyer's as well as the client's right to refuse to disclose and to prevent any other person from disclosing confidential communications between the client and the attorney. For a potential white-collar offender as the client of a law firm, the privilege represents a convenient opportunity for financial crime (Økokrim, 2021: 6):

> It can be difficult to know whether a lawyer knowingly and intentionally assists criminals, or whether he or she is being exploited. At several law firms, there seems to be a lack of understanding of, and knowledge of, money laundering regulations. There is also a big difference in how the regulations are interpreted, and what routines exist to comply with the money laundering act. For example, there is a different understanding of where the line between the money laundering act and the duty of confidentiality lies.

In an outside-in perspective, knowledgeable lawyers and law firms based on integrity and accountability can prevent potential offenses in client organizations, and they can report instances legitimized by the money laundering act in violation of

https://doi.org/10.1515/9783110986686-009

the duty of confidentiality. However, many lawyers and law firms ted to slide on the slippery slope over to the wrong side of the law when there is a profitable client (Økokrim, 2021: 6):

> Among the lawyers who can be linked to crime, few have convictions, even though they have been registered as suspects or charged in several serious cases. There are several lawyers who are charged or suspected of financial crime. In many cases, they are involved in tax evasion, fraud, bankruptcy, accounting crime, financial infidelity /embezzlement or money laundering. A lawyer who has now lost his license has been charged with gross embezzlement of more than NOK 90 million belonging to the lawyer's clients. The embezzlement took place in connection with the settlement of real estate transactions.

Økokrim quoted here is the Norwegian national authority for investigation and prosecution of economic and environmental crime. The public agency is a specialist skills function for the police and the prosecuting functions in the criminal justice system. Økokrim was established in 1989 and is both a police investigative agency as well as a public prosecutors' office. Økokrim (2021: 6) found that secret client accounts can facilitate financial crime:

> Lawyers also facilitate financial crime by using client accounts. The client account is used, among other things, to avoid creditor debt, fraud and money laundering. In one case, a client account was used in a fraud case in such a way that bank loans granted to two companies were paid into a client account. The person who later was convicted of fraud was then given access to the funds in this account. The person in question was the real general manager, but without formal roles and should thus not be able to dispose of the company's funds.

In another case investigated and prosecuted by Økokrim, a lawyer acted as the formal owner of a property through his own company. The prosecuting authority believed that in reality it was one of the lawyer's clients who was the real owner, and that the lawyer was listed as the lawyer to prevent creditors from getting the property as settlement for outstanding debts. Both the district court and the court of appeal agreed with the prosecution's point of view.

A lawyer received millions of Norwegian kroner in a client account which was used, among others, for property purchases. The money originated at actors belonging to a family well known to the police and registered in police systems. Økokrim suspected that the client account was used to launder proceeds from criminal activity via the real estate market.

Lawyers who offer real estate transactions may be well-equipped to prevent and detect white-collar crime in an outside-in perspective. If not reporting to the police, they may contact the client organization for confirmation or disconfirmation of transaction legality.

Lawyers who offer client accounts may prevent creditor evasion by denying access to a company by people and firms who might want to place their assets in the company rather than repay debt. In practice, the lawyer avoids acting as a straw man and avoids being considered a pro forma owner. The lawyer denies access to persons and firms who want to evade values. Økokrim concluded regarding law firms and lawyers that it is highly likely that some lawyers function as facilitators for white-collar crime. Highly likelihood in their assessment is a probability above 90%. The typical lawyer helping facilitate white-collar crime works as partner in a small law firm.

When Russia invaded Ukraine in March 2022, sanctions were imposed on a number of key Russian figures including oligarchs. An oligarch refers to a rich person who is a business leader with substantial political influence. Helpers like law firms, security funds, banks and other financial institutions enabled oligarchs avoid negative consequences of the sanctions (Bamvik, 2022).

Furthermore, Økokrim (2021) found that it was a recurring pattern that lawyers who have lost their legal license to practice as attorneys tend to resume their criminal activity when they get the license back. It was also a recurring pattern that lawyers who had lost their license found other ways to use their competence to commit, or facilitate, crime. It was therefore likely that lawyers who lose their legal license will resume their criminal activity if they get it back, and that lawyers who do not get their license back will find other ways to use their competence to commit, or facilitate, crime. Økokrim here used the term likely, which is a probability of 60% to 90%. In our perspective of outside-in, law-abiding, often larger law firms, can help expose criminals, often smaller law firms, which have been deprived of their legal license permanently or temporarily.

Lawyers and law firms as money laundering enablers were also emphasized by the Norwegian tax administration in the aftermath of the Covid-19 pandemic. The agency wrote in their report (Skatteetaten, 2021: 11):

> Today, there is a greater international awareness of the function of criminal facilitators for threat actors in economic crime. A report published by the OECD in February 2021 states that sophisticated economic crimes often facilitated by professional actors such as lawyers, accountants and financial institutions.

The report by the OECD (2021) emphasized that the majority of professionals are law-abiding and play an important role in supporting compliance and a well-functioning financial system, but nevertheless stated that criminal activities of a limited segment of professionals undermine public confidence in the profession and the legal and economic system. Handling the threat from these professional actors is expected to reduce tax crime by recognizing criminal actors' shift to digitalization after the Covid-19 pandemic. Examples of the most common crime enabling services include (OECD, 2021, Skatteetaten, 2021):

- Establishing companies, foundations, and other business structures – to hide the identity of owners, hide assets, or hide the criminal origin of funds
- Set up offshore structures to hide ownership and income
- Provide false documentation

- Assist in insolvency, bankruptcy, and liquidation by reducing available funds for the creditors of the bankrupt company
- Use of cum-ex schemes to recover unpaid taxes
- Commit financial crime through crypto assets, thereby facilitating money laundering of the proceeds of crime.

The OECD (2021) recommended that tax authorities should establish work processes for identifying and collecting information on facilitators, including definition, measurement of threats, use of indicators and use of data sources for identification (Skatteetaten, 2021).

## Certified Accountant Control

Certified accountants are sometimes asked to create legitimacy for a client company. Accountants can be asked to facilitate money laundering, fictitious invoicing, tax evasion, work-related crime, payment of bribes, as well as disguise of real rights holders and the origin of the funds through complicated corporate structures domestically and globally (Qiu and Slezak, 2019). In a rich country such as Norway, where the state subsidies a number of business sectors, accounting misrepresentation can conveniently lead to subsidies from the government. In many countries, it may be so important to have a bottom line in accounting that satisfies investors and others that crime emerges as potentially acceptable.

Misreporting in accounting is often a convenient way of concealing illegal transactions (Qiu and Slezak, 2019). Lack of transparency makes concealment in accounting convenient (Davidson et al., 2019; Goncharov and Peter, 2019). Managers can withhold bad news by accounting misrepresentation (Bao et al., 2019), since financial statements are a substantive component of a firm's communications with its stakeholders (Gupta et al., 2020). Balakrishnan et al. (2019) found that reduced corporate transparency in accounting is associated with increased corporate tax aggressiveness. Accounting fraud in terms of account manipulation is lacking transparency (Toolami et al., 2019).

Since accounting is no machine that can provide correct answers regarding the financial health of a company, since accounting information has limited representational properties, and since accounting cannot fully inform decision-makers (O'Leary and Smith, 2020), determination of final accounting figures are often left to the discretion of financial managers.

Incentive systems such as bonus arrangements can lead to white-collar crime such as corruption to meet sales targets or other targets on which bonus payments depend. Alternatively, the offender can pretend having met targets by manipulating accounting (Nichol, 2019: 329):

> Bonus contracts have come under a great deal of criticism in the past few years for creating incentives that encourage managers to manipulate accounting information in order to maximize their pay. Such manipulation can range from subtle earnings manipulation to outright fraud.

Økokrim (2021: 8) found that deviant executives who commit criminal activities, for example for fraud, often attempt to use accountants to manipulate accounts, for example to do the following:

> A criminal group uses the same accountant in several cases. This accountant changes the accounts so that the liquidity ratio and profitability look better than they actually are. The manipulated accounts are then used to raise loans on an incorrect basis. Later the company goes bankrupt. The accountant is not listed at the financial supervisory authority of Norway.
>
> Another way accountants can assist offenders is in the event of inadequate follow-up. Such a case was discovered during an investigation. Here it became clear that the external accountant was not critical enough of the documentation handed over, in addition to being creative in keeping accounts. This made the criminal offenses possible. In another case, the accountant neglected his responsibility to prepare documentation for several of the transactions in the company, as well as establish routines for correct accounting.

Among potential offenders, Økokrim (2021) found that some accountants have a reputation of not asking too many questions, or accepting whatever answers they get, and they are therefore popular. It can be difficult to know if such offenses are being committed deliberately. Økokrim (2021) also found evidence of cases where persons who were trained accountants allowed the legitimacy this gives to be exploited by culprits. This happened, for example, through fake invoicing, which is a widespread mode within work-related invoicing as well as in corruption, where the bribed submits a non-real invoice for consulting services. Again, it can be difficult to know whether the accountants in question were unaware of criminal relationships, or an accomplice.

The association of certified accountants might introduce more strict reviews of their members. For example, a few accounting firms seem only to offer their services to criminal actors where they provide crime-as-a-service. One such accounting firm had specialized in assisting business owners draining companies for assets and then files for bankruptcy causing losses to debtors. Another accounting firm had specialized in avoidance of taxes.

Økokrim's (2021) assessment was that accounting firms that only provide services to criminal actors with crime-as-a-service, highly likely (above 90% probability) work as facilitators of financial crime. It seems to be a conscious strategy of labor market offenders to ask accounting firms to produce fake time sheets and invoices to enable payment of salaries in cash where withholding tax is not necessary.

Økokrim (2021) found several cases of accountants who had lost their license but continued to act as accountants anyway. In one case, an accountant without license helped by creative accounting sot that the main person could empty the company of several million. Others did set up their own business and rent out their services from there. Such deviance should not be too difficult to detect and report by the association of certified accountants.

## Auditor Denial of Acceptance

Like certified accountants, certified auditors can give the company legitimacy and can be used to facilitate or commit various forms of financial crime. Økokrim (2021) found that auditors often have chosen to resign from their role at those companies where they have not received sufficient answers to questions. Some auditors are suspected of approving accounts without special control, or they even more actively assist criminals. These auditors are often associated with companies that operate in the gray zone for what is legal. Some auditors accept reporting and being loyal to deviant management (Hurley et al., 2019). In our outside-in perspective, the ideal contribution from auditors would be to deny acceptance of accounts where their queries are not satisfactorily answered and report their findings to the board of directors as well as externally to public authorities.

Concealing illegal transactions may result from the failure of auditors to do their job. Alon et al. (2019) argue that accounting and auditing functions have undergone a legitimacy crisis in recent years. Auditors are supposed to serve as gatekeepers to protect shareholders and other stakeholders, but deviant corporate management tend to hire and control auditors instead of letting auditors report to the board of directors or the supervisory board (Hurley et al., 2019). Skeptical auditors tend to be replaced by less skeptical auditors. Reporting fraud to public authorities will also harm auditors (Mohliver, 2019: 316):

> As organizations, audit firms are often severely penalized for client malfeasance. Yet the individual auditors working for these firms are susceptible to "motivated blindness" stemming from conflicts of interest that bias their moral judgment toward choices that help their clients.

The lack of detection by auditors can also be explained by standardization. Herron and Cornell (2021) found that audit work is standardized which harms auditors creativity, thereby preventing recognition of and responses to fraud cues. Standardization harms an improvisational style of thinking, tolerance for unpredictability, and uncertainty, and open-mindedness that is associated with responses to perceived fraud risk cues.

Shadnam and Lawrence (2011) found that morale collapse increases the tendency to financial crime. In fact, repetition of criminal actions might institutionalize such actions. Dion (2008) found that the larger the corporation, the less deterrence effect from laws on financial crime, which may have to do with increased convenience in concealing crime.

A chief financial officer (CFO) in Norway became divorced and his financial motive became stronger. The growing motive caused him to search for opportunity expansion in the organization. One of his actions was to take control over the auditing process, where he succeeded in controlling that what the auditor presented to the chief executive officer (CEO) and the board of directors. He was thus able to make the organizational opportunity larger. As he noticed that he succeeded in organizational opportunity expansion, his willingness for deviant behavior became higher than it was before.

Hestnes (2017) asked the question in his study of the CFO case: Why did the auditor fail in detecting embezzlement at the company? Normally in a Norwegian context, the auditor is to report annually to the board in the business where the auditor has reviewed accounts. Since the cooperation between the auditor and the CFO went so smoothly, the CEO did not invite the auditor anymore to board meetings. This is where the fourth opportunity expansion occurred. The CFO became the actual person to report external audit results to the board. Mohliver (2019) found that auditor bias towards accepting deviant financial reports increased when there is ambiguity about the appropriateness of a course of action. Financial misreporting that is viewed favorably by the client organization can be recommended by external auditors on the grounds that such reporting is already adopted among companies served by the same auditing firm.

A mechanism for outside-in effects on executive compliance is the threat for both accountants and auditors to be fined and potentially sent to prison. A financial scandal in Norway in a company named Finance Credit caused prison sentences not only for two executives at Finance Credit but also for two auditors from audit firm KPMG. The auditors were incarcerated because they had helped the white-collar offenders create a non-transparent and complicated corporate structure enabling the offenders to make it look like all subsidiaries were financially sound. A similar case in Norway was the auditor for Sponsor Service who was reluctant to criticize and question some of the numbers in the accounts. This auditor ended up in prison as well.

Økokrim's (2021) overall assessment regarding auditors was that auditors associate with crime mainly as passive participants. It was considered highly likely that those companies where white-collar crime occur, that both accounting and auditing suffered from shortcomings. The challenge for the criminal justice system is to determine to what extent such professional service providers facilitate crime.

The financial supervisory authority of Norway has revoked the approval as state-authorized public accountants for, among other things, failure to obtain documentation, lack of documentation of performed audits, for not having acted neutrally by having changed the accounts of clients at their requests, and inadequate assessments when entering into client relationships.

Forensic auditing represents a bottom-up approach to detection of white-collar crime (Baird and Zelin, 2009; Shawver and Clements, 2019; Sonnier et al., 2015).

Forensic auditing is an activity that focuses on the gathering, verifying, processing analyzing, and reporting information within a predefined context in the area of financial irregularities and wrongdoing. Forensic accounting is the tracking and collection of investigative evidence for potential prosecution of financial crime. It is a professional service that is caused by disputes, allegations, and rumors. Forensic auditing refers to examination, review, and evaluation of financial information for use as evidence of wrongdoing by trusted individuals in the organization (Oyerogba, 2021).

## Real Estate Agent Reporting

Økokrim (2021: 12) found that real estate agents are often used as facilitators for money laundering via real estate, including through the use of client accounts as well as illegal borrowing and refinancing, where business enterprises in the real estate market commit financial crime:

> In at least one case, a real estate agent, in collaboration with a bank employee, forged documents for borrowers so that they got a higher mortgage than what they would otherwise get. So far, twenty cases have been uncovered, and findings have been made that indicate money laundering in some of these. Several of the loans are also in default. Two of the real estate agents are linked to the use of drugs and the removal of money from the sale of drugs. One of the two real estate agents also has large cash deposits, as well as deposits and payments to and from own accounts with internet-based gaming companies. The person in question has also set up a real estate company. The bank official has reacted to a number of valuations made by the broker and believes these are too high. Because of their role as real estate agents, they are both in a position to launder money through the real estate market.

A different modus is when the real estate agent facilitates a disproportionately high price assessment of homes. This means that the homeowner can get a higher refinanced mortgage, possibly a higher home loan, than the value of the home indicates. In such a case, the homeowner has then used the borrowed money to buy more homes, and then repeat the process several times (Økokrim, 2021: 12):

> In one case, the culprits probably tried to launder money by hiding real rights holders. The apartment was bought on the open market by a private company where the real estate agent in question stated to be the 100 percent owner. Settlement for payment should come from a separate financial company that should not have a mortgage on the property. The broker was chairman of the board, but not the owner. The real owner was another company well documented in police systems for, among other things, financial crime and money laundering. It was also a subsidiary of this company that was responsible for payment of settlement, not the financial firm specified in the agreement.

Real estate agents were involved in fraud schemes by the convicted white-collar offender Christer Tromsdal in Norway (Hultgreen, 2012). The total number of accomplices in his network was 15 persons. They worked in different organizations, including real estate firms, and they had established a criminal network. Christer Tromsdal has been sentenced for financial crime several times. In June 2015, he was sentenced to six years in prison. Anthony Bratli, a property appraiser, and Terje Hvidsten, a real estate agent, were both at the same time sentenced to four and a half years in prison. At about the same time, Arne Aarsæther, an attorney, was sentenced to four months in prison for handling illegal proceeds for Tromsdal (Borgarting, 2015; Oslo tingrett, 2015b). Christer Tromsdal made frequent media appearances (Kleppe, 2015; Meldalen, 2015).

White-collar offender Christer Tromsdal was running the company Aker Brygge Invest. In our perspective of outside-in, a total of fifteen criminal professionals in various roles might have blown the whistle on him. Even far more people knew about his fraud scheme of property bankruptcy where investors and banks lost money. Real estate agents and other professionals supporting and facilitating the fraud scheme ended up in prison. The fraud was detected by the police as Tromsdal contacted the police to offer his services as a police informant (Dahle, 2011; Hultgreen et al., 2019; NTB, 2015).

Økokrim's (2021) experience with crime service professionals such as real estate brokers is that real estate firms facilitate money laundering via the real estate market using a client account. In the case above concerning the broker who was chairman of the board, but not the owner, more than one million US dollars was transferred from an account in the Middle East to the client account. One of the main shareholders in the real estate firm had access rights to dispose of the money. The broker was later convicted of fraud and violation of narcotics legislation.

Økokrim (2021: 13) wrote in their overall assessment of crime service by professionals at real estate firms:

> It is very likely that several real estate agents are committing systematic and organized financial crime or facilitating this. It will mainly be in the form of money laundering via real estate or by enabling higher mortgages or home loans by using forged documents. It is likely that real estate agents will be exploited for money laundering by hiding real rights holders from the agent.

While Norway has a very long coastline, the attractive real estates for vacation houses and summer guests are located south of the capital of Oslo. In particular, the island of Tjøme is popular. The theme of environmentally harmful construction and expansion of summerhouses serves as an example in relation to convenience theory. The motive is often to climb Maslow's (1943) hierarchy of needs, the opportunity is typically access to resources (Huisman and Erp, 2013), and the willingness for deviant behavior is dependent on neutralization techniques (Sykes and Matza, 1957), lack of self-control (Craig and Piquero, 2016) and other factors. Real estate agents ignored the lack of permits when they were involved in transactions between old mansion owners and new mansion owners. Even when an architect and two municipal case workers were convicted in court for corruption, real estate agents continued helping the rich and mighty people from the capital of Oslo. Økokrim considered prosecuting some of the mansion owners for harming the environment by building enormous mansions along the shoreline that was reserved for wildlife and public access (Feratovic, 2021; Holmøy, 2021).

## Financial Services Detection

The final group of crime service professionals reviewed by Økokrim (2021: 14) was bank and finance clerks:

> In banking and finance, special arrangements for granting loans on the wrong basis are a widespread problem. This occurs in both small and large banking enterprises. Loans are granted on incorrect grounds either through unfaithful employees and/or through the use of forged documents.

In our perspective of combatting white-collar crime through outside-in measures, a bank that discovers attempt at bank fraud should not only consider reporting it to the police but also to the supervisory committee and the compliance officer in the company where someone made the fraudulent attempt. Since police agencies sometimes lack both competence and capacity to investigate, a more preventive measure would be to let the offender organization know of the attempt.

Some white-collar offenders are able to recruit a bank insider for larger fraud transactions. For example, a construction company owned by Norwegians in Dubai needed funding. A woman whose regular position was being a nurse in hospital took on the role of being the rich widow after a deceased entrepreneur. The fake widow told the bank to transfer some of her assets from Norway to Dubai. The internal bank clerk approved the transfer. After the transfer of ten million dollars had taken place, bank management called the real rich widow about the transactions. The real rich widow responded that she had not noticed a reduction on her bank account of ten million dollars (Berge, 2011).

According to Økokrim (2021), some bank employees have committed embezzlement by virtue of their positions. Some employees in banking firms have direct links to criminal actors and environments. For example, a bank executive was invited to a party at a Hells Angels estate. He was offered services by a sex worker that he accepted. Afterwards, pictures of the act were presented to him with a request for a substantial bank loan. He forged documents so that a bank loan was granted to the blackmailer.

Økokrim (2021: 14) found that several employees in banks who are involved in arranging for granting of loans on a misleading and manipulated basis were linked to known criminal actors:

> These have close ties to or are in the same circle of friends as key players in organized crime. A named bank employee in a prominent position must in several cases have granted a loan and given favorable loan terms to criminal actors, as well as persons who are not creditworthy due to bankruptcies. One of the criminal actors associated with the bank employee appears as a central figure in a criminal network. Another bank employee in a prominent position is assumed to be involved in committing fraud in collaboration with known criminal actors.

Banks and other financial institutions help white-collar offenders into tax havens. Tax havens offer convenience for corporate crime. Not only is tax evasion an obvious benefit where corporations can avoid taxes on profits in their domestic markets by transferring profits to tax havens with low or no corporate taxes. Corporations can enjoy secrecy regarding ownership. They can remove traces of corruption by transferring bribes via tax havens, and they can launder money from crime by help of the secrecy in tax havens (Deng et al., 2020; Granda, 2021). In some languages, a tax haven is labeled tax paradise, where a paradise is a place of exceptional happiness and delight (Schmal et al., 2021).

Mannheimer Swartling (2016) described how the Swedish bank Nordea had its subsidiary in Luxembourg illegally backdating contracts and help clients with tax evasion as leaked from the Panama Papers. The bank first denied its link to the Panamanian law firm Mossack Fonseca, which specializes in establishing corporate mailbox companies in tax havens (Associated Press, 2016). Gunn Wærsted resigned from her group executive position at Nordea and chair at Nordea Luxembourg (Trumpy, 2016). Several other Scandinavian banks are also helping their corporate clients in tax havens such as Danske Bank in Denmark (Bruun Hjejle, 2018), Swedbank in Sweden (Clifford Chance, 2020), and Norwegian bank DNB helped Icelandic fishing company Samherji bribe Namibian officials through tax havens (Kibar, 2020a, 2020b; Kleinfeld, 2019, 2020a).

Schmal et al. (2021) use the term tax paradise as a synonym for tax haven when they describe corporate activity in tax havens:

> Multinational firms shift billions of income into tax havens to decrease their taxes. Through the use of transfer pricing and tax-optimizing transactions such as intrafirm debt and royalty payments, firms reduce their tax payments. Using tax havens can be legal. However, financial statement users are concerned that tax havens enable firms to obfuscate information. Tax havens are often related to secretive tax planning schemes because these states often lack transparency and information exchange.

A tax haven or paradise is a state or geographical area with autonomy in tax policy, which offers foreign enterprises zero tax terms or very low tax rates, and a legislation that prevents insight from the outside world. Examples of tax havens include the Bahamas, Bermuda, Cayman Islands, Dubai, British Virgin Islands, Guernsey, Hong Kong, Isle of Man, Jersey, Liechtenstein, Luxembourg, Mauritius, Monaco, Panama, Singapore, and Switzerland. Less well known is that countries such as Ireland and the Netherlands have also been mentioned as tax havens, and that the united state of Delaware might be the most secret tax haven in the world (Schjelderup, 2020).

With this list of tax havens (Schjelderup, 2020), Schjelderup and Sævold (2021) criticized the central bank of Norway (Norges Bank) for a gap between guidelines and practice in handling tax haven matters in an article entitled "Tax planning and the central bank's blind zones" regarding chief executive Nicolai Tangen at the Government Pension Fund Global who had acquired substantial personal wealth in his previous position as investment banker in London:

> Nicolai Tangen's way of organizing his fortune and business can be read as a classic, aggressive tax planning structure. It is startling that Norges Bank does not see that this is a possible perspective. Central bank governor Øystein Olsen writes in the newspaper DN on August 17 that he disagrees with our analysis in his article "In the central bank's blind zones". Our article has been peer-reviewed and published in the journal International Politics. The conclusion is that Norges Bank positioned itself on a traditional line of defense for the use of tax havens in connection with the Tangen employment. We have argued that the central bank thus challenged its own document of expectations on tax, as well as Norwegian official policy on tax and transparency. Norges Bank has been challenged precisely on a vague approach in the area of tax and transparency from its Supervisory Board, the Finance Committee (in the parliament) and the Tax Justice Network that works for tax justice. Olsen refers to the definition of tax havens in his own document of expectations and argues that it provides a broad definition. But it does not acknowledge the criticism that Norges Bank systematically defended the use of Nicolai Tangen's investments in tax havens by pointing to countries such as the Cayman Islands and Jersey having entered into information exchange agreements in tax matters. In response to the criticism of Tangen's use of tax havens before the appointment, Norges Bank's executive board wrote in a letter to the supervisory board on April 29 last year: "The common definition of tax havens is that they have little extent of openness and transparency in combination with no or very low tax rates. However, there are significant differences across these jurisdictions. Both Jersey and the Cayman Islands are members of the OECD global forum on transparency and exchange for tax purposes". It is not unreasonable to interpret the letter from the executive board to mean that states that participate in the OECD's global forum and thus sign information exchange agreements (CSR) are less problematic to use than states that do not participate. In our article, we explain why the information exchange criterion has major shortcomings.

Legitimate access to crime resources at a bank can be illustrated by the case of a chairman of the board who published his autobiography (Olav, 2014, 2015). The chairman used a tax haven where he had an account when he ran business through another company there (Bjørklund, 2018).

Unfortunately, the report by the Norwegian national authority for investigation and prosecution of economic and environmental crime (Økokrim, 2021) did not address the role of banks in enabling white-collar offenders transfer corruption funds and launder money in tax havens. It seems that Økokrim was reluctant to label bank activities as corporate crime or helping white-collar offenders as crime service professionals. Fortunately, the OECD (2021) was willing to label banks professional enablers of crime in tax havens as described in the following.

## Inter-Bank Borders Cooperation

While individual banks attempt to implement anti-money laundering procedures and systems, offenders know how to move illegitimate proceeds between banks across foreign borders. Efforts are made to unite banks against financial crime. One of the initiatives is the fin-crime inter-bank AI platform (Finterai) for financial crime investigation and reporting. The Financial Action Task Force emphasizes the potential of new technologies to make anti-money laundering (AML) and counter terrorist financing (CTF) measures more effective. They mentioned important technology issues such as digital identity and transaction monitoring and reporting. They list new technologies such as artificial intelligence, natural language and soft computing techniques, distributed ledger technology, digital solutions for customer due diligence, and application programming interfaces (FATF, 2021).

The European Commission emphasizes legislation against AML and CTF. The new legislative package includes a proposal for the creation of a new EU authority to fight money laundering. It is part of the commitment to protect EU citizens and the financial system from money laundering and terrorist financing (EU, 2021).

The European Banking Authority launched a public consultation on new guidelines for the role, tasks, and responsibilities of AML and CFT compliance officers. The guidelines also include provisions on the wider governance structure. The guidelines were designed to be applied as a directive in a proportionate manner, taking into account the diversity of financial sector operators that are within the scope of the directive (EBA, 2021).

A number of compliance violations are observed in the European banking sector in recent years. Both Danske Bank in Denmark (Bruun Hjejle, 2018) and Swedbank in Sweden (Clifford Chance, 2020) had compliance violations in their branch offices in Eastern Europe. At the Estonian branch of Danske Bank, non-residents were able to transfer potentially criminal proceeds without appropriate anti-money laundering measures in place. One of the reasons why corporate control functions did not work was because the branch operated computer systems different from computer systems at the headquarters. It was a legacy system from the former owner of the branch office. Not only was the IT platform different, but local bank executives also operated in the local language that executives from the headquarters in Denmark did not understand. The challenge for future real-time anti-money laundering technology is thus a platform that can handle various systems in various languages. The blame for the Danske Bank scandal was attributed to the chief executive officer, and Thomas Borgen had to resign from the position and later faced both criminal and civil charges in Denmark (Milne, 2019a; Milne and Binham, 2018; Klevstrand, 2021). The body of the Estonian chief at Danske Bank was found in the fall 2019 (Milne, 2019b). Chief executive Birgitte Bonnesen at Swedbank faced the same outcome as Thomas Borgen when she had to leave her position because of the absence of relevant anti-money laundering procedures (Milne, 2020). The successor of Thomas Borgen in the CEO chair at Danske Bank, Chris Vogelzang, also resigned because of anti-money laundering matters at the bank (Solgård, 2021).

Wingerde and Merz (2021) summarize a number of other European banks – in addition to Danske Bank and Swedbank – that have money laundering issues recently: UBS in France, ING in the Netherlands, HSBC in France, HSBC in Belgium, Credit Suisse in Italy, Deutsche bank in the UK, Standard Chartered Bank in the UK, Barclays in the UK, BNP Paribas in France, Nordea Bank in Sweden, ING in Italy, UBS in Italy, ABN Amro in the Netherlands, Société Générale in France, Banque Havilland in Luxembourg, Handelsbanken in Sweden, Sonali Bank in the UK, ABLV in Latvia, Raiffeisen Bank in Austria, PrivatBank in Cyprus, FBME Bank in Cyprus, Hellenic Bank in Cyprus, Rabobank in the Netherlands, Santander in Norway, Canara Bank in the UK, RCB Bank in Cyprus, Cyprus Development Bank in Cyprus, Volksbank in the Netherlands, Hypo Vorarlberg Bank in Austria, ING Bank in Belgium, BNP Paribas in France, Central Cooperative Bank in Cyprus, DNB Bank in Norway, ABLV in Latvia, Versobank in Estonia, Pilatus Bank in Malta, Jyske Bank in Denmark, Credit Suisse in Switzerland, Triodos in the Netherlands, Deutsche Bank in Germany, and Gazprombank in Switzerland.

In the Journal of Money Laundering Control, Al-Suwaidi and Nobanee (2021: 396) argue that "there is a significant focus today on the deficiencies of the financial system as the sector continues to boom while facing the growing pains of financial scandals, money laundering and the financing of terrorism around the world". Their review of the literature on AML and CTF are concerned with legal issues rather than technology issues, where they emphasize the ineffectiveness of national laws and international regulations.

Similarly, Jayasekara (2021) argues that the global standards in AML and CTF are not effective. The study emphasizes lack of implementation based on a review of issues from the Financial Action Task Force.

Crime signal detection is a matter of separating real signals from noise signals (Karim and Siegel, 1998). Evidence of system deficiency occurs when the system notices a signal when it is noise (called a false alarm), and when the system notices noise when it is a crime signal (called a miss). Evidence of system efficiency occurs when the system notices a crime signal (called a hit), and when the system notices noise when it is a noise signal (called a correction). The extent system deficiency is the relative fraction of false alarms and misses compared to hits and corrections. Often, it is a matter of detecting a given crime signal against a background of noise that represents a situation of uncertainty (Manning and Kowalska, 2021).

False positives (called a false alarm) in risk analysis result in the misallocation of resources that is human investigation of low-risk or no-risk activity or transactions. Singh and Lin (2021: 476) argue that when "calibration tools are added this only exaggerates the false-positive problem". Other deficiencies mentioned by the researchers are inconsistencies in processes, standards, and applications violating regulatory compliance, absence or malfunction of know-your-customer and customer-due-diligence, and fragmentation of systems that do not interact.

A crime signal or noise signal results from an audit trail that is material and textual consisting of documents, records, and traces that are the created evidentiary residues of a transaction. A failing audit trail lacks transparency and thus traceability (Power, 2021).

In the Journal of Money Laundering Control, Amjad et al. (2021: 2) address the lack of inter-bank cooperation across foreign borders where money laundering may help terrorist financing, bribery, corruption, and sanction violations:

> Banking institutions are mostly used when it comes to money laundering. They provide several services such as depositing, lending money, cashing checks and money or asset transfer from one institution to another without considering the geographical limitation. As globalization is at full force and the world economy is becoming more integrated than before, transferring money across foreign borders is becoming easier. Foreign countries have very tough secrecy laws, allowing sharing of fund without anyone finding out their origin and they also form tax havens to attract the flows. This makes it easier for criminals to transfer funds into a foreign institution without anyone finding out where the funds originated.

The need for inter-bank cooperation across foreign borders is obvious when we list Wingerde and Merz (2021) findings of banks with money laundering issues in Europe recently:

- Austria: Hypo Vorarlberg Bank, Raiffeisen Bank.
- Belgium: BNP Paribas, HSBC, ING.
- Cyprus: Central Cooperative Bank, Cyprus Development Bank, FBME Bank, Hellenic Bank, PrivatBank, RCB Bank.
- Denmark: Danske Bank, Jyske Bank.
- Estonia: Swedbank, Versobank.
- France: BNP Paribas, HSBC, Société Général, UBS.
- Germany: Deutsche Bank.
- Italy: Credit Suisse, ING, UBS.
- Latvia: ABLV, Swedbank.
- Lithuania: Swedbank.
- Luxembourg: Banque Havilland.
- Malta: Pilatus Bank.
- Netherlands: ABN Amro, ING, Rabobank, Triodos, Volksbank.
- Norway: DNB, Santander.
- Spain: Caixaban.
- Sweden: Handelsbanken, Nordea Bank, Swedbank.
- Switzerland: Credit Suisse, Gazprombank.
- UK: Barclays, Canara Bank, Deutsche Bank, Sonia Bank, Standard Chartered Bank.

The lack of inter-bank cooperation across foreign borders might be exemplified by the Norfund scandal in Norway involving DNB bank and the Moldova scandal involving Latvian bank. The method of business email compromise was applied to the enterprise Norfund in Norway making DNB bank transfer USD 12 million not to the designated bank in Cambodia but instead to a bank in Mexico for money laundering. Lack of inter-bank cooperation made it impossible to trace the money beyond the Mexican bank, and the money was lost forever (Teiss, 2020). In Moldova, USD 1 billion disappeared out of several banks, a sum equivalent to 15% of the gross national product in the country. Banca de Economii and other banks transferred the money to Latvian banks where it disappeared forever (Iordachescu and Rodina, 2019).

Most of the literature on AML and CTF apply an offense-based perspective, listing various types of offenses. The theory of convenience applies the offender-based perspective of criminal actors rather than the offense-based perspective of criminal acts. The offender-based perspective emphasizes characteristics of actors such as social and occupational status, power and influence, and access to resources to commit and conceal financial crime (Benson et al., 2021). Convenience theory is concerned with financial motive, professional opportunity, and personal willingness for deviant behavior (Stadler and Gottschalk, 2021).

The convenience of committing money laundering and terrorist financing is explained in the theory in terms of the status of the offender and the offender access to resources. The convenience of concealing money laundering and terrorist financing is explained in the theory by decay (institutional deterioration and inability to control), chaos (lack of oversight and guardianship) and collapse (rule complexity and criminal market forces).

Convenience themes for the offender in the Norfund case are illustrated in Figure 8.1. The lack of inter-bank cooperation contributes mainly to the convenience of concealment in terms of money laundering. In the opportunity dimension of convenience theory, most criminals have no status in society (Pontell et al., 2014), but they have access to tools and vehicles to compromise email accounts and register fake domains and impersonate employees involved in financial transactions (Benson and Simpson, 2018; Ramoglou and Tsang, 2016). Concealing crime in the digital financial world is also a matter of access to resources to quickly move money away from the Mexican account while deleting all traces (Adler and Kwon, 2002). An important opportunity theme is also the lack of digital knowledge in the victim organization Norfund and in police forces in Norway and globally that is indicated by chaos in the figure, where participation in crime networks (Nielsen, 2003) and markets with crime forces (Chang et al., 2005) represent convenient business practice for the criminal organization.

The threat actor managed to change the bank account details in the disbursement notice and convinced Norfund that a Mexican bank was used to avoid using several bank intermediaries in the transaction. The threat actor used Covid-19 as a

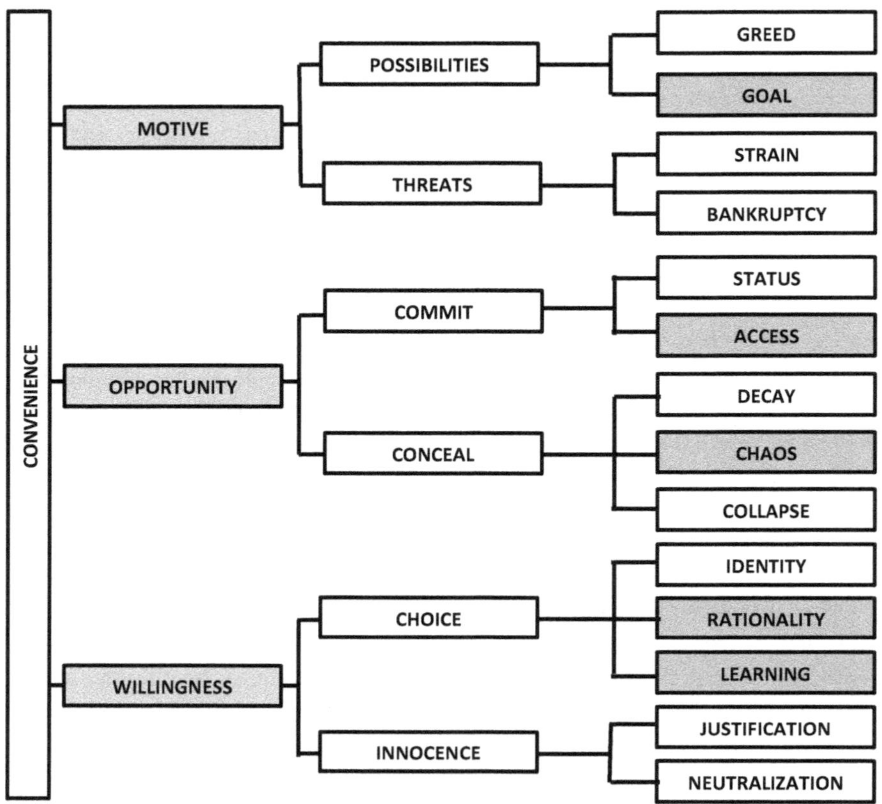


**Figure 8.1:** Convenience themes in the Norfund case with lack of inter-bank cooperation.

factor to convince legitimate Cambodian recipient that the bank transfer was delayed. At the same time, the threat actor sent emails to Norfund confirming that the funds were received in Cambodia, to prevent further investigation on the part of Norfund.

There is a discrepancy between expectations to digital AML and CTF systems (EBA, 2021; EU, 2021; FATF, 2021) and deficiencies of current systems (Al-Suwaidi and Nobanee, 2021; Jayasekara, 2021: Manning and Kowalska, 2021; Power, 2021; Singh and Lin, 2021), causing frequent scandals in the banking sector (Bruun Hjejle, 2018; Clifford Chance, 2020; Klevstrand, 2021; Milne, 2019a, 2019b, 2020; Milne and Binham, 2018; Solgård, 2021).

The idea of an inter-bank platform of artificial intelligence applications for financial crime investigation and reporting addresses deficiencies in current systems as well as convenience themes for offenders. The ability of offenders to manipulate transactions between banks will be drastically reduced by initiatives such as sharing know-your-customer information, real-time communication, and collaboration on investigations. As a result, the frequency of scandals in terms of government fines and executive dismissals is expected to drop.

## Professional Tax Crime Enablers

The organization for economic co-operation and development, OECD (2021), states that white-collar crime like tax evasion, bribery, and corruption are often concealed through complex legal structures and financial transactions facilitated by lawyers, accountants, financial institutions, and other professional enablers of such kinds of crime. These various forms of crime opportunity have significant impacts on government revenue, public confidence, and economic growth. The OECD (2021) report delineates a range of strategies and actions for countries to take to tackle professional intermediaries who enable tax evasion and other forms of financial crime on behalf of their criminal clients. The report highlights the damaging role played by these intermediaries and the importance of concerted domestic and international action in clamping down on the enablers of crime, and includes recommended counter-strategies for deterring, disrupting, investigating and prosecuting the professionals who enable tax evasion as white-collar crime.

OECD (2021: 10) described crime service providers as professional enablers:

> In general, professional enablers of tax crime and other financial crimes are intermediaries with specialized knowledge who play a specific role to facilitate the commission of a tax offence (and possibly other related financial crimes) by others. Professional enablers of tax crime and other financial crimes can include for example: tax professionals, lawyers and legal advisors, accountants, financial advisors, banks and financial institutions, company formation agents, registered agents, notaries, business trustees, trust and corporate service providers, and other promoters of tax evasion schemes.

According to OECD (2021), a professional enabler is typically an individual or entity with professional expertise to perform a specific service to aid their customer in carrying out a tax offence or other financial crime. Most countries do not have a specific definition of a professional enabler. However, the common attributes of a professional enabler include:

- Professional qualifications or training;
- Expertise in taxation, legal or financial processes;
- Experience in setting up tax structures, or structures with cross-border elements; and
- Experience setting up opaque structures for avoiding investigative scrutiny into the clients' tax and economic activities.

Professionals offer various legitimate business services to clients such as legal and accounting advice (OECD, 2021: 11):

> They may also be experts on finding legal loopholes giving room for the creation of "tax-avoidance" strategies. These strategies operate in the so-called "grey areas of the law", allowing professionals to use the inadequacies or ambiguities of a jurisdiction's legal framework to maximize the tax outcomes for their client. The possibility of using "grey areas of the law", while not technically illegal, should be limited by jurisdictions through the enhancement of their tax legislation and by fostering international co-operation.

In the outside-in perspective, OECD (2021: 27) argued that tax authorities can encounter professional enablers across a number of different functions, from those business areas involved in promoting voluntary compliance to those undertaking audits or investigations, through those leading on enforcement activity such as civil penalties and criminal prosecution:

> Lawyers, tax advisors, notaries and accountants are valued gatekeepers to a sound legal and financial system. Their unique sets of skills, together with the professional privileges awarded to them by statutes, put them in a special place within societies. They are experts who are in a position of trust and enjoy certain rights that are not shared by other professions. Jurisdictions should ensure that advisors perform their tasks in accordance with the law, and penalize those few who use their skills, expertise and privileges to design structures with the purpose of breaking the law. This requires that countries have in place a legal framework to support criminal investigators and the justice system in addressing and punishing professional enablers that engage in and facilitate the commission of such crimes.

Among the OECD (2021) suggestions is to target the actions of intermediaries before they become professional enablers. Once professional enablers such as banks have activities, mechanisms to deter and intercept it are necessary. Regulators and professional bodies have to stand up to the challenge of controlling banks across jurisdictions. There is a need for mechanisms of voluntary as well as mandatory reporting of wrongdoing.

The title of the OECD (2021) report is "ending the shell game" and "cracking down on the professionals who enable tax and white collar crimes". Ending the shell game addresses shell companies that are registered in the name of other legal persons in tax havens. Shell companies assist in opening of bank accounts in names that obscure the ownership, both domestic and abroad. Shell companies hold safe custody of incriminating data. Shell companies hold unaccounted funds in offshore jurisdictions, which are the proceeds of crime in overseas jurisdictions.

OECD (2021: 9) made the following recommendations for counter-strategies to combat professional enablers:

- Awareness: Ensure tax crime investigators are equipped with the understanding, intelligence, and analytics skills to identify the types of professional enablers operating in their jurisdiction, and to understand the risks posed by the ways that professional enablers devise, market, implement, and conceal tax crime and other financial crime.

- Legislation: Ensure the law provides investigators and prosecutors with sufficient authority to identify, prosecute, and sanction professional enablers, so as to deter and penalize those found to be professional enablers of tax crime.
- Deterrence and disruption: Ensure there is a coherent and multi-disciplinary strategy for preventing and disrupting the behavior of professional enablers, including engaging in communication, leveraging the role of supervisory bodies and industry sectors, incentivizing early disclosure and whistleblowing and taking a strong approach to enforcement in practice.
- Co-operation: Ensuring relevant authorities are proactively maximizing the availability of information, intelligence, and investigatory powers held by other domestic and international agencies to tackle professional enablers that are sophisticated and operating cross-border.
- Implementation: Appoint a lead person and agency in the jurisdiction with responsibility for overseeing the implementation of the professional enabler's strategy; including to undertake a review of its effectiveness over time and devise further changes as necessary.

The report by OECD (2021) emphasized that the majority of professionals are law-abiding and play an important role in assisting businesses and individuals to understand and comply with the law and helping the financial system run smoothly. Such law-abiding professionals are to be differentiated from a small set of professionals who use their skills and knowledge of the law to actively promote, market, and facilitate the commission of crime by their clients. The report was to support policy makers and law enforcement authorities to address the actions of that small set of lawyers, tax advisors, notaries, financial institutions, and other intermediaries that are professional enablers, with the intent of facilitating wrong-doing by their clients.

## Employees in Health Care Crime

White-collar crime in the health care sector is growing as individual patients as well as public agencies spend a growing amount of money on health care for themselves and for the population. An example is the pharmaceutical industry, which hands out prizes and awards to medical doctors at hospitals. The awards, prizes, and funding for research do frequently resemble regular bribes. In our perspective of outside-in, pharmaceutical officials not involved in bribing should notify hospitals about corrupt medical doctors.

Mulinari et al. (2021) studied responsive regulation to offset pharmaceutical industry illicit behavior in areas such as drug marketing based on self-regulation backed up with threats of government sanctions. The researchers argue for a more probing, critical and government-led regulatory approach instead of the self-regulatory approach. They found extensive abusive business practices, corporate non-compliance, and impression management. They used Astellas wrongdoing regarding off-label promotion of a prostate cancer drug as an example (Mulinari et al. 2021: 71):

> While initially denying wrongdoings, Astellas has fully accepted the findings and rulings, and global company executives have referred to the situation as a "corporate crisis". The company's official explanation for wrongdoings is one of "significant cultural and compliance failings created and caused by the actions and behaviors of some of its very senior managers" in Europe.

Økokrim (2021: 15) found that the criminal activity in the health sector in Norway is particularly evident in the issuance of fictitious medical statements that provide a basis for social security benefits, illegal issuance and sale of prescription medicine, as well as fraud of the reimbursement schemes to the health administration:

> There are several of the actors who have dealt with this type of criminal activity over several years; some have close relationships with known criminal actors and groups. The intention behind the criminal activity of employees in the health service appears to be only profit-motivated. The police have information that indicates that several doctors sell or write sick leave sheet for a fee, as well as write expert reports to help people get disability benefits and compensation from insurance companies. There are concrete examples of doctors who have made large cash deposits into their own personal bank accounts over several years, as well as received suspicious transfers from private individuals. In one case, it is a matter of millions. The money is assumed to be payments received for sick leave messages. The same doctors are in police systems identified with a number of other serious offenses.

Overall, Økokrim (2021) found it highly likely that many doctors will be paid to write fake sick leave reports and, in that way, acquire illegal income, which leads to social benefits being paid on the wrong basis.

## Public-Control Funding Agents

When public authorities are funding activities in the corporate sector, they are supposed to control the allocation of public funds to receivers that qualify for financial support and to purposes for which the funding is intended. For example during the Covid-19 pandemic, states compensated airlines, hotels, restaurants and a number of other businesses that suffered from government lockdown. The funding was to compensate those who reported losses from the lockdown. However, several business areas did not suffer, such as grocery stores that had increased sales because of restaurant lockdown, and online stores experienced growth in sales because of closed or restricted physical stores and shopping malls. Therefore, the latter business sectors were not entitled to government subsidies. Nevertheless, some businesses attempted to gain government support anyway. Virus-related fraud schemes developed quickly in many countries (Kennedy et al., 2021). This kind of fraud can be detected by an outside-in approach where tax authorities and other public agencies monitor money flows and financial performance of subsidies from the government.

Public-control agents can compare different sets of financial books as Wang et al. (2021: 274) did in their research of fraud that was not linked to the virus but to state subsidies for technology innovations in China:

> We look for evidence of whether fraudulent and honest companies depart in their behaviors when they receive external financial resources intended to promote technological innovation. A distinct feature of our setting allows us to overcome the aforementioned empirical challenges to more reliably pinpoint the relationship between fraud and innovation. Rather than relying on a public-control agent's fraud detection actions, we observe fraudulent behaviors directly by comparing two sets of financial books filed by the same set of firms at the same time but to two different state agencies. Although Chinese law requires these two sets of books to be identical, the firms in our data have an incentive to over-report their financial performance in one setting and to under-report their results in the other. This institutional feature allows us to observe whether a company has "cooked its books", but it is independent of the decisions of public-control agents to investigate certain types of actors. This approach enables us to identify the relationship between fraud and innovation without the complications of a public accusation of fraud.

Wang et al. (2021) studied a hand-collected dataset of 467 early-stage high technology firms that applied for government-funded innovation grants in in China. Based on their approach quoted above, they found that more than half of the firms had discrepant financial reporting in a direction that benefitted the firms. They also found that relative to honest firms, fraudulent firms were more likely to receive state grants and were less likely to recruit new employees or produce important innovations in the post-grant period.

Returning to the issue of virus-related fraud schemes, wealthy nations such as Norway provided substantial subsidies to suffering businesses. The internal revenue service in Norway had the task of detecting and reporting suspicions of Covid-19 fraud.

## Professional Crime Supporters

Attorneys at law firms can either take on the role of enablers of or the role of barriers to white-collar crime by their clients (Gottschalk, 2014). Certified accountants at accounting firms can either ignore crime signals or detect and report suspicions when they register transactions for their clients (Qiu and Slezak, 2019). Auditors at audit firms can either ignore crime signals or detect and report suspicions when they review accounting statements from their clients (Herron and Cornell, 2021). Real estate agents can either ignore crime signals or detect and report suspicions of money laundering or fraud when they meet buyers and sellers of real estate (Festovic, 2021). Professionals at financial services institutions can either take on the role of enablers of or the role of barriers to illegitimate loans or investments by their clients (Kleinfeld, 2019, 2020a). Professional intermediaries can either take on the role of enablers of or the role of barriers to transfer of funds to and from tax havens for their clients (OECD, 2021). The pharmaceutical industry, hospitals and other actors within health care either be silently accepted for their occasional wrongdoing or doctors, nurses, and others can blow the whistle whenever they notice wrongdoing (Mulinari et al., 2021).

Surprisingly often in detected white-collar crime cases, there were professional crime supporters who enabled, facilitated, or ignored deviant behavior by white-collar offenders. In the following, empirical evidence of professional crime supporters are collected from investigation reports by fraud examiners. Corporate investigators are in the business of reconstruct past events and sequences of events when there is suspicion of wrongdoing in organizations. They are hired by organizations to reconstruct past events and sequences of events in the client organizations. Investigation reports are the property of client organizations since they have paid for the work by the fraud examiners. Very seldom, the investigation reports become publicly available since client organizations have a variety of reasons for their secrecy (Gottschalk and Tcherni-Buzzeo, 2017).

**Table 8.1:** Investigation reports indicating professional crime supporters.

| Year | Organization | Country | Investigator | Suspect | Wrongdoing | Professional |
|---|---|---|---|---|---|---|
| 2018 | Danske Bank | Denmark | Bruun Hjejle (2018) | CEO | Money laundering | Local audit firm |
| 2018 | Moldova Banks | Moldova | Kroll (2018) | Chair | Bank fraud | Latvian banks |
| 2019 | Oceanteam | Norway | Sands (2019) | CEO | Embezzlement | Legal incentive plan |
| 2019 | Social Security | Denmark | PwC (2019) | Manager | Embezzlement | Family members |
| 2020 | Banedanmark | Denmark | Kammeradvokaten (2020a) | Managers | Corruption | Vendor representative |
| 2020 | Danske Bank | Denmark | Plesner (2020) | Executives | Client fraud | Software company |
| 2020 | Military Property | Denmark | Kammeradvokaten (2020b) | Manager | Corruption | Vendor representative |
| 2020 | Mercy Corps | Congo | Smith (2020) | Manager | Corruption | Vendor representative |
| 2020 | Swedbank | Sweden | Clifford Chance (2020) | CEO | Money laundering | Local audit firm |
| 2020 | Berkley University | United States | State Auditor (2020) | Coach | Corruption | External consultant |

**Table 8.1** (continued)

| Year | Organization | Country | Investigator | Suspect | Wrongdoing | Professional |
|---|---|---|---|---|---|---|
| 2020 | Wells Fargo | United States | Waters (2020) | CEO | client fraud | Financial regulators |
| 2020 | Wirecard Banking | Germany | KPMG (2020) | CEO | Embezzlement | Audit firm |
| 2021 | Apollo Global | United States | Dechert (2021) | CEO | Insider investments | External consultant |
| 2021 | Biathlon Union | Austria | Commission (2021) | President | Corruption | National biathlon |
| 2021 | Nasdaq Clearing | Sweden | Finansinspektionen (2021a, 2021b) | Investor | Manipulation | Investment banker |

Table 8.1 list investigation reports by fraud examiners from recent years that were possible to find for this research. The year of each white-collar crime investigation is listed in the first column. They range from 2018 to 2021. The second column lists organizations where potential wrongdoing occurred. The third column lists the home country of the client organization. The fourth column lists fraud examination firms that where hired by the client organizations in the second column. Most of the investigators in the fourth column are located at low firms. The fifth column lists individuals who were suspected of wrongdoing, and the sixth column lists the suspected wrongdoing.

The final column in Table 8.1 is our major interest in terms of professional crime supporters identified as actors who helped suspected white-collar crime become more convenient:

1. A local audit firm in Estonia ignored lack of money laundering procedures at the local branch office of Danske Bank. CEO Thomas Borgen at Danske Bank had to leave his position (Milne and Binham, 2018) after the bank disclosed the report from Bruun Hjejle (2018). Borgen was charged with white-collar crime by Danish prosecution authorities (Milne, 2019a), and the body of Danske Bank's former Estonian chief executive was found (Milne, 2019b).
2. Banks in Latvia were at the receiving end of funds illegally transferred from Moldova. Politician Ilan Shor left the country when the report from Kroll (2018) was published. The New York Times reported in October 2015 that Moldova "was rocked this year by the discovery that $1 billion had fraudulently siphoned from Moldova's banking system over a period of years, a huge amount for an impoverished country whose entire economic output is only about $8 billion a year" (Nechepurenko, 2015).
3. A consulting firm in the Netherlands designed an incentive plan for executives at Oceanteam enabling them to withdraw money to cover personal expenses.

After the release of the Sands (2019) report, executives at Oceanteam wanted to avoid disclosure of it, even to the company's own shareholders (Strandli, 2019). A letter sent to all shareholders of Oceanteam on March 30, 2020, illustrated the dispute, dissatisfaction, and reluctance to distribute the private policing report, as the letter emphasized the lack of trust that major shareholders and the company placed in the Sands (2019 report.

4. Family members helped create accounts where embezzled money could be laundered (PwC, 2019). BBC (2020) reported the following year: "A Danish court is due to deliver its verdict in the case of a woman accused of stealing 117 million Danish kroner (£13m; $17m) of government funding. Britta Nielsen worked at Denmark's social services board for 40 years, distributing funding to people in need".
5. Vendor representative offered favors and gifts to employees who happened to select that vendor. Investigative journalist at a Danish newspaper learned about potential fraud at Banedanmark, a governmental body under the ministry of transportation and housing in Denmark. The state-owned company is responsible for tracks, signals, and safety systems for the railroad traffic. They renovate the rail network and build new lines. They monitor rail traffic and steer trains in and out of stations and across the entire rail network. The Danish newspaper Berlingske reported in 2020 that they had started their inquiries in 2018 and that Banedanmark had reported suspects to the police two years later (Jessen and Jung, 2020): "Banedanmark suspects employees of bribery and illegal circumstances. Banedanmark has reported an employee and a contractor to the police for potential bribery. This is happening on the basis of a request for access to documents by Berlingske in 2018. The minister takes the matter very seriously". Banedanmark hired Danish law firm Kammeradvokaten (2020a) to investigate allegations against 23 named individuals who were former and current employees at the state-owned company. The individuals were suspected of bribery, abuse of office, and theft.
6. A software company developed a system where money on old client accounts was confiscated by the bank (Plesner, 2020). Danske Bank admitted in September 2020 that they had known for years about the bank's practice of collecting outdated and excessive debt from customers. Denmark's financial watchdog Finanstilsynet (2020) launched the previous month an inquiry into how Danske Bank had wrongly collected debt from up to 106,000 customers since 2004. The bank blamed IT system errors (Reuters, 2020). While CEO Thomas Borgen had to leave his position and was charged with white-collar crime in the money laundering scandal (Bruun Hjejle, 2018; Milne, 2019a, 2019b; Milne and Binshan, 2018), CEO Jesper Nielsen and then CEO Chris Vogelzang had to leave their positions at Danske Bank because of the fraud against bank customers. The former chief executives all faced further criminal proceedings in Denmark (Ulvin, 2021).

7. Vendor representative offered favors and gifts to an employee who happened to select that vendor (Kammeradvokaten, 2020b). Dennis Bechmann Engmann, who was previously head of the building department at Karup Airport, was sentenced by the court in Viborg to two years in prison. The verdict was the end of the case of bribery in the Ministry of Defense's property management agency (Julsgaard, 2020). In 2015 and 2016, Dennis Bechmann Engmann made extensive renovations of his house in Møldrup and an extension of the building at a total value of 1.7 million kroner (about USD 240,000). The building work was completed free of charge by one of the vendors who did construction work for the Ministry of Defense's property management agency.
8. Local service providers offered foreign aid officials bribes when they selected those providers (Smith, 2020). Mercy Corps is a charity. The international non-government organization (NGO) experienced a scam in the Democratic Republic of Congo (DRC). The scam involved corrupt aid workers, business owners, and community leaders (Kleinfeld, 2020b): "Together they zeroed in on the humanitarian sector's flagship rapid response programmes – the main mechanism for helping displaced people in Congo, where hundreds of millions of dollars of foreign aid are spent every year".
9. A local audit firm in Estonia ignored lack of money laundering procedures at the local branch office of Swedbank. Swedbank carried out bank transactions of more than 37 billion Euros (about US$40 billion) with a high risk for money laundering over a five-year period according to private policing in terms of an internal investigation by fraud examiners from law firm Clifford Chance (2020). The investigation report suggests that the Swedish bank actively targeted high-risk individuals in the Baltic region and points to failings from both top management and the board (Milne, 2020).
10. An external consultant who ran a California-based edge college and career network helped rich parents bribe athlete coaches at prestigious universities. The University of California was investigated by the auditor of the state of California. The California state auditor found that qualified students faced an inconsistent and unfair admissions system that had been improperly influence by relationships and monetary donations (State Auditor, 2020). Several rich and mighty people were involved in the corruption scandal (Puente, 2020; Taylor, 2020).
11. Financial regulators were reluctant to intervene when bank clients were fraudulently assigned cards and accounts at their expense (Shichor and Heeren, 2021). Waters (2020) at the U.S. House of Representatives investigated Wells Fargo in the United States. Examiners draw conclusions stating that Wells Fargo's board and management prioritized financial and other considerations above fixing the deviant issues identified, Wells Fargo's board did not hold senior management accountable for repeated deviance, and management gave inaccurate and misleading testimony (Rothacker, 2016; Shearman Sterling, 2017; Wieczner, 2017).

12. Audit firm confirmed that money had disappeared but was reluctant to trace it. The background for the investigation of Wirecard by KPMG (2020) was to examine the validity of various accusations that were presented in the press and on the internet (Chazan and Storbeck, 2020a, 2020b). Among these allegations, it was suggested that Wirecard has, among other things, recorded higher revenues through fictitious customer relationships, suspicious loan relationships through what is called merchant cash advance, over reporting of profits in the Singapore branch and in the United Arab Emirates, and a suspicious transaction by a company in India (McCrum, 2019). The allegations were concerned with deficiencies in the accounts and mysterious collaborations with third-party companies in countries such as Singapore, the United Arab Emirates, and India (McCrum, 2020).
13. Financial advisor helped design fraud scheme for insider investments. The media reported in 2020 that "the billionaire who stood by Jeffrey Epstein", "Dechert's Leon Black investigation: things you may have missed", "what a sad tale of sycophants: Wall Street is not buying Leon Black's Epstein story", "Jeffrey Epstein's deep ties to top Wall Street figures", "billionaire Leon Black is leaving Apollo following scrutiny over ties to Jeffrey Epstein", and "billionaire Leon Black, revealed to pay Jeffrey Epstein $158, is stepping down" (Gara and Voytko, 2021). These headlines emerged as law firm Dechert (2021) concluded an investigation on behalf of Apollo Global Management' board. Jeffrey Epstein committed suicide in jail in August 2019 after conviction as a sex offender abusing underage female prostitutes (Sampson, 2020). The suspected fraud was concerned with Black's involvement with Epstein.
14. A national biathlon union invited the president to experience favors and adventures that emerged as bribes (Commission, 2021). Anders Besseberg was president of the International Biathlon Union (IBU) from 1992 until he was laid off in 2018 on the basis of accusations of wrongdoing (Ellingworth and Dunbar, 2018). During those years, the sport of biathlon evolved from being a sport for people who were particularly interested to becoming one of the most popular winter sports on television. Besseberg is considered the architect of the various successful forms of competition in biathlon such as hunting start, joint start, and mixed relays. He lifted the sport of biathlon to new heights during his period as president. By being in the position of president over such a long time, he became a powerful individual with great influence internationally. There were no restrictions on being the union president and how many periods he could be in such a central position without being replaced. Besseberg has been a central figure in shaping the business, culture, ethics, structure, and compliance of right and wrong at IBU as an organization. The suspected fraud was concerned with the president receiving favors and bribes from Russian biathlon union officials.

15. Investment banker ignored red light signals for risky gambling in different energy prices. Finansinspektionen (2021a, 2021b) found deviations at the company so serious that they fined the company $36 million. Nasdaq Clearing appealed the fine as the company disagreed with several of the fundamental assessments that underpinned the decision as well as its conclusions.

# 9 Corporate Scandal Accounts

A corporate scandal is "an unexpected, publicly known, and harmful event that has high levels of initial uncertainty, interferes with the normal operation of an organization, and generates widespread, intuitive, and negative perceptions" externally (Bundy and Pfarrer, 2015: 350). In a typical scandal, "the press (or a whistleblower) raises the alarm, expressing outrage which manifests itself as a moral panic" (Smith et al., 2022: 4). The event is regarded as legally, morally, or socially wrong and causes general public outrage. Scandals are negative surprises that are shocking and can cause moral panic. Scandals are publicized transgressions that run counter to established norms, typically resulting in condemnation and discredit including bad press, disengagement of key constituencies, the severance of network ties and decrease in delivering to key performance indicators (Piazza and Jourdan, 2018). Scandals cause public calls for examinations (Smith et al., 2022: 3):

> Scandals are a key mechanism used by media, pressure groups and social movements to demand inquiries and investigations into alleged corruption, incompetence and immorality.

As a scandal evolves, the corporation has to make statements to explain unanticipated negative conduct in the form of accounts of incidents (Gottschalk and Benson, 2020). A typical element of scandal accounts is the emphasis on corporate compliance. The scandalized enterprise might experience various forms of compliance pressure, conformity pressure, and obedience pressure. Obedience pressure is considered a form of social influence pressure, alongside the two other types of social influence pressure: compliance pressure and conformity pressure (Baird and Zelin, 2009: 2):

> Compliance pressure is similar to obedience pressure, except that compliance pressure can come from one's peers as well as from superiors, while obedience pressure must come from an authority figure. Conformity pressure refers to pressure to conform to perceived or societal norms.

At Samherji in Iceland, bottom-up notification occurred when an employee blew the whistle on his employer. Corporate greed at the headquarters led to convenient corruption in Namibia, where Samherji obtained profitable offshore fishing rights. The strong goal-orientation of the company was the motive, the opportunity was access to influential people including Namibian government ministers, and the willingness was the common local culture of corruption (Amundsen, 2021; Ekroll et al., 2019; Kibar, 2020a, 2020b; Kleinfeld, 2019, 2020a; Reuters, 2019; Schultz, 2019; Schultz and Trumpy, 2019a, 2019b). The whistleblower at Samherji was Johannes Stefansson who told WikiLeaks and then Al Jazeera. Samherji (2019a, 2019b, 2020a, 2020b) first denied wrongdoing. A statement and apology was eventually published by Samherji (2021).

https://doi.org/10.1515/9783110986686-010

At Telia in Sweden, detection of corruption occurred in a bottom-up approach as an employee in a competing telecom enterprise blew the whistle on his employer (Deloitte, 2016; Hovland and Gauthier-Villars, 2015; Trumpy, 2016). Several telecom enterprises were involved in corruption in Uzbekistan to obtain profitable mobile phone licenses. The strong goal-orientation of companies such as Telia was the motive, the opportunity was access to the daughter of the Uzbek president, and the willingness was common corrupt culture in the telecommunication industry. Telia's initial denial of wrongdoing eventually changed into a partial acknowledgment in combination with a scapegoating discourse (Schoultz and Flyghed, 2020a, 2020b, 2021a, 2021b).

The interesting topic in this chapter is how the various corporations dealt with accusations and allegations of misconduct in terms of corporate scandal accounts where corporations have to make some kind of statements publicly in response over time. In addition to Samherji and Telia, this chapter presents Lundin Energy in Sweden (Schoultz and Flyghed, 2020a, 2020b), Wells Fargo in the United States (Shichor and Heeren, 2021), Astellas in Japan (Mulinari et al., 2021), and the big four auditors Deloitte, EY, KPMG, and PwC (Dunne et al., 2021). Furthermore in this chapter, the cases of Danske Bank in Denmark (Bruun Hjejle, 2018), Olympus corporation in Japan (Deloitte, 2011), Toshiba Corporation in Japan (Deloitte, 2015; Demetriades and Owusu-Agyei, 2021), Fuji Xerox in New Zealand (Deloitte, 2017), NNPC in Nigeria (PwC, 2015), Telenor in Norway (Deloitte, 2016), Nordea bank in Sweden (Mannheimer Swartling, 2016), Lehman Brothers in the United States (Jenner Block, 2010), General Motors in the United States (Jenner Block, 2014), WorldCom in the United States (PwC, 2003), and Enron corporation (Wilmer Cutler Pickering, 2003) are briefly reviewed towards the end of the chapter, as research information regarding their early and late accounts of scandals is available. An account is a statement made by an actor to explain unanticipated or untoward behavior that is subject to some sort of evaluative inquiry by other actors (Gottschalk and Benson, 2020).

## Icelandic Samherji in Namibia

The bottom-up whistleblower told WikiLeaks (Kibar, 2020a, 2020b) and then Al Jazeera (Kleinfeld, 2019, 2020a). According to Reuters (2019), Samherji transferred more than $70 million through a shell company in the tax haven Marshall Islands from 2011 to 2018. Samherji transferred the money through accounts in the Norwegian bank DNB. The bank's largest shareholder is the Norwegian state, which holds 34% stake in the bank (Ekroll et al., 2019; Kibar, 2020a, 2020b). Starting with DNB in Norway, the broadcasting corporation Al Jazeera investigated allegations and published the report entitled "Anatomy of a bribe: A deep dive into an underworld of corruption – An Al Jazeera investigation into the corrupt power brokers and global business elites defrauding the Namibian people" (Kleinfeld, 2019). The alleged corruption payments from the Icelandic fishing corporation Samherji traveled via the Norwegian bank DNB to state officials in Namibia to obtain fishing rights off the coast of Namibia (Amundsen, 2021; Schultz, 2019; Schultz and Trumpy, 2019a, 2019b).

Samherji is a seafood company in Iceland. The country's largest fishing group was accused of paying bribes to trawl an African country's waters (Samherji, 2019a, 2019b, 2020a, 2020b). Financial Times reported in November 2019 that two ministers in Namibia had resigned and that Samherji's chief executive had temporarily stepped down over allegations the company paid bribes for fishing quotas in the southern African nation's maritime waters (Samherji, 2019b). The whistleblower at Samherji was Johannes Stefansson who told WikiLeaks and then Al Jazeera.

Johannes Stefansson came to Namibia in Africa in 2011, where he was assigned the task by the Icelandic seafood company Samherji of looking for business opportunities. To complete the mission, he involved himself in questionable payments to politicians and businesspeople in Namibia and Angola. After a while, he developed a bad conscience and felt guilty of wrongdoing. He decided to give notice of the situation. The police arrested the former minister of fisheries in Namibia, Bernhard Esau, and indicted him for corruption and money laundering in November 2019. Stefansson provided information to WikiLeaks and then Al Jazeera, where investigative journalist James Kleinfeld interviewed local sources in Namibia. Kleinfeld (2019) then wrote a report on the "Anatomy of a bribe: A deep dive into an underworld of corruption". Iceland public broadcasting, similar to BBC in the UK, interviewed the whistleblower and cooperated with Al Jazeera. Al Jazeera's investigative unit secretly filmed officials in Namibia demanding cash in exchange for political favors. It was a story of how foreign companies plunder Africa's natural resources. Using confidential documents provided to Al Jazeera by WikiLeaks, "Anatomy of a Bribe" exposed the government ministers and public officials willing to sell off Namibia's assets in return for millions of dollars in bribes. Al Jazeera journalists spent three months undercover posing as foreign investors looking to exploit the lucrative Namibian fishing industry. The country's minister of fisheries demonstrated a willingness to use a front company to accept a $200,000 'donation'. Exclusive testimony from the whistleblower, who worked for Iceland's biggest fishing company, revealed that his employer seemingly instructed him to bribe ministers and even the president in return for fishing rights worth hundreds of millions of dollars.

The prosecuting authority in Namibia claimed in December 2019 that the accused officials in the country had received 103 million Namibian dollars – equivalent to 6 million US dollars – in kickbacks to ensure the Icelandic company access to fishing quotas. According to court documents, a large number of false invoices had been made to hide the payments (Kibar, 2020a).

Samherji in Iceland hired fraud examiners at law firm Wikborg Rein in Norway to investigate all these allegations. The report of investigation was completed in the summer of 2020, but Samherji as the client organization would not disclose the report and denied everybody insight into it.

The broadcasting corporation Al Jazeera investigated allegations and published the report entitled "Anatomy of a bribe: A deep dive into an underworld of corruption", "An Al Jazeera investigation into the corrupt power brokers and global business elites defrauding the Namibian people", and "The storm is brewing – We are preparing ourselves for war" (Kleinfeld, 2019):

> Since Al Jazeera first presented the accused parties with evidence of their alleged wrongdoing, the response has been swift and overwhelming: Minister of Fisheries Bernhard Esau and the minister of justice have both resigned from their cabinet positions; James Hatuikulipi has resigned as the chairman of Fishcor and has also resigned from his job as the managing director of Investec Asset Management. In the run-up to elections in Namibia, the Fishrot affair has caused outrage in the country, leading to protests in the capital, Windhoek, with hundreds of people marching to the Anti-Corruption Commission demanding decisive action against corruption in the country. On the day of the elections on November 27, most of the Namibians implicated in the investigation were arrested on charges of corruption, money laundering and fraud.
>
> All the Namibians featured in the Al Jazeera investigation deny all wrongdoing. Sacky Kadhila told The Namibian newspaper that he knew from the start that our undercover reporters were "fake businessmen". "I played along . . . in order to confirm my suspicions," he wrote. He added that he had reported the matter to the president's lawyer, Sisa Namandje, who in turn claimed he had alerted police.
>
> In Iceland, the scandal has led to the suspension of Samherji's longtime CEO.

Al Jazeera is an independent news organization funded in part by the Qatari government. In 2006, Al Jazeera Satellite Network was changed to a public utility and private corporation by a public memorandum and articles of association in accordance with the provisions of Qatar Law and was re-named Al Jazeera Media Network. The investigative journalist who wrote the above report continued his investigations in Namibia where he detected corruption allegations because of a 5G deal with Huawei. Bribes were offered to politicians to ensure Chinese tech giant Huawei would win an exclusive 5G telecommunication network in Namibia (Kleinfeld, 2020a).

Two years long, from 2019 to 2021, executives at Samherji in Iceland denied wrongdoing and blamed Johannes Stafansson for the wrongdoing in Namibia. However, on June 26, 2021, Samherji published a statement and apology on its website (www.samherji.is):

> Samherji firmly rejects the allegations of bribery but accepts the criticism that in the circumstances, it was necessary to pay more attention to how payments were made, who they were made to and on what basis, who had the authority to give instructions about them and where they should be received. It is also clear that the underlying agreements behind the payments should have been precise and formal (. . .)
>
> "It is my and Samherji's firm position that no criminal offences were committed in Namibia by companies on our behalf or their employees, apart from the conduct that the former managing

> director has directly confessed to and acknowledged. Nonetheless, as Samherji's top executive, I am responsible for allowing the business practices in Namibia to take place. It has upset our staff, friends, families, business partners, customers and others in our community. I am very sorry that this happened, and I sincerely apologize to all those involved, both personally and on behalf of the company. Now it's important to ensure that nothing like this happens again. We will certainly strive for that", says Thorsteinn Már Baldvinsson, CEO of Samherji.

The apology here by the CEO is limited to not having oversight and guardianship in Namibia against opportunistic employees such as Johannes Stefansson. The actual corruption is not admitted but rather attributed to the whistleblower.

The statement by Samherji (2021) claimed to present the main findings by examiner Elisabeth Roscher at law firm Wikborg Rein in Norway. The corporate statement made indirect references to the investigation report as there are no quotes in the statement. The contents of the investigation report might thus have been subject to manipulation by Samherji before publication of the so-called main findings. Maybe Samherji avoided text in the report of investigation that directly criticized Samherji and potentially made the firm legally liable. Maybe Samherji chose text in the investigation report that blamed others for incidents in the wrongdoing. Maybe Samherji (2021) in their statement selected findings that they easily and conveniently could comment.

## Swedish Telia in Uzbekistan

The bottom-up whistleblower told his employer Telenor in Norway that VimpelCom was financially involved with the daughter of the Uzbek president while VimpelCom was applying for mobile phone licenses in Uzbekistan. The Norwegian telecommunication company Telenor owned one-third of the telecommunication company VimpelCom in the Netherlands where the Norwegian Telenor employee currently was working. Two Telenor executives in Norway interviewed the whistleblower about the allegations of corruption in Uzbekistan by VimpelCom (Deloitte, 2016; Hovland and Gauthier-Villars, 2015; Trumpy, 2016).

After a while, the scandal of corruption in Uzbekistan spread to competing telecommunication companies such as Telia in Sweden. Several telecom enterprises were involved in corruption in Uzbekistan to obtain profitable mobile phone licenses. The strong goal-orientation of companies such as Telia was the motive, the opportunity was access to the daughter of the Uzbek president, and the willingness was common corrupt culture in the telecommunication industry. Telia's initial denial of wrongdoing eventually changed into a partial acknowledgment in combination with a scapegoating discourse (Schoultz and Flyghed, 2020a, 2020b, 2021a, 2021b).

Telia bribed the daughter of the president in Uzbekistan to obtain licenses for mobile phone communication in the country. When detected, Telia agreed to pay $965 million to resolve charges relating to violations of the Foreign Corrupt Practices

Act in the United States. At the same time, the public prosecutor in Sweden charged three executives at Telia of bribery in connection with the company's entry in Uzbekistan (Schoultz and Flyghed, 2020a, 2021b).

Telia were not the only company bribing Gulnara Karimova, the daughter of Uzbek president Islam Karimov. The Dutch telecommunication company VimpelCom did the same, and they had to enter into a deferred prosecution agreement with the US Department of Justice, where VimpelCom admitted, accepted, and acknowledged that it was responsible for acts of its officers, directors, employees, and agents. The Norwegian chief executive at VimpelCom, Jo Lunder was charged for corruption by Norwegian police. Two executives at Telenor in Norway had to leave their positions after ignoring whistleblowers from VimpelCom, where Telenor had a substantial share of the ownership (Deloitte, 2016).

Corruption is defined as the giving, requesting, receiving, or accepting of an improper advantage related to a position, office, or assignment (Ashforth et al., 2008). The improper advantage does not have to be connected to a specific action or to not doing this action (Artello and Albanese, 2021). It will be sufficient if the advantage can be linked to a person's position, office, or assignment. An individual or group is guilty of corruption if they accept money or money's worth for doing something that he is under a duty to do anyway, that he is under a duty not to do, or to exercise a legitimate discretion for improper reason. Corruption is to destroy or pervert the integrity or fidelity of a person in his discharge of duty, it is to induce to act dishonestly or unfaithfully, it is to make venal, and it is to bribe (Lord et al., 2018). Corruption involves behavior on the part of officials in the public or private sectors, in which they improperly and unlawfully enrich themselves and/or those close to them, or induce others to do so, by misusing the position in which they are placed. Corruption is an undesirable and destructive aspect of social life (Pertiwi, 2018). Corruption covers a wide range of illegal activity such as kickbacks, embezzlement, and extortion. Corruption entails "mistreatment of suppliers, customers, or competitors" (Kolthoff, 2020: 434).

In 2006, Telia sought to expand into the central Asian telecommunications market (Schoultz and Flyghed, 2020b: 4):

> The growth strategy was well-anchored in Telia and among the company's owners, which include the Swedish state. Telia entered Uzbekistan in 2007, a country controlled by the authoritarian President Islam Karimov and his family (up until his death in 2016), who over the years has been shown to have very little respect for human rights. Uzbekistan was known as a country in which it was almost impossible to implement international investments without the involvement of the governing regime. In information presented to the Telia board in 2007, Uzbekistan was described "as the most difficult and politically most uncertain country" but was at the same time understood to be the "commercially most interesting".
>
> As a result of the region's human rights record, Telia's presence in Uzbekistan was from the start criticized by human rights organizations, investors and the Swedish media. The criticism related to Telia's partner in Uzbekistan and this partner's connections with president Karimov,

> also to claims that Telia's equipment was being used for the purpose of surveilling the political opposition in several authoritarian countries.

Telia's response to the allegations involved a wide range of neutralizations and denials. The company stated that they were aware of the corruption problems in Uzbekistan while at the same time giving assurance s that the company had zero tolerance for corruption (Schoultz and Flyghed, 2020b).

The Swedish Telia corruption case was detected by investigative journalists at the Swedish public broadcasting corporation in the wake of the Dutch VimpelCom scandal involving Norwegian Telenor. Then the Telia affair in Uzbekistan became a public scandal in 2012 (Schoultz and Flyghed, 2020b: 5):

> Following revelations focused on how the company was participating in surveillance operations conducted by the secret services linked to several oppressive regimes, the investigative TV shows moved on to look at the 2007 acquisition by Telia of a 3G license, frequencies and number series, in order to become established as a telecom operator in Uzbekistan. Information was presented describing extensive financial transactions with a letter-box entity, Takilant. The journalists could show that Takilant was owned by an assistant to the president's daughter, Gulnara Karimova. By the time that Telia purchased the license in Uzbekistan, Gulnara Karimova's racketeering activities in the telecommunications market had been documented in several high-profile news publications.

Telia attempted to conceal corruption in criminal market structures dominated by corruption. Criminal market structures cause external collapse. Collapse represents a convenient situation for everybody ready to commit white-collar crime. Some industries have criminal market structures, where a corporation simply adapts to illegitimate practices (Chang et al., 2005; Geest et al., 2017).

The financial motive for Telia was to make money in Uzbekistan by providing mobile phone services in the country. In many organizations, ends justify means (Campbell and Göritz, 2014). If ends in terms of ambitions and goals are difficult to realize and achieve in legal ways, illegal means represent an alternative in many organizations (Jonnergård et al., 2010). Among most executives, it is an obvious necessity to achieve goals and objectives, while it is an obvious catastrophe failing to achieve goals and objectives. Welsh and Ordonez (2014) found that high performance goals cause unethical behavior. Dodge (2009: 15) argues that it is tough rivalry making executives in the organization commit crime to attain goals:

> The competitive environment generates pressures on the organization to violate the law in order to attain goals.

Individual executives would like to be successful, and they would like their workplace to be successful. Being associated with a successful business is important to the identity of many executives. They explore and exploit attractive corporate economic possibilities in both legal and illegal ways, so that their organization can emerge just as successful, or as even more successful, than other organizations.

Profit orientation becomes stronger in goal-oriented organizations whose aim tends to be an ambitious financial bottom line. A strong emphasis on goal attainment might indeed lead organizational members to engage in illegal acts (Kang and Thosuwanchot, 2017).

## Swedish Lundin Energy in Sudan

This is a case of outside-in detection of suspected corporate crime. The outsiders were non-government organizations working in aid functions in Sudan during the civil war that eventually lead to the separation of South Sudan. The civil war caused the deaths of thousands of people, the forced displacement of almost two hundred thousand people, and numerous cases of rape, torture, and abduction. Villages were put on fire. According to the outside-in sources, executives at Lundin Energy knew that such crime was committed, that Lundin Energy enabled some of it, took no effective action to stop their occurrence, and worked alongside their perpetrators to secure oil and gas activities. Communities were allegedly violently displaced from areas where Lundin Energy planned to operate (BHR Resource Center, 2018).

Schoultz and Flyghed (2020a: 739) suggest that corporate accounts of wrongdoing slide over time from "we didn't do it" to "we've learned our lesson". On this slippery slope of slow confession that can last for years, corporate spokespersons may visit various justification and neutralization statements such as denial of the act, denial of responsibility, and diffusion of responsibility, over to moral indifference, avoidance and minimization of the allegation, condemnation of the condemner, and finally apology. In an apology, the actor admits violating a rule, accepts the validity of the rule, and expresses embarrassment and anger at self.

Lundin Energy is a business enterprise in oil and gas headquartered in Sweden that explores for, develops, and produces natural resources. In June 2010, the Swedish prosecution authority initiated an investigation into Lundin's activities in southern Sudan from 1997 to 2003 in an area called Block 5A, where the energy company operated as part of a consortium formed with the Malaysian company Petronas, the Austrian company OMV and the Sudanese company Sudapet. During the police investigation in Sweden, Lundin created its own website for the legal case to deny any wrongdoing (www.lundinsudanlegalcase.com, downloaded July 14, 2021):

> None of Lundin's representatives committed or were complicit in any violations of international humanitarian law by the Government of Sudan or associated militia, and we know that Lundin did nothing wrong.
>
> Lundin and its representatives have cooperated continuously and proactively with the investigation since it began in 2010, and we continue to have significant concerns about the fairness and legal basis of this case.

> Our firm belief is that Lundin was a force for development in Sudan and did everything in our power to advocate for peace by peaceful means in the country.

Two distinct techniques of guilt removal are implicit in this quote. First, the company expressed concern about the fairness and legal basis. Implicitly they attacked the Swedish prosecution authority and condemned their behavior. It is a matter of condemning the condemner, which is a frequently applied neutralization technique. Outsiders do not understand relevant behavior. The offender tries to accuse critics of questionable motives for criticizing them. According to this technique of condemning the condemners, one neutralizes own actions by blaming those who create problems for the offender. The offender deflects moral condemnation onto those ridiculing the misbehavior by pointing out that they engage in unfair proceedings. The offender condemns procedures of the criminal justice system, especially police investigation with interrogation, as well as media coverage of the case.

The other distinct technique visible in the quote is the statement that Lundin was a force for development and peace in Sudan. Implicitly, Lundin argued that they did so much good that they should be excused if they made some mistakes. It is a matter of an acceptable blunder quota. *It was a necessary shortcut to get things done*. The offender argues that what he or she did is acceptable given the situation and given his or her position. The company claims that after having done so much good for so many for so long time, others should excuse them for more wrongdoings than other people deserve forgiveness. Others should understand that the alleged crime was an acceptable mistake. This is in line with the metaphor of the ledger, which uses the idea of compensating bad acts by good acts. That is, the individual believes that he or she has previously performed a number of good acts and has accrued a surplus of good will, and, because of this, can afford to commit some bad actions. Executives in corporate environments neutralize their actions through the metaphor of the ledger by rationalizing that their overall past good behavior justifies occasional rule breaking.

Not only did Lundin post their own self-defense on the Internet, but they also hired Bedford Row International to present a defense of Lundin in Sudan in the form a report. The report had its own website (www.reportlundinsudan.com, downloaded July 14, 2021) and was written by the lawyers Steven Kay, Gillain Higgins, John Traversi, and Rupert Boswall in the UK:

> This report finds that the allegations and basis for the Lundin investigation are seriously flawed.

The investigation report claimed that the report was independent of the company Lundin Energy as the client. The report attacked the sources of information on which the Swedish prosecution apparently based the case against the company. Again, it was an attempt of condemning the condemners as some of the information originated from non-governmental organizations (NGOs) operating in Sudan. NGOs claimed that Lundin had been involved in crime against humanity, including death shootings and the burning of villages.

In October 2018, the Swedish prosecuting authority received approval in principle to indict the chief executive of Lundin Energy (formerly Lundin Petroleum) and the chairperson of the board, Alexander Schneiter and Ian Lundin. The charges related to aiding and abetting war crime occurring between 1999 and 2003 in Sudan, now South Sudan. Both denied the allegations.

Alex Schneiter resigned from his position and the company at the end of 2020 (Lorentzen, 2020). The survival of the company Lundin Energy was apparently more important than the protection of Alex Schneiter in his chief executive position. Research shows that after an initial protection of suspected executives, corporations tend to separate, distance, and disassociate themselves from accused, previously trusted officials during a white-collar scandal (Gottschalk and Benson, 2020).

In their analysis of the Lundin Energy case, Schoultz and Flyghed (2020b: 7) found that the initial account of the scandal was characterized by appeal to higher loyalties, denial of knowledge, and condemnation of the condemner:

> The vice president of exploration, Alexander Schneiter, who had lived in Sudan during the ten-year period that the company had been present in the country, had not seen any of the phenomena witnessed by the various aid and human rights organizations. "I have instead seen the opposite. How villages have grown up along the road and how people's conditions have improved as a result of having better communications. Our presence means a form of security for the population". Nor had the company's CEO, Ian Lundin, "seen any burning villages, only tribes that are fighting one another". Representatives of Lundin Petroleum used denial of knowledge, in the form of an interpretative denial, which involves assertions of not having known what was happening at the time.

The next account of the Sudan scandal was characterized by condemnation of the condemner and literal denial. Schoultz and Flyghed (2020b: 8) found that Lundin's actions in relation to its critics were to take a more aggressive form particularly against publication of a report by the European coalition on oil in Sudan:

> The coalition received an e-mail from the chairman of the Lundin board, Ian Lundin. "Lundin responded by stating that it considers the report to be defamatory and it reserved the right to claim damages if it were to be published". This form of response, where the corporation legally counteracts an accusation of crime through the threat of initiating lawsuits against their accusers, is not necessarily a form of neutralization but a way of avoiding the allegations.

The third phase of public accounts by Lundin was characterized by denial of responsibility, condemnation of the condemner, and cooperation. Two weeks after the publication of the European coalition report, the prosecutor in Stockholm initiated a criminal investigation into suspicions of violations of international law relating to the activities of Lundin's activities in Sudan (Schoultz and Flyghed, 2020b: 9):

> A few days later, a statement was released by the company's deputy chief legal officer denying all responsibility: "The prosecutor's press release speaks of a criminal investigation into

> alleged offences against international law that will be attempting to ascertain which individuals may be connected to Sweden. Lundin Petroleum is not involved in this".

This quote indicates that the company was ready to separate, distance, and disassociates itself from the potentially blamed executive Schneiter already in 2010 if considered necessary for company revival. Schneiter was the potential scapegoat, but it took a decade before the scapegoat was dismissed from the company. The long period of time might be explained by the similarly long time Swedish investigators and prosecutors were working on the case. At the time of writing about this case, in the summer of 2021, there is still no court hearings scheduled with Ian Lundin and Alexander Schneiter as defendants. While a company cannot be incarcerated, it can certainly be fined substantially in monetary terms. The deputy chief legal officer attempted in the quote above to acquit Lundin as a company from any suspicion. However, Swedish prosecutors had included the company in their criminal charges.

The fourth and final phase of public accounts by Lundin was characterized by minimizing the allegations where the company approach was to downplay the seriousness of the accusations against the company (Schoultz and Flyghed, 2020b: 9):

> In November 2016, the Swedish prosecution authority determined to notify Ian Lundin, chairman of the board and Alex Schneiter, the company's CEO, that they were suspected of aiding and abetting aggravated crimes against international law. Lundin's press officer immediately made a statement. "It is common in the context of a Swedish criminal investigation to be notified that one is a suspect when you meet the prosecutor. This does not mean that there will be a prosecution. We are entirely convinced that there are no grounds for any of the allegations of incorrect behavior by representatives of Lundin".

Lundin accounts so far have not (yet) been of the kind of "we've learned our lesson" (Schoultz and Flyghed (2020a: 739). Rather, the focus continued on the path of condemning the condemners. If Lundin and Schneiter end up as defendants in Swedish court, and they are convicted to prison, and in addition, Lundin Energy as a company is assigned a substantial fine for wrongdoing in Sudan, then it is not unlikely that the public statement will be that they have learned a lesson.

Human rights violations motivated by white-collar crime profits in South Sudan were studied by a commission (Council, 2021: 1):

> Even prior to gaining independence in July 2011, human rights violations and related economic crimes in southern Sudan had a direct, negative impact on the capacity of the State to meet its core, socio-economic obligations, such as healthcare, education, and the Sustainable Development Goals, with poor and extremely poor civilians including women and children disproportionately affected.

A significant proportion of oil revenues continued to be diverted and stolen in South Sudan (Council, 2021).

## Wells Fargo in the United States

Bottom-up reporting of suspected wrongdoing sometimes finds its way out of the organization before exposure of the potential scandal. Employees might report their suspicion to a trusted lawyer that formally approaches the employer with the notification that the lawyer as the employee's representative has in legal custody. An alternative external destination for whistleblowing is the media, which happened in the case of Wells Fargo in the United States. Wells Fargo's deviant sales practice first came to public attention and thereby the bank's attention through articles in the Los Angeles Times that spotlighted troubling practices engaged in by some employees in Los Angeles (Rothacker, 2016; Shichor and Heeren, 2021; Wieczner, 2017).

The message was that Wells Fargo had a widespread fraudulent business practice related to an intense pressure for increasing sales of bank products. In the corporate accounts of the scandal, the bank quickly seemed to admit wrongdoing (Shichor and Heeren, 2021: 97):

> Wells Fargo claimed that it "has responded swiftly to the crisis" after the settlement was made public. This "response" included the refunding of $2.6 million in fees that were wrongly levied on customers and the firing of 5,300 lower level employees who were involved in the above practices, which included among other offenses, the forging of signatures on applications for the opening of many accounts.

The settlement with various agencies in the United States was for Wells Fargo to pay $185 million. However, the quote above was an attempt to attribute blame to lower level employees for wrongdoing that was initiated from the top level of the bank. The quote that Wells Fargo responded swiftly was an attempt of making 5,300 employees scapegoats for corporate wrongdoing. A scapegoat is a person who is blamed for the wrongdoings, mistakes, or faults of others (Gangloff et al., 2016), in this case the wrongdoings of top management. The chief executive had introduced improper and unethical sales practices violating specific statutory provisions, according to an internal review report by corporate investigators from law firm Shearman Sterling (2017). Wells Fargo's Community Bank had aggressive sales practices where bank customers received services that they had not ordered. The law firm conducted a fraud examination and wrote an investigation report about management and employees in the sales model perspective. The report was 113 pages.

However, the initial corporate account as illustrated by the above quote was also referred to by Rothacker (2016):

> Wells Fargo has said it fired 5,300 employees for secretly opening unauthorized deposit and credit card accounts – conduct that resulted in $185 million in fines announced Thursday – but the bank isn't providing many details.
>
> The head of the community bank during the period under scrutiny was Wells Fargo veteran Carrie Tolstedt, who announced in July that she had decided to retire at the end of the year at age 56.

There was no corporate responsibility account so far. There was no personal responsibility account so far by CEO Carrie Tolstedt in 2016. The earliest media coverage of the scandal we found in the newspaper 'Charlotte Observer' published September 10, 2016 by Rothacker (2016) as quoted above. Charlotte was Wells Fargo's biggest employee hub with more than 23,000 employees in a wide variety of business lines. Already the heading of the newspaper article caught our attention; "Banking – Wells Fargo gives few details about firing".

However, the following year, Shearman Sterling (2017) mainly attributed blame to the retired chief executive. The investigators wrote that Wells Fargo's decentralized corporate structure gave too much autonomy to the Community Bank's senior leadership, who were unwilling to change the sales model or even recognize it as the root cause of the problem. Executive management rather than lower-level managers now got the blame. The investigators wrote that Carrie Tolstedt, head of the Community Bank, and certain of her senior leaders paid insufficient regard to the substantial risk to Wells Fargo's brand and reputation from improper and unethical sales practices even as they failed to recognize the potential for financial or other harm to customers. The investigators concluded that Tolstedt was extremely ambitious and caused the misconduct with her sales model.

The investigators found that Tolstedt reinforced a culture of tight control over information about the community bank division, including sales practice issues. She retired before the accounting fraud scandal became public. Fraud investigators from law firm Shearman Sterling (2017: 2) presented their root cause analysis:

> The root cause of sales practice failures was the distortion of the Community Bank's sales culture and performance management system, which, when combined with aggressive sales management, created pressure on employees to sell unwanted or unneeded products to customers and, in some cases, to open unauthorized accounts. Wells Fargo's decentralized corporate structure gave too much autonomy to the Community Bank's senior leadership, who were unwilling to change the sales model or even recognize it as the root cause of the problem. Community Bank leadership resisted and impeded outside scrutiny or oversight and, when forced to report, minimized the scale and nature of the problem.

Shearman Sterling (2017: 20) mention Carrie Tolstedt 141 times in their 113-pages report, all of the time in critical terms:

> The scorecards, instituted by Tolstedt when she took over the Community Bank, measured how an employee or manager was performing compared to the sales plan. Scorecards were segmented by business drivers and updated on a daily basis, and employees and managers could check their progress against the sales plan at any time and were actively encouraged to do so. Certain managers made meeting scorecard requirements their sole objective, a tactic referred to as "managing to the scorecard." As a result, employees reporting to these managers were consistently pressured to meet scorecard goals.

While investigators blamed Tolstedt, she still blamed individual employees (Shearman Sterling, 2017: 103):

> Tolstedt emphasized that a large organization could not be perfect, and that the sales practice problem was a result of improper action on the part of individual employees.

While the initial blame one year earlier was on individual employees, the communicated corporate account was now to blame Tolstedt for having introduced a sales model that caused inappropriate sales practices. As a corporation, Wells Fargo was still denying responsibility for the misconduct. However, not only did Tolstedt resign, also Wells Fargo's CEO John Stumpf resigned shortly after because the account fraud scandal continued as an ongoing controversy.

In the current research perspective of addressing the issue of how accounts based on neutralizations and justifications evolve over time as events from exposure of a corporate scandal move along, we see a shift in the blame (Lee and Robinson, 2000; Resodihardjo et al., 2015; Xie and Keh, 2016), but no shift in corporate responsibility. Denial of responsibility continued. According to Sykes and Matza (1957), this is a common neutralization technique where the corporate offender disclaims responsibility for action and argues that the corporation is not responsible for what happened. The corporation as an alleged offender here claims that the corporation does not meet one or more of the conditions of responsible agency. The corporation committing a deviant act defines itself lacking responsibility for own actions. In this neutralization technique, the corporation rationalizes that the action in question is beyond corporate control. The offender may view the corporation as a billiard ball, helplessly propelled through different situations. The corporation denies responsibility for the event or sequence of events. This technique denies responsibility where the corporation accepts that wrongdoing has occurred but denies their own involvement or responsibility. The corporation may refer to some other actor as the responsible party or explain how a number of social actors jointly produced the misconduct. The corporation can also deny intent as a way of denying responsibility by referring to an event as an accident, where the corporation had no intent of producing harm. Similarly, the corporation can deny control over the situation where wrongdoing occurred. The corporation can transfer responsibility to others by the blame game or by scapegoating. The corporation will try to change expectations by referring to their limited formal responsibility.

However, the Community Bank at Wells Fargo was held responsible based on two laws, the Sarbanes-Oxley Act and the Dodd-Frank Act (Shichor and Heeren, 2021: 105):

> Both laws have provisions for clawbacks of compensation, which is a notable feature of the penalties imposed on Wells. In addition, both laws require corporations to be concerned about internal governance, including the operation of the Board, corporate risk and compliance, and improved shareholder input. Sarbanes-Oxley reinforces these concerns by criminally penalizing any interference by a corporation which obstructs a governmental investigation of the corporation. This kind of provision seems to have played an important role in the ongoing revelations about the misdeeds of Wells Fargo.

The misconduct represented in the investigation report included lack of customer consent and generally bank employees opening unauthorized personal checking or savings accounts for existing customers. Furthermore, there was falsification of bank records, generally falsifying customer identification or contract information or forging customer signatures, funding manipulation, and employees funding an account held by a customer with their own money or money from another account held by that customer. There was also the creation of unnecessary accounts, generally employees opening accounts, which served no customer financial need. There was a growing conflict over time between vision and values and the emphasis on sales goals.

In our perspective of convenience theory, the financial motive was the sales-driven organization and the threat of "poor performance in many instances led to shaming or worse" (Shearman Sterling, 2017: 30). Some executives were "calling their subordinates several times a day to check in on sales performance and chasing those who failed to meet sales objectives" (Shearman Sterling, 2017: 7). The organizational opportunity structure for account fraud in the community bank division had several elements, including distortion of sales culture and performance management system, aggressive sales management, and creation of open unauthorized accounts. Furthermore, a decentralized corporate structure gave too much autonomy, and corporate control functions were constrained by the decentralized organizational structure. "Wells Fargo's decentralized organizational structure and the deference paid to the lines of business" contributed to the persistence of an environment focused on sales rather than service-oriented financial advice" (Shearman Sterling, 2017: 8). The personal willingness existed because everyone could blame others in convenient ways.

The words "convenient" and "blame" are mentioned in the investigation report (Shearman Sterling, 2017: 5): "It was convenient instead to blame the problem of low quality and unauthorized accounts and other employee misconduct on individual wrongdoers and poor management in the field", rather than the sales model by the senior management.

## Japanese Astellas in Europe

In this case, there was first an outside-in notification that was later followed by a bottom-up notification. The outside-in notification was by a customer who had attended a company event. The bottom-up notification was by an employee who could provide detailed evidence of suspected wrongdoing. Both notifications from whistleblowers were concerned with a meeting held by the Japanese pharmaceutical company Astellas that attempted to promote an off-label medicine for prostate cancer.

Mulinari et al. (2021) studied the Japanese pharmaceutical firm Astellas. At a meeting in Milan, Italy with over one hundred doctors from mostly European countries present, Astellas executives attempted to promote an off-label prostate cancer drug enzalutamide. An anonymous Astellas Europe employee reported the incident to the Prescription Medicines Code of Practice Authority (PMCPA) in the UK. Astellas was then suspended. Like in so many other cases presented in this book, Astellas executives initially denied wrongdoings. Later, they accepted investigation findings and punishment rulings (Mulinari et al., 2021: 71):

> The company's official explanation for wrongdoings is one of "significant cultural and compliance failings created and caused by the actions and behaviors of some of its very senior managers" in Europe. It its report, The PMCPA attributed Astellas's gross misconduct and dishonesty to "multiple organizational and cultural failings" within the company, and to a corporate culture that prioritized "the bottom line" over compliance obligations and ethical norms.

The priority of compliance suffered under the priority of the bottom line in terms of profits. When the bottom line is struggling and not meeting investor expectations, compliance is indeed potentially violated in many corporate settings as presented in this book. Furthermore, as emphasized in several case studies in this book, also Astellas applied the procedure of scapegoating (Mulinari et al., 2021: 75):

> According to Astellas Europe, "the email indicated that there was a conscious decision by one individual" (. . .), but that "as an organization" Astellas had been completely unaware of the email up until this point. Hence, the company submitted there "was no dishonesty or deliberate attempt to mislead" – except by this single rogue employee. Astellas Europe also stated that, "immediate action had been taken to address the conduct of this senior member of staff.

However, when facing permanent expulsion from the UK's pharmaceutical industry trade body ABPI, Astellas said it "deeply regrets" safety failings, which was another deviant incident at the company (Megaw and Neville, 2017):

> In a highly unusual move, the Association of the British Pharmaceutical Industry imposed a second consecutive 12-month suspension on the company, citing a series of "shocking" breaches of guidelines that the trade group said, "raised serious concerns with regard to patient safety and public confidence in the pharmaceutical industry". The ABPI first suspended Astellas last year after complaints, that it had purposely misled the PMCPA, the industry's self-regulatory body in the UK. Subsequent re-audits of Astellas' UK and European businesses found they had failed to provide enough oversight and training of nurses and had not supplied complete prescribing information for a number of medicines (. . .)
>
> Astellas said in a statement: "We deeply regret our failings, and in light of this we have reinforced our focus on patient safety. We are committed to providing the highest standards of care for everyone who relies on our medicines and services".

A code-of-conduct document of forty-five pages can be downloaded from the Astellas homepage. There the company claims that it is important to be aware of and fully comply with applicable laws, regulations, and industry code. The conduct document covers integrity, respect, responsibility, fairness, and transparency. Nevertheless, the company has several times recently been exposed for violations of laws, regulations, and industry code. "The Japanese drug company Astellas has had its knuckles rapped for wrongdoing four times in less than three years" (BMJ, 2019). "Astellas had colluded to deliberately mislead and not tell the truth" (Mulinari et al., 2021: 72). The code-of-conduct document was signed by the Kenji Yasukawa, president and CEO at Astellas.

The Milan gathering was officially an advisory meeting where attendees received payments that later resembled corruption (BMJ, 2019):

> Over 100 oncologists and urologists from EU countries, as well as Turkey, Russia, and South Africa, had been invited to attend Astellas's "Pan-European Uro-oncology Advisory Board Meeting". All attendees were paid €1000 (£894;$1139) except for those from southeastern Europe, who were paid €500, and two speakers who were each paid €1500.

An employee at Astellas, who had worked in the drug industry for some time, quickly realized that all was not quite right. Astellas did not hold an advisory meeting. Rather, the company used the meeting to promote to prescribers the off-label use, for an additional indication, of its prostate cancer drug enzalutamide and to assess the impact of potential promotional claims – despite the meeting's purportedly scientific nature. The whistleblowing employee spoke to the BMJ (2019) on the condition of anonymity because the person still worked in the pharmaceutical industry.

## Deloitte – EY – KPGM – PwC

Deloitte (2017), EY (2019), KPMG (2020), and PwC (2015) are examples of fraud examination reports by corporate investigators from the big four auditors. These reports are often valuable contributions to reconstructing events and sequences of events when there is suspicion of white-collar crime. By interviewing suspects and witnesses, by reviewing documents, and by following digital leads such as emails and social media, corporate investigators from the big auditing firms attempt to present to their client organizations reports that serve to help make client decisions about the matters.

Here in our perspective of denial of wrongdoings we focus on the auditors themselves. Dunne et al. (2021) examined how big four auditors respond to public scrutiny, and how they employ impression management at a public inquiry. Impression management refers to attempts to influence the perceptions of others about the company by regulating and controlling information in social interactions. The researchers found that big four auditors had come under public scrutiny for issuing unqualified audit reports to financial institutions that subsequently collapsed (Dunne et al., 2021: 2):

> We view this public scrutiny as an "identity-threatening predicament", in the sense that Big Four Auditors' reputation, legitimacy and image were at risk. Big Four auditors also faced a potential financial risk from possible lawsuits were the inquiry's deliberations to reveal

> negligence on their parts. In addition, their predicament was that regulators would introduce more restrictive rules curtailing auditors' operational freedom, for example, curbing Big Four dominance. There was also a contagion effect risk that the public inquiry could spill over into a wider discourse on the profession. Therefore, a lot is at stake for the Big Four under scrutiny.

In their analysis of the big four firms, Dunne et al. (2021: 5) applied the following five defensive impression management strategies:

1. Denial. Denial involves individuals or organizations claiming to be innocent of a negative event. Denial ensures an impression of infallibility, so important in many presentations, is maintained. In this paper, denial refers to Big Four auditors denying that any action or inaction on their part contributed to audit failure or to the severity of the banking crisis.
2. Disassociation. Disassociation involves individuals or organizations distancing themselves from negative perceived events or people. In this paper, disassociation refers to Big Four auditors distancing themselves from their clients and the financial regulator.
3. External attribution. External attribution involves individuals or organizations attributing responsibility for negative outcomes to external factors. Two negative outcomes – audit failure and the severity of the banking crisis – prompted Big Four auditors' appearance at the public inquiry. In this paper, the two variants of external attribution are: (a) attribution to client; and (b) attribution to financial regulator.
4. Justification. Individuals or organizations use justification when they identify an external cause for a negatively-received action or event. In this paper, the three variants of justifications are: (a) explanation of audit; (b) explanation of financial statements; (c) unforeseeable banking crisis.
5. Selectivity. Individuals or organizations use selectivity to highlight facts that portray them in a positive light. In this paper, selectivity refers to Big Four auditors selectively quoting aspects of reports that portray them in a positive light.

Furthermore, in their analysis of the big four firms, Dunne et al. (2021: 6) applied the following five assertive impression management strategies:

1. Enhancement. Individuals or organizations use enhancement to accentuate the desirability of a positive event for which they were, at least partially, responsible. Given the context of the public inquiry, there are few positive events for Big Four auditors to enhance. However, one positive event involves the improvements to financial reporting and auditing since the banking crisis. In this paper, enhancement refers to Big Four auditors accentuating the desirability of these improvements.
2. Exemplification. Exemplification involves projecting an image of integrity or moral worthiness. In this paper, the two variants of exemplification are: (a) reflection; and (b) independent and ethical. Reflection refers to Big Four auditors demonstrating that they have reflected on the causes of the banking crisis and

suggesting ideas to prevent its reoccurrence. Independent and ethical refers to Big Four auditors describing how independence and ethics guide their work.

3. Integratiation. Integratiation involves attempting to gain an audience's approval through flattery. In this paper, integratiation refers to Big Four auditors flattering the inquiry members or the work of the inquiry.
4. Internal attribution. Internal attribution involves individuals or organizations attributing positive events to their own actions. In this paper, internal attribution involves Big Four auditors describing how the annual audit improves financial reporting.
5. Self-promotion. Individuals or organizations use self-promotion to highlight their competencies and expertise. In this paper, the two variants of self-promotion are: (a) expertise; and (b) quality. Expertise refers to Big Four auditors describing their expertise and experience. Quality refers to Big Four auditors describing the quality of their work.

Written statements by each big four auditor was analyzed by Dunne et al. (2021). They found more frequently defensive impression management strategies than assertive strategies. The most frequent defensive strategies were justification and disassociation.

## Comparison of Corporate Cases

The six case studies presented above are compared in Table 9.1. Three cases were detected by bottom-up notification, while three cases were detected by outside-in coverage. The early corporate accounts of the scandals were typically employee blame, denial of wrongdoing, scapegoating, and justification. The late corporate accounts were typically oversight failure, executive blame, scapegoating, regrets, and dissatisfaction. The executive destiny after scandals was survival in the positions for some (Samherji, Astellas, and Big Four), while others were dismissed from their positions and the organization (Telia, Lundin, and Wells Fargo).

Table 9.2 presents a condensed version of how the accounts of other scandals changed from initial exposure to findings in examination reports by corporate investigators. Typically, accounts move from denial of wrongdoing, followed by obfuscation, and then denial of responsibility.

The first corporate response to exposure of a scandal is never an outright admission of wrongdoing and an acceptance of responsibility. Rather, the initial response tends to take one of three forms: (1) deny wrongdoing, (2) acknowledge but obfuscate the nature of the wrongdoing, or (acknowledge but deny responsibility for some kind of wrongdoing (Gottschalk and Benson, 2020). In Table 9.2, five firms appeared to simply deny any wrongdoing at first, including Fuji Xerox in New Zealand, NNPC in Nigeria, along with Lehman Brothers, WorldCom, and Enron in the

**Table 9.1:** Comparison of corporate scandal detection.

| Corporation Name | White-Collar Crime | Executive Deviance | Corporate Control | Early Corporate Account | Late Corporate Account |
|---|---|---|---|---|---|
| Samherji seafood in Iceland | Corruption in Namibia | Corporate greed | Bottom-up by local employee | Employee blame | Oversight failure |
| Telia telecom in Sweden | Corruption in Uzbekistan | Criminal market forces | Bottom-up by competitor employee | Denial of wrongdoing | Executive blame |
| Lundin Energy in Sweden | Human rights violations in Sudan | Civil war alliances | Outside-in by local NGOs | Denial of wrongdoing | Scapegoating |
| Wells Fargo banking in the USA | Customer fraud in the USA | Goal orientation | Outside-in by the media | Employee blame | Executive blame |
| Astellas pharmaceuticals in Japan | Patient fraud in Europe | Market manipulation | Bottom-up by company employee | Scapegoating | Regrets |
| Big Four audit firms globally | Audit failure in bank crisis | Opportunistic threats of bankruptcy | Outside-in by the media | Justification | Disassociation |

United States. For example, a representative for Fuji Xerox said "the company had always been confident there were no grounds for action" after the Serious Fraud Office decided to take no action, while NNPC accused its accuser (a government official) of ignorance and political motivations. Finally, senior executives at Lehman, World Com, and Enron, at first simply denied that there was any accounting or financial problems at their firms. In these cases, there is no acknowledgement that something untoward may have happened and no mention of organizational deficiencies or irregularities, a pattern that changes with obfuscation.

As examples of obfuscation of wrongdoing consider that Dansk Bank's initial response to charges of money laundering by one of its subsidiaries referred to "deficiencies in controls and governance", and Toshiba reported it was "looking into irregularities," while Olympus admitted "it had covered up losses" but "declined to provide details" of its ethically challenged accounting practices. General Motors acknowledged that ignition switch failures had led to deadly crashes but then obscured this fact by referring to speed, driving conditions, failure to wear seat belts, and substance abuse by drivers. Obfuscations such as these mentioned fall somewhere between outright denials of any wrongdoing versus an acknowledgement of wrongdoing. Rather than simply denying wrongdoing, these accounts tend to obscure

**Table 9.2:** Comparison of early and late accounts of corporate scandals.

| Corporation Name | Early Corporate Account | Late Corporate Account |
|---|---|---|
| Denmark: Danske Bank's Estonian branch involved in money laundering scandal. | "The Danish bank has admitted to 'major deficiencies in control and governance' at its Estonian branch." (Moscow Times, 2017).<br>"In press release of 21 September 2017, Danske Bank acknowledged that it was "major deficiencies in controls and governance that made it possible to use Danske Bank's branch in Estonia for criminal activities such as money laundering". The press release referred to the findings of a "root-cause analysis" prepared for the bank by US-based consultancy Promontory Financial Group, LLC ("Promontory")." (Bruun Hjejle, 2018). Not yet admitting bank services for money laundering. | "With regard to the Non-Resident Portfolio, it has been found that, from 2007 through 2017, a number of former and current employees, both at the Estonian branch and at Group level, did not comply with legal obligations forming part of their employment with the bank. Most of these employees are no longer employed by the bank. For employees still with the bank, the bank has informed us that appropriate action has been or will be taken. We are not in a position to share an assessment of an individual unless requested by the individual in question. We have been requested by the Board of Directors, the Chairman and the Chief Executive Officer ("CEO") to share their assessments. According to assessments made, the Board of Directors, the Chairman and the CEO have not breached their legal obligations towards the bank." (Bruun Hjejle 2018). Admitting bank services for money laundering by non-residents in Estonia. |

| | | |
|---|---|---|
| Japan: Olympus Corporation in Japan involved in inappropriate accounting practices scandal. | “Olympus’ admission that it had covered up losses on securities investments dating back to the 1990s by booking them as acquisition fees of up to $1.4bn between 2006 and 2008 has once again thrown the spotlight on the weak corporate governance of Japanese companies. The company declined to provide details of how it kept those losses off its books for so long, but the revelation that a practice most closely associated with the bursting of Japan’s bubble economy in the 1990s had been going on as recently as a few years ago, stunned the investment community.” (Nakamoto, 2011). Tobashi still not mentioned. | “Olympus used SG Bond Plus Fund for ‘tobashi’ of part of the losses it suffered as the result of failures in financial management techniques in the 1990s. To cover up losses to which ‘tobashi’ had been used, Olympus and OFUK purchased warrants attached to FA and dividend preferred shares in association with the Gyrus acquisition; ultimately Olympus planned to use Funds for back-flow of funds.” (Deloitte, 2011). Tobashi scandal. |
| Japan: Toshiba Corporation in Japan involved in inappropriate accounting practices. | ”Toshiba withdrew its earnings guidance and scrapped its year-end dividend payout on Friday, saying it had found improper accounting on some of its infrastructure projects. The announcement came after the company said last month that it was looking into irregularities that had come to light in an internal probe. Since then, shares of Toshiba have fallen 5.7 per cent. The company declined to provide further details on which infrastructure projects were being questioned.” (Inagati, 2015). Disclaim knowledge of the irregularities. | “For some projects, it has been found that certain members of top management were aware of the intentional overstating of apparent current-period profits and the postponement of recording expenses and losses, or the continuation thereof, but did not give instructions to stop or correct them. Moreover, with regard to some projects for which the percentage-of-completion method was used, it has been recognized that, although the Company requested approval to record provisions for contract losses, certain top management either rejected it or instructed the recording to be postponed.” (Deloitte, 2015). Fake completion rates encouraged by executives. |

(continued)

**Table 9.2** (continued)

| Corporation Name | Early Corporate Account | Late Corporate Account |
|---|---|---|
| New Zealand: Fuji Xerox in New Zealand involved in inappropriate sales and accounting practices. | "The Serious Fraud Office will take no action against office products firm Fuji Xerox after closing its inquiry into the company's affairs. Several senior industry players were understood to have been interviewed by the market watchdog. But yesterday, Fuji Xerox said it welcomed the SFO's decision. Fuji Xerox New Zealand managing director Gavin Pollard said the company had always been confident there were no grounds for any action, and it was pleased the matter was closed. 'We co-operated fully with the SFO with its inquiries on a voluntary basis as we were eager to resolve this matter as quickly as possible'. NZ First began putting pressure on the Government about the company in October, questioning whether Northland schools were encouraged to sign certain printing contracts." (Hamish, 2016). Denied all allegations only one year before fraud examiners exposed misconduct. | "In the interviews in this Investigation, a number of interviewees (APO-related people) said the pressure from FX to attain business results (especially to achieve sales) was very intense. In particular, people who were involved in budget allocations and personnel evaluations at FXAP from around 2009 through 2015 uniformly made statements to the effect that with the economic decline and slowdown of growth in Japan, there were expectations from all of FX for the China and Asia region to act as a driving force to restore business performance, and the regions attracted their attentions (. . . .) That the APO Finance Department, in addition to having accounting and finance check functions, also performed the role of performance management, can be raised as one of the main causes of the inappropriate accounting practices carried out at FXNZ and FXA." (Deloitte, 2017). Investigators blame top management in Japan and New Zealand for the misconduct. |
| Nigeria: National petroleum company NNPC in Nigeria withheld transfers of oil revenues to the government. | "The NNPC claimed that the country's chief banker was ignorant on matters of oil earnings and remittances. It accused Mr. Sanusi of Nigeria's version of the capital sin: Playing politics." (Reporter, 2013). A former governor of the Central Bank of Nigeria, Lamido Sanusi, raised the allegation that a huge amount had disappeared. | "For the period reviewed, we identified possible errors in the computation of crude oil prices at the NNPC that resulted in a $3.6 million shortfall in incomes to the Federation account." (PwC, 2015). Sanusi at alleged $49.8 billion, while investigators only found $3.6 million missing. |

| | | |
|---|---|---|
| Norway: Telenor in Norway had ownership in VimpelCom in the Netherlands that was involved in corruption in Uzbekistan. | "Norwegian telecom giant Telenor was allegedly involved in a corruption scandal in Uzbekistan with ties to President Islam Karimov's daughter, Norwegian media reported Saturday. According to documents published by Norway's Klassekampen daily, VimpelCom, an Uzbek firm partially owned by Telenor, paid $25 million (20 million euros) in bribes to obtain telecom licenses in the Central Asian nation. The money allegedly went from a subsidiary of VimpelCom to Takilant Limited, owned by Gayane Avakyan, a friend of Karimov's oldest daughter, Gulnara Karimova. 'Bank statements document how the money was transferred from a previously unknown company in the British Virgin Islands as VimpelCom purchased licenses to the mobile market in the former Soviet state,' Klassekampen wrote on its website. Telenor owns 33 percent of VimpelCom and has 43 percent of the voting rights in the company. 'We are a minority shareholder in VimpelCom, so it's up to VimpelCom to take responsibility for answering any questions that relate to their operations', Telenor communications head Glenn Mandelid told AFP. 'Telenor has zero tolerance for corruption, both when it comes to our own operations and also to the companies that we are part owners in'." (Agence France, 2014). Denial of responsibility to act. | "In due consideration to what is stated above, we are notwithstanding of the opinion that certain employees at Telenor at certain point in time should have handled the 2011 concerns differently. The individuals in question are senior employees of Telenor and with high-ranking leadership positions and/or with professional education and experience. Due to this, our assessments of such individuals have been based what we believe should be expected of such individuals as leaders, as Telenor Nominees and as individuals with professional background and experience. The facts and circumstances in this case do in our view not solicit an approach where the actions and decisions of individuals are assessed against formal legal frameworks." (Deloitte, 2016). Criticism of lack of action, but no crime. |

(continued)

**Table 9.2** (continued)

| Corporation Name | Early Corporate Account | Late Corporate Account |
| --- | --- | --- |
| Sweden: Nordea in Sweden had a subsidiary in Luxembourg revealed by the Panama Papers in backdating documents. | "Nordea, the Nordic region's biggest bank, says it doesn't help wealthy customers evade taxes in response to reports linking it to the Panamanian law firm at the center of a media investigation into offshore accounts." (Associated Press, 2016). The Panama Papers disclosed involvement in tax havens, but the bank first denied responsibility for what customers might do in tax havens. | "The investigation has found deficiencies in the procedures regarding renewal of Powers of Attorney (POA). In at least seven cases the investigation has shown that backdated documents have been requested or provided during the last six years, which is illegal when it aims at altering the truth." (Mannheimer Swartling, 2016). The Panama Papers disclosed involvement in tax havens, and the investigation documents law violations in the Luxembourg branch of Nordea. |
| USA: Lehman Brothers went bankrupt because of alleged risky management. | "Lehman's shares fell $7.51, or 19 percent, to $31.75 after Chief Executive Officer Richard Fuld said in a statement that the Federal Reserve's decision to lend to brokers and accept securities as collateral "improves the liquidity picture and, from my perspective, takes the liquidity issue for the entire industry off the table." (Onaran, 2008). This was half a year before CEO Fuld had to file for bankruptcy. Obviously, he knew that it would not work, but his communicated account was that liquidity was fine again. | "The business decisions that brought Lehman to its crisis of confidence may have been in error but were largely within the business judgment rule. But the decision not to disclose the effects of those judgments does give rise to colorable claims against the senior officers who oversaw and certified misleading financial statements – Lehman's CEO Richard S. Fuld, Jr., and its FCOs Christopher O'Meara, Erin M. Callan and Ian T. Lowitt." (Jenner Block, 2010). Fraud examiners directly blame the top executives for their decision-making and misleading financial statements. |

| | | |
|---|---|---|
| USA: General Motors' reluctant to correct ignition switch failure for financial reasons. | "The company said it knows of five front-impact crashes in which six people died and air bags did not deploy in vehicles. GM said affected vehicles' ignition switches can turn off in a crash. That causes the engine to shut down, and as a result, air bags fail to activate. 'All of these crashes occurred off-road and at high speeds, where the probability of serious or fatal injuries was high regardless of air bag deployment,' GM spokesman Alan Adler said. 'In addition, failure to wear seat belts and alcohol use were factors in some of these cases.' (. . .) GM said the National Highway Traffic Safety Administration never investigated the issue. The automaker learned of it through field reports." (Shepardson and Burden, 2014). They claim they learned of the ignition switch failure from field reports, but the later investigation tells that many knew of the failure long before field reports of accidents emerged. | "From the outset, the Cobalt ignition switch had significant problems that were known to GM personnel. Designed to be a new generation ignition switch first introduced in the Saturn ion, the switch was so plagued with problems that the engineer who designed it labeled it then 'the switch from hell'. (. . .) In 2005, various committees within GM considered proposed fixes, but those were rejected as too costly. (. . .) Despite learning about what GM's outside counsel called a 'bombshell' in April 2013, it was not until February 2014 that GM issued the first recall." (Jenner Block, 2014). GM did not fix it for cost reasons. |

(continued)

**Table 9.2** (continued)

| Corporation Name | Early Corporate Account | Late Corporate Account |
|---|---|---|
| USA: WorldCom went bankrupt after inappropriate accounting. | "In a conference call with investors and analysts, Ebbers and other executives sought to dismiss concerns about WorldCom's accounting practices, debt load and cash flow. The CEO also said he will not sell WorldCom shares to pay down his personal debt." (Porretto, 2002). One year later, WorldCom was bankrupt, accounting practices were wrong, and Ebbers had sold shares to pay down his personal debt. | "Numerous individuals – most of them in financial and accounting departments, at many levels of the Company and in different locations around the world – became aware in varying degrees of senior management' s misconduct. Had one or more of these individuals come forward earlier and raised their complaints with Human Resources, Internal Audit, the Law and Public Policy Department, Andersen, the Audit Committee, individual Directors and/or federal or state government regulators, perhaps the fraud would not have gone on for so long. Why didn't they? The answer seems to lie partly in a culture emanating from corporate headquarters that emphasized making the numbers above all else; kept financial information hidden from those who needed to know; blindly trusted senior officers even in the face of evidence that they were acting improperly; discouraged dissent; and left few, if any, outlets through which employees believed they could safely raise their objections." (PwC, 2003). A corporate culture where executives did what Ebbers told them to do. |

| USA: Enron Corporation went bankrupt after inappropriate accounting practices. | "Absolutely no accounting issue," Lay told analysts, "no trading issue, no reserve issue, no previously unknown problem issues" is behind the departure. There will be 'no change in the performance or outlook of the company going forward', he added" (Deseret News, 2001). Skilling left the company, but accounting scandal denied by Lay. | "Individually, and collectively, Enron's Management failed to carry out its substantive responsibility for ensuring that the transactions were fair to Enron–which in many cases they were not–and its responsibility for implementing a system of oversight and controls over the transactions with the LJM partnerships. There were several direct consequences of this failure: transactions were executed on terms that were not fair to Enron and that enriched Fastow and others; Enron engaged in transactions that had little economic substance and misstated Enron's financial results; and the disclosures Enron made to its shareholders and the public did not fully or accurately communicate relevant information. We discuss here the involvement of Kenneth Lay, Jeffrey Skilling, Richard Causey, and Richard Buy." (Wilmer Cutler Pickering, 2003). Top executives were the architects of the accounting scandal that led to bankruptcy. |
|---|---|---|

what has happened by avoiding references to individuals or to personal agency and instead speaking of the organization as if it existed separately from people and as if it were like a faulty piece of software that has bugs that need to be fixed. That something untoward may have happened, however, is acknowledged.

Two firms – Telenor in Norway and Nordea in Sweden, and in fact similar to Wells Fargo in the United States – appeared to acknowledge that something untoward had happened but they denied responsibility for it. For instance, Telenor acknowledged that corruption involving a company that it partially owned (VimpelCom) was occurring in Uzbekistan, but it described itself as a "minority shareholder" that had no say over day to day operations. Nordea acknowledged that some of its wealthy customers may have used Panamanian accounts to avoid taxes but asserted that it did not help them do this. Similarly, Wells Fargo initially blamed its scandal on wayward and greedy employees who had financial motivations.

In all of the cases cited above, the initial accounts were not successful in that they did not completely quell media, public, or legal interest in the various scandals. Rather, enough negative publicity was generated that the firms felt it necessary, for example, to sponsor an independent investigation by outsiders and to have a report of the investigation results issued by the outside entity. Although the investigation accounts often included descriptions of deviant corporate cultures and weak corporate control structures, they differed from the initial accounts in that they were more likely to be personalized and more critical of top executives in the various firms.

Beginning with the firms that originally denied wrongdoing, the report for Fuji Xerox admitted to "inappropriate accounting practices" being carried out in New Zealand and blamed these practices on pressure from headquarters that was transmitted by managers to salespeople and accountants. NNPC eventually admitted some wrongdoing in its accounting practices but minimized its seriousness. In the investigation reports for firms located in the United States, two admitted serious wrongdoing (World Com and Enron) and blamed high level executives for failing to carry out their substantive responsibilities to their companies. The report for Lehman Brothers concluded that senior officers were only guilty of making poor business decisions.

The investigation reports for firms that appeared to engage in obfuscation varied in their admission of wrongdoing and where blame was placed. At Danske Bank, money laundering in its Estonian branch was acknowledged and former and current employees were blamed, but senior officials, including the Board and CEO, were cleared of responsibility. Olympus admitted the use of the maligned accounting practice of 'tobashi' to cover losses, but the individuals who should be held responsible was not identified. At Toshiba, top management figures were blamed for allowing unethical accounting practices to continue even after top management became aware of them (Demetriades and Owusu-Agyei, 2021). The final report on the scandal at General Motors blamed the legal department for not acting sooner to force a recall when knowledge of the ignition switch problems first became available.

Finally, of the firms that originally acknowledged untoward behavior related to their organizations but denied responsibility, all of them eventually admitted wrongdoing. Nordea admitted deficiencies in procedures regarding the backdating of documents that helped wealthy clients to avoid some taxes. Wells Fargo admitted wrongdoing in its community bank, but shifted blame from low level employees to senior leaders, in particular Carrie Tolstedt. The final report on the Enron scandal admitted wrongdoing and blamed senior managers.

Some scandals continued beyond presentation of examination reports by corporate investigators. At Danske Bank, chief executive Thomas Borgen had to resign after the money laundering scandal in Estonia (Milne, 2019a, 2019b) despite the fact that fraud examiners from law firm Bruun Hjejle (2018) did not blame him in their report. The following year, Danish prosecutors charged the former CEO for potential crime in the money laundering scandal. Some shareholders also decided to launch financial charges against the retired CEO (Klevstrand, 2021).

# 10 State-Corporate Crime

A common perspective is to think of the state with its public agencies as the guardianship against corporate wrongdoing. When corporate wrongdoing occurs, then the state has its criminal justice system to create control by investigating, prosecuting, and convicted offenders. The state is supposed to have an oversight over what the corporate sector is doing, introduce regulations wherever it seems needed, and punish those who violate laws and regulations. The state is in the role of protecting the vulnerable and avoiding victimization of innocent people and organizations.

A very different perspective is to think of the state as a criminal actor, often operating alongside cooperation. This is labelled state-corporate crime. The concept of state-corporate crime takes as its starting point the mutually beneficial and reinforcing relationships between state institutions and private corporations (Bernat and Whyte, 2020). The wealthy and powerful in the upper class of society define their own corporate and bureaucratic identities in terms of what is right and what is wrong for them, sometimes in a state-corporate alignment (Rothe, 2020; Rothe and Medley, 2020).

The long-lasting influence of Edwin Sutherland upon criminological, sociological, and more recently also on management thinking is observable across the globe, but in particular in the United States and Europe (Friedrichs et al., 2018). Sutherland (1939, 1983) exposed crime by individuals who people thought of as almost superior, and people who apparently did not need to offend as a means of survival. Sutherland's influence lifted insights from street crime into elite crime labelled white-collar crime and further into state crime.

Businesspersons and professionals frequently commit serious wrongdoing and harm with little fear of facing criminal justice scrutiny. It can be true that poverty and powerlessness is a cause of one kind of crime while excessive power can be a cause of another kind of crime.

Sutherland exemplified the corporation as an offender in the case of war crime where corporations profit heavily by abusing the state of national emergency during times of war. Corporate form and characteristics as a profit-maximizing entity are shaping war profiteering. War profiteering is organizational crime by powerful organizations that may commit environmental crime, state-corporate crime, and human rights violations. Corporations break the law, and they get away with it, according to Sutherland (Müller, 2018).

A recent example of state-corporate crime is opium production in Afghanistan. The vast majority of the world's opium manufactured into heroin comes from Afghanistan, with production and exports centered in areas controlled by the Taliban, who have taxed the drugs during their 20-year insurgency. The income from narcotics financed arms and other equipment that enabled Taliban to take power over the whole country, including the capital Kabul, in August 2021. According to Goodhand (2005),

https://doi.org/10.1515/9783110986686-011

the opium economy has existed in Afghanistan for several decades, where there are historical roots of poppy cultivation. Opium from Afghanistan is manufactured into heroin in Kosovo and sold, for example, in Oslo, Norway to users at a price of the equivalent of two hundred US dollars per gram. The price of a kilo is thus two hundred thousand US dollars that represent the value of a new Tesla car in Norway.

State-corporate crime is not limited to white-collar offenses. When Russia went to war against Ukraine in 2022, the West introduced economic sanctions against Russia. However, because of the substantial black economy in Russia with mafia organizations linked to the state, the sanctions became less effective (Grønningsæter, 2022).

## Alignment of Mutual Interests

Interdependent interests and incentives connect state affairs with corporate affairs (Ken and León, 2021: 4):

> By "the state", we refer to a bureaucratic, fragmented, and crowded ensemble of institutions and actors that organize social, economic, and political relations of power, despite competing priorities.

Ken and León (2021) studied state-corporate harm in the U.S. pork packing industry during the Covid-19 pandemic. In 2020, when over 67,000 meatpacking and processing workers were infected with the virus, the state allowed and encouraged this industry to harm worker health and lives to continue to slaughter pigs.

The powerful in the upper class of society define their own identity in terms of what is right and what is wrong for them, sometimes in a state-corporate alignment (Tombs and Whyte, 2020; Zysman-Quirós, 2020). If they themselves break their own laws, then there is a need to change the laws rather than punish law violators (Petrocelli et al., 2003).

Denial of responsibility for crime depends on the situation. For example, in a state-corporate alignment, the corporation can attempt to blame the state (Bernat and Whyte, 2020; Rothe, 2020; Rothe and Medley, 2020; Tombs and Whyte, 2020; Zysman-Quirós, 2020). In the case of profit-driven environmental crime, the corporation can claim that multiple factors cause pollution and other kinds of harm (Böhm, 2020; Budo, 2021; Lynch, 2020; Wingerde and Lord, 2020). Furthermore, the corporation can blame a too complex regulatory environment (Braithwaite, 2020; Lehman et al., 2020).

Whyte (2014: 237) argues that the perspective of state-corporate crime brings the important role of the state into the study of social harm caused by corporations:

> The state-corporate crime framework allows us to place at the centre of our analysis an understanding of how the state, in various ways, produces corporate crime, or at the very least, assists in the production of corporate crime – corporate crime is not something that simply

> happens when states are not vigilant enough, nor is it simply the unintended consequence of normally benign functions of administration.

Laws and regulations have conventionalized and normalized several types of corporate crime, ensuring that the capital, in the form of the corporation, continues to prosper regardless of its damaging effects on the capacity for society to develop and reproduce (Oliveira and Silveira, 2020: 12):

> Historically, corporations have obtained political power and favoring regulatory laws, have monopolized or mapped markets, and have transformed themselves into powerful institutions through special privileges granted to them. Therefore, the strictly legal definition of corporate crime conceals the destructive character of capitalism. Likewise, the concept of 'state-corporate crime' developed in the literature conceals this issue; it reinforces the neoliberal discourse by stating that it is a crime initiated or facilitated by the state.

Convenience dynamics in white-collar crime can take place at different levels such as the individual, the organizational, and the national level. Dynamics also take place between these levels. For example, dynamics of state-corporate crime occurs between the national and organizational levels (Bernat and Whyte, 2020: 127):

> This growing body of literature on state-corporate crimes takes as its starting points the mutually reinforcing relationships between state institutions and corporations.

In system dynamics terms (Randers, 2019; Sterman, 2018), a mutually reinforcing relationship is a positive feedback loop, where increased state involvement in corporate crime will cause increased corporate involvement in state crime. Over time, a positive feedback loop can cause exponential growth in state-corporate crime. The opposite of a positive feedback loop is a negative feedback loop, where for example increased corporate crime causes a reaction in terms of reduced state crime that in turn reduces corporate crime.

## The Regime of Public Permissions

Osoria (2021) studied state-corporate crime caused by the Covid-19 pandemic in Puerto Rico. He applied the framework of the regime of permission to describe the dynamics of state-corporate crime in capitalist societies as a lens to analyze the intertwined relationship between exceptionality, corruption, and state-corporate crime. The regime of permission suggests that the state neither controls nor intervenes against corporate crime as long as corporate activity is considered beneficial to the state (Whyte, 2014: 244):

> Corporate power in this sense is wholly reliant upon a series of regimes of permission, including the permission to trade as a separate entity, investment regimes which permit limited liability, the application of the separate entity in criminal law, the permission for corporations to

> act as holders of "rights" and so on. Crucially, within those regimes of permission we also find the co-ordinates of impunity – a corporate veil which shields owners from civil liability and a de facto corporate veil which shields both owners and managers from criminal liability.

The framework of the regime of permissions suggests that corporations are permitted by the state to commit crime for which they are not considered liable. Lack of liability is a concept that features across regulatory offenses, financial crime, and environmental crime that disable the attribution of liability to corporations in criminal courts. Rather than controlling order in the market economy, regulatory agencies attempt to mitigate problems that are the product of state regimes of permission.

Haines and Macdonald (2021: 298) found that regimes of permission to enable business activity, and regulation to control it, can be intertwined in the case of licenses granted to enterprises:

> This in turn shapes which forms of business activity are supported, and which resisted. In this context, licensing emerges as a key aspect of regimes of permission that needs more attention. Just as corporate law creates personhood out of a legal fiction, licenses pertaining to land use create a fiction of the visceral connection between the fate of humanity and the fate of the planet we inhabit.

Osoria (2021) found that the regime of permission during the Covid-19 pandemic in Puerto Rico led to permission for corporate corruption, tax fraud, and human rights violations. Since Puerto Rico has a number of manufacturing facilities for Covid-19 vaccines, pharmaceutical corporations were permitted by the state to extract large profits from the production without the corporations exercising any sort of social responsibility. The state's only concern was for the corporations to produce as many vaccines as possible by leaving transnational corporations such as Abbott and Roche completely unregulated and not liable for any wrongdoing.

As argued by Tombs and Whyte (2020: 17), corporations can have no meaningful existence without the state:

> They can have no legal basis for their function as the primary institution through which capital is reproduced and can have no infrastructure or indeed political allies or representatives in government.

Whyte (2014) distinguished between state-initiated crime and state-facilitated crime. State-initiated crime is the active involvement of state agencies in the production of particular criminal processes and events. It can also mean the failure of state agencies to control corporate crime. Corporate crime occurs at the direction of, or with the explicit or tacit approval of, the government. State-initiated corporate crime thus represents a criminal conspiracy. State-facilitated crime implies the failure of state agencies to control corporate crime. There is no attempt to restrain deviant business activities, and the state is unwilling to pursue any effective regulation due to shared state-corporate goals.

An example of state-initiated corporate crime was the illegal family separation of immigrants to the United States. While the state initiated family separations, private enterprises made money on taking care of separated family members in detainment camps. State-initiated crime occurred when private companies employed by the government engaged in organizational deviance as instructed by, and with tacit approval from, government actors. This kind of state-corporate crime is wrongdoing at the intersection of government and business. Contracts were granted to non-profits with known histories of abuse and negligence. Most contracts were granted to multimillion dollar enterprises that made substantial profits on their detainment camps implementing illegal state immigration policy (Barak, 2021).

## Modern Profitable Slavery

Both the mistreatment of workers in the pharmaceutical industry in Puerto Rico (Osoria, 2021) as well as the mistreatment of workers in the meat industry in Iowa (Ken and León, 2021) might be characterized as modern profitable slavery. Marmo and Bandiera (2021) identified modern slavery as forced labor and debt bondage in the protective equipment industry. Worker passports were confiscated, workers had six 12-hour day shifts, some workers were children, there were illegal deductions from salaries, and over-crowded accommodations with up to 24 people per room. The debt bondage occurred because there were substantial recruitment fees where workers had a hard time with down payments.

The Australian company Ansell denied wrongdoing in their accounts of the scandal (Marmo and Bandiera, 2021: 1):

> We reflect on how Ansell has moved from declaring no knowledge, to conceding very little in terms of its own responsibility in "causing or contributing" to modern slavery.

Marmo and Bandiera (2021) argued that the power of states and corporations, under neoliberal globalization, has combined to produce the conditions that give rise to modern slavery. States and reporting entities are benevolent actors who have legalized market practices that cause modern slavery. Corporate crime is normalized through state practices. States have been key agents in the production of modern slavery. Corporations have taken advantage of their power over national and international law, as well as the discrepancy and gaps between various legislations.

Marmo and Bandiera (2021) introduced the perspective of capitalism with social conflict to explain modern slavery. In capitalism, there is social conflict between the ruler and the ruled. The social conflict perspective suggests that the powerful and wealthy in the upper class of society define what is right and what is wrong (Petrocelli et al., 2003; Siegel, 2011). The rich and mighty people can behave like "robber barons" because they make the laws and because they control law enforcement (Chamlin, 2009; Kane, 2003; Haines, 2014; Sutherland, 1983; Veblen, 1899;

Wheelock et al., 2011). The ruling class does not consider white-collar offences as regular crime, and certainly not similar to street crime (Hagan, 1980; Lanier and Henry, 2009a, 2009b; Slyke and Bales, 2013).

In Marxist criminology, capitalism is a criminogenic society, i.e., a society that tends to produce criminality. Capitalism is a system of economic production in which power is concentrated in the hands of a few, with the majority existing in a dependency relationship to the powerful (Lanier and Henry, 2009b: 259):

> This class-based economic order is maintained by a criminal justice apparatus that serves the interests of the wealthy at the expense of the poor. Those who challenge this system of production are destined for social control, especially if they are seen as a serious threat to the system.

Nevertheless, crime by individuals in the elite tends to be prosecuted if offenses are detected and evidence of wrongdoing is present (Brightman, 2009), as long as they are not too powerful (Pontell et al., 2014) and do not have too excellent defense attorneys. Sometimes, but not very frequently, does the ruling class punish their own.

The social conflict perspective views financial crime as a function of the conflict that exists in society (Siegel, 2011). The perspective suggests that class conflict causes crime in any society, and that those in power create laws to protect their rights and interests. For example, embezzlement by employees is as a violation of law to protect the interests of the employer. However, it might be argued that an employer must and should protect own assets. Bank fraud is a crime to protect the powerful banking sector. However, in the perspective of social conflict one might argue that a bank should have systems making bank fraud impossible. If an employee has no opportunity to commit embezzlement, and if a fraudster has no opportunity to commit bank fraud, then these kinds of financial crime would not occur, and there would be no need to have laws against such offenses. Furthermore, law enforcement agencies protect powerful companies against counterfeit products, although the companies should be able to protect themselves by reducing opportunities for the production of counterfeit products.

The social conflict perspective holds that laws and law enforcement are used by dominant groups in society to minimize threats to their interests posed by those whom they perceive as dangerous and greedy (Petrocelli et al., 2003). Crime is defined by legal codes and sanctioned by institutions of criminal justice to secure order in society. Crime is defined as acts that are considered bad and that should be punished. The ruling class thus defines crime by identifying what they think is bad and what they think should be punished. The ruling class secures order in the ruled class by means of laws and law enforcement. Conflicts and clashes between interest groups are restrained and stabilized by law enforcement (Schwendinger and Schwendinger, 2014).

According to the social conflict perspective, the justice system is biased and designed to protect the wealthy and powerful. The wealthy and powerful can take substantial assets out of their own companies at their own discretion whenever they like, although employed workers in the companies were the ones who created the values. The superrich can exploit their own wealth that they created as owners of corporations as long as they do not hurt other shareholders. Employees have no right to object. It is no crime to take out values from own enterprises and build private mansions for the money. This is no crime by the owners. Even when the owners just inherited the wealth created by earlier generations, they can dispose freely of it for private consumption. Similarly, top executives who are on each other's corporate boards grant each other salaries that are ten or twenty times higher than regular employee salaries. As Haines (2014: 21) puts it, "financial practices that threaten corporate interests, such as embezzlement, are clearly identified as criminal even as obscenely high salaries remain relatively untouched by regulatory controls". Furthermore, sharp practices such as insider trading that threaten confidence in equities markets have enjoyed vigorous prosecution, since the powerful see them as opaque transactions that give an unfair advantage to those who are not members of the market institutions.

## State-Enabled Economic Crime

State-facilitated economic crime refers to those activities of the state that fail to constrain criminal, economically motivated behaviors (Rothe, 2020). State-facilitated crime implies the failure of state agencies to control corporate crime. There is no attempt to restrain deviant business activities, and the state is unwilling to pursue any effective regulation due to shared state-corporate goals. State-initiated economic crime is the active involvement of state agencies in the production of particular criminal processes and events with financial benefits. It can also mean the failure of state agencies to control corporate crime. Corporate crime occurs at the direction of, or with the explicit or tacit approval of, the government. State-initiated corporate crime thus represents a criminal conspiracy (Whyte, 2014). The term state-enabled economic crime is introduced here to combine both state-facilitated and state-initiated crime. However, state-enabled economic crime is limited to offenses that have an economic motive to serve a purpose that is in line with the white-collar crime terminology of financial crime by privileged individuals.

Yet another term here is state crime that refers to an act or omission of an action by actors within the state that results in violations of domestic and international law, human rights, or systematic or institutionalized harm of its or another state's population (Rothe, 2020). This definition is problematic, as it leaves the common definition of crime as violation of law. Crime is defined by legal codes and sanctioned by institutions of criminal justice to secure order in society.

In the state crime definition, crime is defined as acts that are considered bad and that should be punished, irrespective of whether or not the actions are sanctioned by law. Rothe (2020) listed a number of acts all across the globe that he labeled state crime, such as state actions in China, Israel, and Russia against their own population. However, the opinion of wrongdoing might vary, where some may find Chinese boarding schools for the Uighur population acceptable, the Israeli control of Palestinians acceptable, and the Russian control of political opposition acceptable. Therefore, what I think is wrong and should be punished is a bad framework in criminology. Hence, crime as a term is here restricted to violation of the law of both national and international caliber. This legalistic constraint is of course not unproblematic as emphasized by Bradshaw (2014: 165) in the case of environmental crime as white-collar offenses:

> Most simply, environmental crime can be defined from a legalistic perspective as "any act that violates an environmental protection statute". However, many scholars of environmental crime argue that the field must move beyond legalistic definitions, be they criminal, civil, or regulatory. In consideration of broader philosophical issues, crimes against the environment can alternatively be defined as "an act committed with the intent of harm or with a potential to cause harm to ecological and/or biological systems and for the purpose of securing business or personal advantage".

This is a fascinating approach to the definition of crime, where both intentional and unintentional harm qualify for the term, in addition to a speculation into the motive of an advantage. However, to include more than legalistically relevant incidents, one might argue that if an act is to be classified as crime, the classifier should agree and argue for a future situation where the act has been included in laws. The requirement of labelling an act as crime should thus be in terms of legalistic coverage in the future.

The problematic approach of non-legalistic definition of state-corporate crime might be illustrated by professional wrestling where Corteen (2018: 53) concluded that:

> The harms and crimes within the professional wrestling industry can be examined as state crime due to state inaction regarding the harmful health and safety activities.

Well, professional wrestling was legal in the United States despite serious harms and deaths among participants. But it was no crime in that country. In other countries at that time, both professional wrestling and professional boxing was illegal and thus state-corporate crime if the state facilitated or showed inaction regarding the harmful health and safety activities in those countries.

The restriction on the term crime to law violation is in line with the social conflict perspective. The ruling class secures order in the ruled class by means of laws and law enforcement. Conflicts and clashes between interest groups are restrained and stabilized by law enforcement (Schwendinger and Schwendinger, 2014).

State-enabled economic crime is thus financially motivated crime that can provide the state as well as corporations illegitimate gain by violation of the law. State-enabled economic crime is illegal actions that occur when one or more institutions or political governance body pursue a goal in direct cooperation with one or more entities of economic production and distribution (Rothe, 2020: 9):

> It should be noted that all crimes carried out by either the state or by corporations (state crime, corporate crime) involve some level of implicit or explicit cooperation between states and corporations. In many circumstances, disentangling "state interests" from "corporate interests" is highly problematic due to the intersecting agendas of those at the top of both the state and corporate hierarchies and the multiple "interlocks" reflected in movements in and out of high-level state and corporate positions.

Environmental destruction can serve as example of state-enabled economic crime. The case is concerned with rich and mighty people who build mansions on the shoreline of Tjøme Island in Norway. Wildlife and public access are the victims. Municipal officials were reluctant to intervene when architects, lawyers, and construction companies made substantial profits on environmental crime (Blix, 2021; Holmøy, 2021).

## Construction Industry Case

Davies (2021) found that construction industries provide significant opportunities for criminal processes to occur, including fraud, tax evasion, poor health and safety, and underpayment of workers. Construction is well known for being vulnerable to criminal activities that are perpetrated by both states and businesses. Widespread subcontracting, short-term projects, non-standard work, poor health and safety practices, and substandard accommodation facilities all contribute to worker mistreatment and undercutting of serious entrepreneurs. The development of new infrastructure for the Qatar 2020 Fifa world cup is an example, where more than six thousand migrant worker deaths are due to poor safety practices (McCarthy, 2021):

> 6,500 migrant workers have died in Qatar since it was named Fifa world cup host. These laborers are from five countries in South Asia, with 2,711 of those who died hailing from India (. . .)
>
> Like other countries in the region such as Saudi Arabia and the UAE, Qatar is highly reliant on migrant workers, the majority of whom tend to voluntarily come from Asia and part of Africa. Qatar's population stood at 2.6 million in 2017, of which 313,000 were Qatari citizens and 2.3 million were migrant workers. The country has been plagued by allegations of human rights abuse and labor violations for years with international organizations consistently reporting that migrant laborers have been subject to serious exploitation and abuse (. . .)
>
> Qatar has undertaken a massive construction program to prepare for the World Cup including building seven stadiums, a new airport as well as broad additions to its public transportation network.

Davies (2021) generally found evidence globally of the states' role in terms of active collusion and more passive facilitation. There is a rich tradition of political and economic interdependence between states and corporations in the construction industry. The systematic mistreatment of workers is one of the key elements of state-corporate crime in this industry. Whether construction of private and commercial buildings, civil engineering infrastructure including roads, bridges, and tunnels, or electrical and electronic installations, the white-collar offenders all adapt to criminogenic market forces in the construction industry.

What makes the Qatar case particularly interesting in the perspective of white-collar crime is the corruption that led to the unexpectedly awarded hosting rights for soccer's biggest tournament to Qatar (McCarthy, 2021). Media reports have suggested that the reason why Fifa world cups ended up in Russia in 2018 and in Qatar in 2022 was corruption. Members of the executive committee at Fifa did not only receive bribes from the winning nations Russia and Qatar, but also from losing competitors such as Australia. On December 2, 2010, the executive committee of the international football association Fifa, using an anonymous voting procedure, determined the hosts for the 2018 and 2022 Fifa world cup tournaments. Allegations of corruption related to the voting process had surfaced even before the final vote that December day in Zürich in Switzerland. Ever since, there have been persistent allegations of misconduct with respect to the selection process. In 2017, British newspaper The Guardian reported that a Fifa official allegedly took bribes to back Qatar's 2022 world cup bid (Laughland, 2017):

> Julio Grondona, a senior vice-president at Fifa and head of the Argentinian football association until his death in 2014, allegedly told the witness, Alejandro Burzaco, an Argentinian sports marketing executive, that he was owed the money in exchange for his vote, which helped Qatar secure the lucrative tournament.

Three years earlier, in 2014, the Garcia report was completed. The Garcia (2014) report was an investigation produced by Michael Garcia and Cornel Borbély into allegations of corruption in world association football. Fifa appointed Garcia and Borbély in 2012 to investigate ethical breaches at Fifa, which is world football's governing body. The two examiners quickly focused on persistent public accusations of bribery in the 2018 and 2022 world cup bids, which Russia and Qatar respectively won in 2010. Fifa kept the Garcia report secret for several years before it leaked to a German newspaper, which caused Fifa subsequently to release the report to the public in 2017.

## Housing Market Bubble Case

In Spain, the state first helped the private sector develop an expanding housing market where banks had ample state-supported opportunities to provide mortgages to new homeowners. Then as the housing market bubble burst, and banks did not get their repayments of mortgages from homeowners, the state compensated the banks financially. The state also helped the banks in terms of eviction of all those homeowners who had failed with repayments of mortgages. Finally, the state helped banks take over the ownership of all those homes (Bernal et al., 2014: 221):

> The apparent commonality of interests between state institutions (national and autonomous governments, town councils and entities of surveillance and control – Bank of Spain),

> corporations which comprise part of the financial system (banks, savings banks, financial credit establishments and cooperatives) and companies involved in real estate (companies of constructions and real estate agencies) had guaranteed the maximization of profitability through real estate, thus generating wealth and expanding political power.
>
> Thus, a society has been created where the cooperation between the state and the corporations has been made explicit: parliament and the government modified the Land Act, as well as environmental and mortgage-lending regulation; the Bank of Spain gave up control over financial markets and, thanks to the introduction of bulk mortgage loans and the speculation within the debt markets and of its derivatives, finance corporations accrued benefit at an exponential level. As a consequence, money flowed from everywhere. However, the latter was none other than a mirage. The whole economy was built on weak foundations that would eventually collapse with disastrous consequences.

The bailouts of private banks through state funds and an enormous cut in welfare created large increases in social equalities. Poor people entered the speculative home market and lost everything after eviction. One reason for the speculative market was the re-zoning of protected lands that implied converting them into developable urban lands. Another reason was the financial expansion where lower-class families had mortgage loans conveniently granted to them. The more there were sales of land and homes, the more people entered the market. At one point in time, there were more newly constructed houses in Spain than in France, Germany, and the UK put together. The prices of real estate increased, the mortgages increased, and the activities on the home market in terms of both supply and demand was formidable. Then the bubble burst, low-income families sold their homes with substantial loss, or they suffered from eviction by the banks.

Bernal et al. (2014: 224) offered the following analysis of the national crisis in Spain:

> We believe that the conceptual frameworks of both social harm and state-corporate crimes can, in their combination, produce important insights into certain social phenomena. For us, it is imperative to recognize the fact that the harms caused against the Spanish population are not natural nor inevitable effects, but they derive from a mode of economic organization and a social structure within which the omissions and the actions of the state and of the corporations play decisive roles. According to our interpretation, the latter produced harms and inequalities because of the markets, which derive directly from the state tolerance, absolving the international financial institutions from accountability for their decisions and allowing private enterprises to act freely, without being sanctioned for breaking the law (. . .)
>
> As a result of processes of dispossession due to unpaid debts, Spain is going through an intense situation leading to the loss of homes for hundreds of thousands of families. The situation is becoming worse because, in Spain, even with home loss, debtors still retain a certain part of the debt.

Bernal et al. (2014) argued that the decay in the banking sector in Spain might be characterized by speculating banking and swindler banking, via eviction banking, and to armed banking. Speculating banking contrived to generate the housing market bubble, swindler banking used the state to socialize the losses, eviction banking expelled the victims of consumption out of their houses, and armed banking gained enormous profits from financing arms manufacturing where the funds came from the socialized losses.

## Industrial Fishing Piracy Case

Piracy is an act of robbery by ship, typically with the goal of stealing valuable goods. Standing (2015) used the term pirates about state-corporate criminals in African fisheries. Icelandic fishing company Samherji bribed Namibian government officials to obtain fishing quotas. Corruption money was transferred through Norwegian bank DNB and tax havens to the corrupt ministers. The story of Samherji told earlier in this book certainly deserves the label of piracy (Amundsen, 2021; Kibar 2020a, 2020b; Kleinfeld, 2019, 2020a; Reuters, 2019; Samherji, 2021).

The industrial fishing piracy as state-corporate crime studied by Standing (2015: 177) was along the coast of Senegal.:

> Despite its economic importance, the fishing sector in Senegal is facing considerable ecological problems. The growth of the fisheries sector has been unsustainable, and there has been chronic overcapacity for decades, partly stimulated by government investment in local fisheries development, including fuel and boat building subsidies. Overcapacity has meant Senegalese fishers have migrated throughout West Africa and the government of Senegal has negotiated bilateral access agreements for its domestic fishing sector with Mauritania, Gambia, Guinea-Bissau and Cape Verde.

While the fishing pirates at the coast of Namibia came from Iceland, the fishing pirates at the coast of Senegal came from Russia. They had super trawlers target small-pelagic fish species authorized by corrupt Senegalese officials. An official at the central office of the Ministry for maritime affairs in Dakar claimed to know nothing about these boats, saying they were probably illegally fishing in Senegalese waters (Standing, 2015: 178):

> Yet in late 2010, more Russian and East European flagged trawlers were docked in the Dakar port for refueling and servicing, making it more difficult for the authorities to avoid giving out information on their legal status (. . .)
>
> The Russia-Senegal cooperation agreement may have been an outcome of a "military co-operation pact" that the governments of Russia and Senegal signed in 2007. At the time this agreement was signed, the foreign minister of Russia, Sergey Lavrov, claimed that as a consequence of the renewed co-operation between the two countries, "our wish is to sign a fishing accord with Senegal".

Senegalese law prohibited foreign trawlers in their waters to protect local fishing boats. The legality of providing authorization to the super trawlers was in conflict with licensing rules, where all fishing licenses should be presented to an industry advisory board that was a multi-stakeholder committee designed to bring accountability to the licensing process.

Standing (2015: 186) analyzed the role of the state in corporate crime in the fishing sector:

> The case from Senegal reveals the ways in which states are implicated in the harms caused by corporations, either through direct facilitation or through omission. To simplify, there is the role of the state at the local level where fishing takes place – that is, the host countries to foreign fishing firms, and the role of foreign governments – the home countries of multinational fishing enterprises. At the host level, a straightforward problem comes with bribery and extortion (. . .)
>
> It is difficult to find examples where home governments of distant water fishing fleets proactively prosecute or punish firms for crimes in foreign waters, or simply facilitate host countries in their investigations. In Senegal, the Russian government has used various tactics, including bullying, threat of litigation and the use of financial inducements, to advance the interests of its firms and avoid excessive regulation or prosecution.

Standing (2015) concluded that the concept of state-corporate crime applies to the fisheries sector. The state denies allegations and enters into agreements that benefit political and business elites at the expense of local fishing boats who have the legal right to catch fish in local waters. The fish pirates are actors who commit unsustainable acts for short-term illegal profits.

## Gulf of Mexico Oil Spill Case

After an oil spill in the Gulf, British Petroleum had to compensate victims of the accident. The total compensation was $11 billion. As suggested by the theory of convenience, a financial motive, an organizational opportunity, and a personal willingness can explain deviant behavior by members of the elite in society to gain from the compensation program. In the case of the BP Deepwater Horizon settlements, attorneys were both presenting claims on behalf of victims as well as approving claims on behalf of petroleum company BP. It was a profitable assignment for attorneys, and some attorneys made it even more profitable for themselves by kickbacks and by both applying for and approving compensations.

The Wall Street Journal reported in 2014 that BP has been complaining for a year that money it has promised to pay to financial victims of the Deepwater Horizon disaster has been doled out to unworthy, uninjured claimants (Fowler, 2014):

> In courthouse filings and newspaper ads, BP has targeted companies it says were not really harmed by the accident and their lawyers, as the oil giant's estimate of the tab ballooned from $7.8 billion to $9.4 billion. Now the oil company is taking aim at the guy doing the doling: Patrick Juneau, who was appointed by a federal judge in New Orleans to administer claims under a settlement between BP and lawyers for businesses along the Gulf Coast. Last week BP

> wrote a letter to former FBI Director Louis Freeh, who at the request of the court has been looking into alleged mischief and fraud in the Deepwater Horizon claims office. The company asked him to turn over reams of documents – including any related to Mr. Juneau's knowledge of alleged wrongdoing.

The article refers to Freeh (2013), who had written an independent external investigation report of the Deepwater Horizon court supervised settlement program. Concerns regarding improper roles of attorneys in presenting claims had caused the investigation. In the report, Freeh (2013: 9) argues that; "the nature and seriousness of this type of conduct varied in degree but was pervasive and, at its extreme, may have constituted criminal conduct".

The report by Freeh (2013) is interesting, because it examines misconduct and potential crime among white-collar offenders in the legal profession. When attorneys commit financial crime, their offenses belong to the white-collar category because attorneys satisfy many of the key characteristics. Sutherland (1939) who introduced the concept of white-collar crime specifically focused on emphasizing the respectability of white-collar offenders, stating that persons of the upper socio-economic class commit all kinds of financial crime. The ability of white-collar offenders to commit crime relates directly to their privileged position, the social structure, and their orientation to legitimate and respectable careers (Friedrichs et al., 2018).

Kang (2015) reported on the consequence for attorneys Andry, Lerner, and Sutton:

> A Louisiana federal judge sanctioned three attorneys on Thursday for misconduct in connection with BP PLC's Deepwater Horizon settlement, disqualifying them from participating in the settlement program and referring their case to the court's disciplinary committee. An investigation by court-appointed special master Louis J. Freeh released in September 2013 found that Lionel H. Sutton III, a former staff attorney for the Court Supervised Settlement Program, may have committed fraud when he referred claims to a New Orleans law firm".

This sanction was in line with Freeh's (2013: 87) recommendation that the criminal justice system "should determine whether Mr. Sutton's actions and lack of disclosures in connection with the Romeo Papa claim constituted criminal conduct".

The alleged fraud by trusted attorneys occurred in the aftermath of the oil spill a few years earlier. It was on April 20, 2010, that the Deepwater Horizon oil rig owned by Transocean exploded in the Gulf of Mexico, killing 11 people and injuring 17. Following the explosion, the rig toppled into the Gulf two days later, thereby unleashing millions of barrels of oil that caused tremendous environmental harm.

Bradshaw (2014: 163) analyzed the alleged cover-up after the environmental catastrophe in terms of state-corporate crime:

> Developing the concept of state-corporate environmental crime, this article examines the government and corporate response to the 2010 Gulf of Mexico oil spill. US federal responders functioned in coordination with BP and an extensive array of privately contracted oil spill response organizations to systematically conceal the environmental damage caused by the spill

> through various means. State-corporate responders applied unprecedented amounts of toxic chemical dispersants in an effort to hide the oil, blocked public and media access to response operations, and relied upon a network of federal, state and local law enforcement agencies alongside private security firms to enforce the ban. In combination, these efforts constitute a state-corporate cover-up of environmental crimes in the Gulf of Mexico oil spill.

The following year, Bradshaw (2015) documented criminogenic industry structures in the offshore oil industry. Participation in criminal networks can be attractive (Nielsen, 2003), especially if criminogenic market symptoms cause markets with crime forces to be the usual way of doing business (Chang et al., 2005).

## Dynamic Symbiosis Processes

Tombs (2012) identified three processes of dynamic symbiosis that tie states and corporations into increasingly tight relationships. The first process is concerned with state complicity in crime resulting from failings in law and regulation. States appear complicit in corporate crime production through omissions or a serious of failures over time to intervene. The state is unable to put into place more effective legal regimes, the state is unable to enforce adequately existing laws, and the state is unable to respond effectively to violations of existing laws. The state has given up and is reluctant to try to intervene again.

The second process is concerned with ways in which states may be aligned in corporate crime production through their formal, often intimate, relationship with the corporate sector (Tombs, 2012: 180):

> These relationships take various forms, such as, states' (local, regional, national) effective role as joint partners with the private sector in various forms of economic activity, as out-sources and contractors of economic activity, and as key purchases of corporate goods and services. They generally proceed through contracts, new regulatory regimes, regulatory reform, or a combination of each.

In Norway, multinational companies have taken over elderly care for the state (Skurdal, 2020a). A number of nursing homes are operated by profit-seeking enterprises. Violations of the legal rights of patients in state-funded, privately-run nursing homes are reported continuously in the media (Helgheim, 2021; Skurdal, 2020b). However, in a municipal Norwegian nursing home, law violation occurred as employees made no attempts to resuscitate patients (Kristiansen, 2019). A scandal in Sweden revealed poor care and anxious elderly and relatives in private nursing homes. Legal rights of service quality and security for the elderly were violated (Holmquist, 2011). When scandals are detected in private health care institutions, the state sees no alternative in reversing the privatization process. It is a process of dynamic symbiosis that ties the Norwegian state and corporations into increasingly tight relationships (Helgheim, 2021).

In addition to frequent violations of patient rights in private nursing homes funded by the state, employees in the nursing homes tend to suffer from substandard working conditions where they have to work long hours, pay for bad accommodation, and they are denied the right to protest (Helgheim, 2021; Skurdal, 2020a). This is linked to a code of silence, where employees in nursing homes do not report violations of patient rights in terms of security, safety, and service.

Another arrangement illustrating the second process of alignment between state and corporation mentioned by Tombs (2012) is the private finance initiative introduced in many countries. It was a matter of private financing of public infrastructural and service provision which generated long-term public debt to consortia of private contractors. The so-called public-private partnership combined a public procurement program, where the state buys financing from the private sector as well as the goods and services needed for completion of projects.

The third and final process of dynamic symbiosis suggested by Tombs (2012: 183) is long-term creation of criminogenic markets as free markets did never exist and cannot exist:

> States help to constitute capital, commodity, commercial and residential property markets, help to produce different kinds of "human capital", constitute labor markets, and regulate the employment contract; the state plays a role in constituting economic enterprises through specifying rules of liability, often specifying the rules of incorporation. In other words, regulation is a necessary function of a state even in the quintessential market economy, even while advocates of global neo-liberalism consistently deny such a role for the state and regulation. While "the ideological notion of latent or implicit markets when only need freeing figures strongly in neo-liberal rhetoric", this contrasts with the overwhelming empirical and theoretical evidence attesting to markets as social constructions.

Criminogenic markets emerge out this complex set of regulation imposed on corporations. Lehman et al. (2020: 1442) defined rule complexity in terms of components and connections:

> First, a rule is more complex to the extent that it comprises more components that together describe the actions and outcomes necessary for compliance. A rule with a high number of components contains more detail and requires more actions to constitute compliance. Second, a rule is more complex to the extent that it has more connections to or functional dependencies upon other rules in the same system. A rule with a high number of connections refers to actions or outcomes that may be affected by activities pertaining to another rule or set of rules.

Regulation complexity can create a situation where nobody is able to tell whether an action represented a criminal offense. It is impossible to understand what is right and what is wrong. Some laws, rules and regulations are so complex that compliance becomes random, where compliance is the action of complying with laws, rules and regulations. The regulatory legal environment is supposed to define the boundaries of appropriate organizational conduct. However, legal complexity is often so extreme that even specialist compliance officers struggle to understand what to recommend to business executives in the organizations (Lehman et al., 2020). Then regulatory inspection does not work for compliance (Braithwaite, 2020). Business executives can thus find the large grey zone in legal matters a convenient space for misconduct and crime.

Dynamic symbiosis processes can take place in various forms of state-corporate crime. When Russia and Qatar applied for and were assigned the football world championships in 2018 and 2022 respectively, an investigation report by Garcia (2014) documented widespread corruption in the allocation of the championship to those two states. It was on December 2, 2010, that the executive committee of the international football association FIFA, using an anonymous voting procedure, determined the hosts for the 2018 and 2022 FIFA world cup tournaments. The year before the games in Qatar, several national football associations discussed a potential boycott of the game. However, both associations and their national governments were reluctant to act. For example, in Norway, where the national football team had not yet qualified for the tournament, both football leaders and politicians were speaking loud about boycott because of corruption (Strøm, 2021).

A different kind of dynamic symbiosis process took place when the Kingdom of Norway wanted to gain a seat on the Security Council of the United Nations. The country spent three million US dollars on the campaign. The money was spent on travel, representation, promotional materials and profiling, training and professional preparation, salaries for temporary staff and special envoys who were specially engaged to promote the candidacy (Melgård and Oterheim, 2020). The mixture of government officials and hired representatives make the spending classification into corruption quite appropriate.

While the Norwegian government was skeptical to the Qatar games because of corruption, the Norwegian government itself got involved in corruption to get a seat on the Security Council. The only relevant bottom-up approach to such wrongdoing is the public in general protesting and investigative media in particular reporting.

Similarly, when people in the audience visit museums and notice antiques that obviously have been stolen from other countries and traded on illegal markets, then the only relevant bottom-up approach to such wrongdoing by both state museums and private museums is the public in general protesting and investigative media in particular reporting. Hanrahan (2021) found that most museums practice active non-compliance with the regulations and restrictions on acquiring antiquities as internal and external collections policies are ignored.

## Covid-19 Pandemic State Crime

The concept of state crime is not confined to legally recognized states but can include any authority that exerts political and military control over a substantial territory. State institutions and their officials commit crime. The State Crime Journal published in 2021 a special issue on the Covid-19 pandemic and state crime with the following titles of research articles in the special issue:

1. State crime, structural violence and Covid-19.
2. Do prisoners' lives matter? Examining the intersection of punitive policies, racial disparities and Covid-19 as state organized crime.
3. State crime, native Americans and Covid-19.
4. Dying for the economy: Disposable people and economies of death in the global north
5. Violating food system workers' rights in the time of Covid-19: The quest for state accountability.
6. The Covid-19 pandemic in Puerto Rico: Exceptionality, corruption and state-corporate crimes.
7. Covid-19 and the U.S. health care industry: Towards a "critical health criminology" within state crime studies.
8. Amplified vulnerability and reconfigured relations: Covid-19, torture prevention and human rights in the global south.
9. The harms of state, free-market common sense and Covid-19.

The number six article about the regime of public permissions in Puerto Rico by Osoria (2021) was presented earlier in this chapter. Most of the other articles have little or nothing to do with white-collar crime. The number seven article by Friedrichs and Weis (2021) might be of interest, since Friedrichs is a white-collar crime researcher who has labeled white-collar criminals as trusted offenders. The crime suggested in the number seven article is homicides in hospitals as a consequence of individual and corporate financial greed. For example, the chief executive in a small city hospital was reported to have earned $8 million in compensation the year before the pandemic.

The hospital CEO was not being rewarded for enhancing the quality of patient care at the hospital, or for coming up with a cure for serious illnesses (Friedrichs and Weis, 2021: 127):

> He was solely being rewarded for his perceived skill (and board of trustees' connections) in overseeing the realization of the best possible financial return for shareholders (and disproportionately, for top executives) in the corporation he headed. The hospital itself was classified as "for profit", which is of course one dimension of the widespread critique of the U.S. health care system, which has a huge private profit-seeking sector, unlike almost all other "advanced" Western countries.

The homicide potential in the hospital resulted from nurses having to go directly from treating covid patients to treating cancer patients, who are especially endangered by a Covid-19 infection. The nurses moved between units with patients who had been diagnosed with Covid-19 disease and other units where patients could easily be infected (Friedrichs and Weis, 2021: 127):

> Asked by reporters, the nurses alleged that medical staff, as well as patients, were not provided with the necessary protective equipment and that preventive procedures were not in place. A statement issued on behalf of the hospital's CEO took exception to these allegations, and representatives for the hospital claimed that the accusations were instigated by the health workers' union "for its own purposes".

In line with the homicide potential in private hospitals as a result of a profit-seeking sector (Friedrichs and Weis, 2021), the title of article number four might be relevant as is addressed the issue of dying for the economy. The economy is worth dying for, at least if it is not your life, but elderly people. Texas lieutenant governor Dan Patrick went on Fox News saying (Beckett, 2020):

> Older people would rather die than let Covid-19 harm US economy. Lieutenant governor Dan Patrick tells Fox News: "Do we have to shut down the entire country for this? I think we can get back to work".

While to most people this seems like crazy talk, Darian-Smith (2021) argued that the loss of some individuals' lives in order to sustain a buoyant economy is a rationale acceptable to many in the corporate sector as well as their pro-business political partners. She found that the profit-over-people doctrine is a rationale that has undergirded the global political economy for centuries and insidiously pervaded all elements of social life through neoliberal ideology for several decades already.

Darian-Smith (2021) found among political as well as business leaders there were some indifferent to life in the context of Covid-19. It did not amount to any carefully planned genocide equivalent epidemics in other parts of the world, but there was in the United States an underlying rationale of a kind of hierarchy of killability. In July 2021, the United States had the largest number of deaths from the Covid pandemic with 615,000 people.

## Bottom-Up Outside-In Control

The bottom-up and outside-in approaches to detection and prevention of white-collar offenders in cases of state-corporate crime will typically involve non-government organizations (NGOs) such as the League of United Latin American Citizens. This advocacy group learned from bottom-up insiders that workers at U.S. pork packing plants were being made to work despite being infected with the Corona virus. Several died. The workers had no masks or other protection measures. The state allowed and encouraged this industry to harm worker health and lives to continue to slaughter pigs (Ken and León, 2021).

The League of United Latin American Citizens filed a complaint with the Iowa Office of Safety and Health Administration in the case of a 61-year-old man named Jose Andrade-Garcia who worked at a plant in Iowa (Ken and León, 2021: 1):

> The plant safety manager said the complaint "lacked merit". Six weeks later, Andrade-Garcia died. His children and grandchildren set up a GoFundMe page to help transport his body for burial in Michoacán, Mexico, where he had planned to return after retirement to care for his elderly mother. Along with Andrade-Garcia, 318 meatpacking and processing workers around the US died due to coronavirus in 2020.

Osoria (2021) studied a similar case of state-corporate crime during the Covid-19 pandemic. The state regime of permission in Puerto Rico led to permission for corporate corruption, tax fraud, and human rights violations. Since Puerto Rico had a number of manufacturing facilities for Covid-19 vaccines, pharmaceutical corporations were permitted by the state to extract large profits from the production without the corporations exercising any sort of social responsibility. The state's only concern was for the corporations to produce as many vaccines as possible by leaving transnational corporations such as Abbott and Roche completely unregulated and not liable for any wrongdoing.

The outside-in reaction to corporate wrongdoing in Puerto Rico occurred when an interim secretary of state in the island, Quinones de Longo, resigned and presented her allegations of financial crime and human rights violations in the local pharmaceutical industry (Osoria, 2021: 116):

> The Puerto Rican House of Representatives investigated the allegations made by Quinones in a series of public hearings and published a report on June 29, 2020. The report identified the following pattern of irregularities and negligence in the management of the pandemic: (1) the irregular and fraudulent procurement of medical equipment; (2) the role of governmental employees in the purchase of medical equipment; and (3) the effects of fraudulent transactions in Puerto Rico's preparedness for the pandemic. It is interesting to note that the report does not mention the revolving doors, or that many of those involved in these transactions were former governmental employees with close ties to the ruling party.

More stories of state-corporate crime during the Corona virus pandemic can probably be told. One way of analyzing the offense occurrences is to use the situation of exception as a framework. The situation of exception allows public agencies to decide which laws and rights do or do not apply in certain situations. In Puerto Rico, the governor granted immunity from criminal charges to medical facilities and professionals during the pandemic (Osoria, 2021). All over the world, it seemed that supply of medicines, foods, and other goods and services to meet the basic needs of people had such a high priority during the pandemic that violations of human rights, worker safety regulations, corruption laws, and other offenses were ignored in the state-corporate relationships.

In the case of illegal family separation of immigrants, public outcry of the abhorrent conditions caused an outside-in end to the state crime of separation except when parents had criminal histories or were being prosecuted for criminal offenses (Barak, 2021: 112):

> Despite this, the government used minor offenses – such as parking violations or driving with an expired license – to separate additional migrant families. In violation of official policy, some families legally seeking asylum at ports of entry were also separated.

The slavery contracts in the protective equipment industry were detected in an outside-in approach by investigative journalists (Marmo and Bandiera, 2021: 2):

> The most recent and visually compelling of these was the investigation into the supply of personal protective equipment (PPE) on the UK's National Health Service (NHS) conducted by the BBC's Channel 4, televised in July 2020, which exposed extreme forms of labor exploitation akin to slavery for the purpose of meeting higher PPE production targets.

The state-corporate environmental crime on Tjøme Island in Norway was detected in a bottom-up approach from two citizens on the island. They were surprised by the privatization of the shoreline and started to review public documents for each summerhouse construction site. They found that all applications by skilled architects and attorneys on behalf of the rich people had been reluctantly approved by state clerks. Eventually, both a state planner and an architect were convicted to prison for corruption. The rich and mighty mansion owners were forced to demolish buildings and improve the landscape (Blix, 2021; Holmøy, 2021).

The state-corporate crime in the case of the construction industry in Qatar was detected by outside-in reports from investigative journalists in the UK newspaper The Guardian (McCarthy, 2021). While Qatar officials initially denied any worker deaths at world cup construction sites, the media focus caused several football nations to present the threat of boycott if not working conditions improved. Then Qatar officials acknowledge problems and claimed to have implemented measures in the spring of 2021. The deaths of more than six thousand immigrant workers were caused by poor and non-existent safety practices on construction sites (Davies, 2021).

The state-banks conspiracy in Spain, where the state helped the banks with funding for lost repayments of mortgages from homeowners, and also helped banks with eviction of homeowners so that the banks were the legal owners of the homes, became an issue by outside-in detection (Bernal et al., 2014: 226):

> After the press widely publicized three of these latter suicide cases, the government was pressured to take certain measures. It finally passed the RD-Act 27/2012, which established a 2-year moratorium on the evictions. However, the reality is that, due to this law's restrictive conditions, none of these three widely publicized suicide cases would have been prevented, and less than 10 per cent of those facing eviction would have been able to find any benefits from it.

Industrial fishing piracy in Namibia was detected in a bottom-up notification from an internal whistleblower (Kleinfeld, 2019, 2020a). Industrial fishing piracy in Senegal was detected in an outside-in notification from the non-government organization Coalition for fair fisheries arrangements. The coalition conducted field work in Senegal, follow-up conversations with local experts at international meetings and through emails, and it interpreted various published reports (Standing, 2015).

The Gulf of Mexico oil spill needed no bottom-up or outside-in notification. It was visible to everyone when it happened. However, the following attempts to conceal the damage needed investigative attention such as the research article by Bradshaw (2014). Federal responders were reluctant to intervene as British Petroleum quickly contracted private oil spill response organizations and public relations professionals. BP acted deliberately to hide the impact the spill was having on wildlife. As the oil made landfall, the images of dead and dying animals quickly surfaced in the media. Then federal, state, and local law enforcement in cooperation with private security soldiers recruited by BP prevented public and media access to the spill.

Admiral Allen officially announced a ban on civilians and media within 65 feet of cleanup equipment, workers and animals on July 1, 2010 (Bradshaw, 2014: 174):

> Penalties for violating the "safety zone" included a Class D felony violation, a US$40,000 fine and possible jail time. Shortly thereafter on 6 July, a spokesperson for Admiral Allen released a statement elaborating that the zone was implemented due to concerns over vandalism. The enforced zones were not a complete ban on media access, as the Coast Guard would consider applications for permission to enter the safety zones, though they would be decided on a case-by-case basis. In the instances that press were granted access, it was done with strict oversight from BP and the Coast Guard. Photographers were escorted by BP officials on boats and aircraft contracted by BP, thereby granting BP control over what could be seen.

As Bradshaw's (2014) analysis demonstrated; states and corporations often work in collaboration to conceal their deviant activities through censorship of information. With increasing privatization and liberalization globally, the state is unwilling and unable to protect the public from the environmentally harmful offenses of corporations. In the absence of state oversight and guardianship, it is vital that citizens, journalists, ideal organizations become involved in bottom-up and outside-in notification.

The state-corporate crime in Scandinavian nursing homes was detected in an outside-in approach by relatives of the elderly. Sons and daughters notice that their parents are treated badly in private nursing homes operated by profit-seeking multinational corporations. When investigative journalists – often in local media – cover a specific story, then the individual in focus quickly tends to receive improved treatment (Helgheim, 2021; Holmquist, 2011; Skurdal, 2020a, 2020b). However, the system does not change. It is a process of dynamic symbiosis that ties the Scandinavian states and corporations into increasingly tight relationships (Tombs, 2012).

The state-corporate crime in private hospitals in the United States owned by corporations was detected by bottom-up notification from nurses who had to move between hospital units potentially infected with the Corona virus and potentially able to infect very vulnerable groups such as cancer patients. The nurses told media reporters that they as well as the patients were not provided with the necessary protective equipment and those preventive measures were not in place (Friedrichs and Weis, 2021).

# 11 Responsibility Attribution

Trusted chief executives and others in the elite in white-collar crime will vary in terms of others' attribution of responsibility on them and punitiveness for financial crime. For example, Fleckenstein and Bowes (2000) suggested that trust should be understood as a fiduciary responsibility in religious organizations. A fiduciary responsibility implies putting others' interests ahead of own interests, with a duty to preserve good faith and trust. Violating the fiduciary responsibility by putting own interests ahead of others' interests by committing occupational or corporate crime as a white-collar offender can cause different attribution of responsibility for financial crime.

## Perspectives on Responsibility

As described by Kim et al. (2009), situational attribution of responsibility is assigned to the trustee by the trustor. When situational attribution is low, then the individual response might be defensive. When the situational attribution is high, then the individual might be accommodative. While a defensive response accepts no or little responsibility for an incident, an accommodative response acknowledges the individual's causal role in the incident. Denials and excuses are examples of defensive responses, while apologies and promises are examples of accommodative responses. In-between there is justification, where the actor admits responsibility for the act in question but denies its pejorative and negative content (Schoen et al., 2021: 730):

> People use justification mechanisms to protect their sense of self. People who sincerely believe that they are a specific kind of person but routinely demonstrate behaviors that indicate otherwise may avoid cognitive dissonance and maintain their sense of self by using justification mechanisms that allow them to "explain away" their behavior.

The individual's causal role in an incident is dependent on the social role in the offense, where Schmidt et al. (2022) distinguished between offending autonomously, offending from obedience, or co-offending with others. Their review of the literature on responsibility attribution in organizational settings showed that the social role in an offense affects assessments of responsibility for deviance.

CEO power and influence, actions, and decisions are supposed to be monitored by owners, shareholders, or board directors (Veltrop et al., 2021). However, Hambrick et al. (2015) found that boards often fail in their monitoring responsibilities. One reason is that many board members are missing some of the following attributes: independence, expertise in the domain, bandwidth, and motivation. Hambrick et al. (2015: 324) expressed surprise that investigative journalists succeed while board members fail:

https://doi.org/10.1515/9783110986686-012

> On the face of it, this study applauds the role of the press as governance watchdog, but it also raises deeper questions: If journalists could spot these frauds using public sources, why couldn't the companies' boards have detected them? For that matter, why couldn't the boards have spotted the frauds when they were first being perpetrated? And what kind of tone did these boards set that would prompt their companies' CEOs and other executives to engage in such acts and think they could get away with it?

When boards fail in their monitoring responsibilities, lower attribution of responsibility for white-collar crime on chief executives might occur. While Porter et al. (2004) argued that being a CEO means bearing full responsibility for an organization's success or failure but being unable to control most of what will determine it, the attribution of responsibility is not obvious in situations of white-collar crime and corporate scandals. CEOs are in positions of power and formal responsibility (Galvin et al., 2015), but they are not necessarily made accountable for misconduct, wrongdoing, and crime that undermine their organizations.

A frequent neutralization technique for avoidance of guilt feeling is to disclaim responsibility, where the chief executive perceives not being responsible for what happened or not happened. The offender here claims that one or more of the conditions of responsible agency did not occur. The person committing a deviant act defines self as lacking responsibility for his or her actions. In this technique, the person rationalizes that the action in question is beyond his or her control. The offender may view self as a billiard ball, helplessly propelled through different situations with various stakeholders (Jordanoska, 2018; Kaptein and Helvoort, 2019; Sykes and Matza, 1957).

When a chief executive acknowledges responsibility, then the person accepts being accountable. Accountability refers to liability, answerability, and blameworthiness. Accountability is the acknowledgment and assumption of responsibility for actions and decisions. Accountability refers to situations in which someone is required or expected to justify actions and decisions. Accountability is concerned with holding someone responsible to someone for something (Smith, 2009).

The opposite of responsibility is irresponsibility (Alcadipani and Medeiros, 2020; Tang et al., 2015). High social status in privileged positions creates power inequality compared to those without any status in their positions. The perspective of power inequality suggests that, for example, family members in family firms wield significant influence in their firms (Patel and Cooper, 2014). Family members often have legitimate access to firm resources that nonfamily executives in the firm cannot question. Individuals with high social status in privileged positions can cooperate to create a business climate of "organized irresponsibility" (Berghoff, 2018: 425):

> The term implies that management had conspired to prevent efficient controls and therefore facilitated and promoted corruption.

Berghoff and Spiekermann (2018: 291) found that white-collar crime is often systemic and part of a culture, either of a corporate culture inside the firm or of a culture in the firm's environment:

> In the first case, the corporation's control mechanisms are typically weak, intentionally or unintentionally, which is an obstacle to the prevention and the investigation of economic crimes. Individual responsibility is therefore hard to ascertain. Defendants routinely deny responsibility and point to their superiors who made them commit crimes, or to their inferiors who engaged in shady practices without their knowledge or authorization.

A bottom-up approach to address individual irresponsibility is focused deterrence, which is to communicate the likelihood and severity of sanctions to potential offenders. Explicit sanction communication is meant to increase the perceived certainty of punishment. Rorie and West (2022) suggested that when potential white-collar offenders are explicitly told that a behavior is prohibited, then they will be less likely to engage in that specific behavior since they will perceive potential punishments as more certain, and they will perceive the potential punishments as more severe.

Attribution theory explains how individuals attribute responsibility for both own and others' behavior (Fisse and Braithwaite, 1988). The central premise is that attributions of responsibility depend on whether individuals view the causes of behavior as a result of internal or external factors. If individuals determine that a behavior results from internal factors in terms actor personality characteristics and actor disposition, then they typically will attribute the behavior to the actor. Alternatively, individuals can attribute the behavior to other people or the situation such as social structure or organizational context. The strength of attribution in terms of responsibility can depend on a number of factors such as causality, knowledge, intentions, and seriousness (Gailey and Lee, 2005). Attribution is concerned with how individuals make judgments about responsibility (Piening et al., 2020: 335):

> Attributions of responsibility involve a series of yes-no judgments in which individuals first determine whether a negative event has been caused by internal or external factors. If the event is attributed to internal causes, the process continues to determine whether the cause was controllable or not, whereas in case of external causality, the organization cannot be held responsible, so the process stops.

A successful attribution of blame elsewhere is a matter of blame game performance. The blame game is concerned with misleading attribution to others (Eberly et al., 2011). Linked to the blame game is shaming, where the offender expresses social disapproval of the innocent in the organization, thereby attempting to gain social control on perceptions of transgression. Shaming implies stigmatization and disapproval (Amry and Meliala, 2021). The blame game in an organizational setting can enable the chief executive to disclaim responsibility for wrongdoing (Hurrell, 2016; Keaveney, 2008; Lee and Robinson, 2000; Resodihardjo et al., 2015; Xie and Keh, 2016). How blame is assigned is especially important for understanding legal culpability, punishment outcomes, and corporate regulation (Schmidt et al., 2022).

The attribution perspective implies that white-collar offenders are able to attribute causes of crime to everyone else but themselves in the organization. Attribution theory is about identifying causality predicated on internal and external circumstances

(Eberly et al., 2011). External attributions place the cause of a negative event on external factors, absolving the account giver and the privileged individual from personal responsibility. Innocent subordinates receive blame for crime committed by elite members (Lee and Robinson, 2000). According to Sonnier et al. (2015: 10), affective reactions influence blame attribution directly and indirectly by altering structural linkage assessments:

> For example, a negative affective reaction can influence the assessment of causation by reducing the evidential standards required to attribute blame or by increasing the standards of care by which an act is judged.

When scandals first emerge into public view, corporations often do not fully understand them as negative events, as there is uncertainty regarding exactly what happened, the potential significance of the events, and how stakeholders and outside observers will respond to it. Most importantly, there is a concern whether an individual or the corporation as a whole will face responsibility and sanctions (Bandura, 1999; Schoultz and Flyghed, 2016, 2019, 2020a, 2020b, 2021a, 2021b). Scandals have become a key mechanism used by news media, pressure groups, and social movements to demand inquiries and investigations into alleged corruption, incompetence, and immorality.

All crises are uncertain events that generate initial negative reactions. According to Bundy and Pfarrer (2015: 352), an effective response strategy should match external observers' situational attributions of the crisis to prevent cognitive dissonance among observers:

> A crisis with higher situational attributions of responsibility should be matched with a response strategy that accepts more responsibility, and a crisis with lower situational attributions of responsibility should be matched with a response strategy that accepts less responsibility (. . .) An organization that is under conforming by being defensive in response to a crisis with higher situational attributions risks being perceived as unethical and manipulative.

Bandura (1999) identified the ways that corporations can disengage themselves from the harmful consequences of their actions. Moral disengagement can occur by belittled labeling, advantageous comparison, displacement of responsibility, diffusion of responsibility, disregard or distortion of consequences, and dehumanization of victims.

Bundy and Pfarrer (2015) suggested that the more an organization's response strategy matches evaluators' situational attributions of crisis responsibility, the lower the mean and variance of social approval loss. Furthermore, for an organization with higher social approval, a response strategy that accepts less crisis responsibility, relative to an average-approval organization, will generate a lower mean and variance of social approval loss than a response strategy that accepts the same or more crisis responsibility. Third, for an organization with lower social approval, a response strategy that accepts less crisis responsibility, relative to an average-approval organization, will generate a lower mean and variance of social approval loss than a response strategy that accepts the same or more crisis responsibility. Finally, managers of a higher- or lower-approval organization will be more likely to accept less crisis responsibility, relative to managers of an average-approval organization.

## Empirical Attribution Study

Schmidt et al. (2022) conducted an empirical study of responsibility attribution. Their five proposed dimensions of responsibility were predictive of responsibility attributions, and their path analysis showed offender role and offense environment affecting how the five dimensions of responsibility affect attributions. They drew on the attribution literature to construct a multidimensional model of responsibility attribution and punishment. From this model, they derived hypotheses that might predict how organizational culture and offender social role affects the antecedents of, and overall, attribution of responsibility and subsequent punishment.

The five dimensions applied in the research were; (1) causality (i.e., was the actor directly involved), (2) knowledge (i.e., was the actor aware or could foresee consequences), (3) intentionality (i.e., was the action intentional), (4) moral wrongfulness (i.e., how wrong was the action), and (5) coercion (i.e., was free will inhibited). These five dimensions influence the extent of attribution of responsibility that in turn influences the extent of punishment (Schmidt et al., 2022: 2):

> For the multidimensional model to be applicable to the evaluation of white-collar crime, we argue that a link between attribution of responsibility (AOR) and punishment must be added. Previous research shows that responsibility attributions predict punitive attitudes. Specifically, greater dispositional attributions increase punitiveness, while greater situational attributions decrease it. For instance, research shows dispositional attributions predict greater punitiveness towards violent corporate offenders and greater support for harsher punishment (i.e., capital punishment). Research shows greater situational attributions predict less harsh punishments (i.e., rehabilitative over retributive types of punishments). Thus, we would expect attributions of responsibility to directly affect punishment, with greater attributions linked to greater punishment.

The five independent variables and the two dependent variables were measured in terms of the following statements by Schmidt et al. (2022) in their vignette survey among university students:

- Causality – the extent to which the actor was directly involved, was at fault for what happened, could have avoided what happened, and the wrongdoing was preventable.
- Knowledge – was the actor aware or could foresee consequences, was aware of the potential consequences for what happened, was able to foresee the harm of own action, and recognized the seriousness of own action.
- Intentionality – was the action intentional, the actor intended to commit wrongdoing, the action was no accident, and the actor planned the action in advance.

- Wrongfulness – how wrong was the action, what the actor did was wrong, the actor was not acting morally, the actor was deceitful in the action, the actor was not justified in the action, the action was serious.
- Coercion – was free will inhibited, did other people influence the person to act, was the person coerced in the action, and was someone else besides the person responsible for the wrongdoing.
- Responsibility – the person acted of own will, the person is blameworthy, and the person is responsible for what happened.
- Punishment – the extent of a monetary fine ranging from nothing to one million US dollars.

As the positivity of most estimated coefficients in the Schmidt et al. (2022) research indicated, the greater the offender is deemed to have been directly involved (causality), aware of the consequences (knowledge), acted intentionally, and deemed morally wrong, the more responsibility attributed to the actor. Further, if the offender was deemed to have been influenced by others (coercion) in committing financial crime, the offender was deemed less responsible as evidenced by a negative coefficient. Finally, attribution of responsibility was statistically significant in predicting recommended fine. The greater the attribution of responsibility, the greater was the recommended fine.

## Fraud Investigation Reports

A fraud examiner is a financial detective in the private policing business undertaking internal investigations in client organizations. The fraud examiner conducts commercial inquiries by undertaking factual reviews of documents, interviews with whistleblowers and suspects, and other investigative steps. The client expectation is that fraud examiners will uncover and verify the facts of the case, reconstruct past events and sequences of events, and thereby allowing the client to make informed decisions to either litigate or resolve matters on a commercial basis (King, 2021; Meerts, 2020).

A corporate investigation serves the purpose of finding answers to questions such as: What happened? When did it happen? How did it happen? Who did what to make it happen or not happen? Why did it happen? An important task for a corporate investigator is to assess attribution of responsibility by discussing issues such as causality, knowledge, intentionality, wrongfulness, and coerciveness (Button, 2020; King, 2020a, 2020b; Wood, 2020).

The outcome of an internal investigation by fraud examiners is a fraud investigation report. The investigation report is handed over to the client who pays for the work. The report thus becomes the property of the client who normally prefers to keep the report secret for various reasons (Gottschalk and Tcherni-Buzzeo, 2017).

Sometimes, reports become publicly available, and then they can serve as an empirical source for the study of attribution of responsibility.

For the current research, it was possible to retrieve fifteen recent fraud investigation reports as listed in Table 11.1. The table consisting of parts a and b lists year of report publication, the corporate investigator that were typically partners in law firms or auditing firms, the client organization where there was suspicion of wrongdoing, and the suspected white-collar person.

The first entry in Table 12.1 is concerned with the corporate investigation report by law firm Bruun Hjejle in Denmark. The law firm conducted a corporate investigation into alleged violations of money laundering procedures at Danske Bank's branch office in Estonia. Thomas Borgen, the chief executive officer at the bank, had to leave his position and was later sued by shareholders and investigated by Danish police (Hecklen et al., 2020; Högseth, 2019; Milne, 2019a, 2019b; Milne and Binham, 2018). At the time of writing, Danish police had closed their investigation without charging Borgen for wrongdoing, while shareholders were still in the process of preparing a case against him (Klevstrand, 2021; Solgård, 2021). On the scale for punishment from 1 (not serious) to 11 (very serious) the number 6 in the table represents an assessment of not going to prison while civil procedures are pending. Corporate investigators at Bruun Hjejle (2018) did not blame Borgen for the violations of procedures in Lithuania, therefore responsibility on the scale from 1 (no responsibility) to 11 (complete responsibility) is assigned stage 2 in Table 1. Furthermore, the investigation report leaves the impression that Borgen did not know, and therefore stage 2 in the table for knowledge. However, the intention to have a branch office was to have profitable clients from Russia who were well-known violators of legal principles, thereby justifying stage 8 for intention in the table. Finally for Borgen, money laundering is assessed at seriousness stage 9, since money laundering today is sometimes linked to terrorist financing. In 2022, the media reported that Thomas Borgen had found employment at the Norwegian investment firm Reiten & Co. In addition, he planned to pursue a doctoral degree where his dissertation would be to study implementation of business strategy (Bøe, 2022).

The second entry in Table 11.1 is concerned with the corporate investigation report by audit firm Kroll in Moldova. The New York Times reported in October 2015 that Moldova "was rocked this year by the discovery that $1 billion had fraudulently siphoned from Moldova's banking system over a period of years, a huge amount for an impoverished country whose entire economic output is only about $8 billion a year" (Nechepurenko, 2015). Ilan Shor, at that time a 28-year-old Moldovan business executive and the mayor of Orhei organized the swindle. Shor was chairperson of the board of Banca de Economii (Rosca, 2015). The Times of Israel reported in 2019 that Ilan Shor was sentenced to 7.5 years for fraud and money laundering (Iordachescu and Rodina, 2019; Liphshiz, 2019). However, at the time of writing, he never returned to Moldova to serve his time in prison. Since he escaped prison, punishment is assigned stage 7 in the table. Kroll (2018) did blame Shor completely for the disappearance of funds, therefore is responsibility assigned stage 11 in the table. Corporate investigators argued in their report that Shor had complete knowledge and complete intention (thus stage 11 in the table for both variables). The crime was serious at stage 9 since the scam threatened to ruin the financial situation in Moldova.

The third entry in Table 11.1 is concerned with the corporate investigation report by law firms Sands in Norway regarding the company Oceanteam in the Netherlands. It was a minority shareholder in Norway who requested the investigation (Riisnæs, 2018). The corporation Oceanteam was in the business of providing support for offshore contractors all over the world through its fleet of large offshore vessels and its expertise in marine equipment, cable logistics and design engineering (Strandli, 2019). Haico Halbesma, chief executive officer, Hessel Halbesma, chairperson of the board, as well as three board members faced accusations of fraud against Oceanteam (OT). Sands (2019) found that in general, fraud examiners observed an extensive lack of control of invoices and timesheets from executives and board members. Relevant functions had not controlled board members' timesheets, and the same applied to the CEO. For example, in 2015, Hessel Halbesma invoiced 3.600 additional hours of a total of EUR 1,080,000. Travel bills and other remunerations were extremely high. For example, Hessel Halbesma had travel expenses of EUR 333.000 in 2013 (Sands, 2019: 9):

> In our review of Hessel Halbesma's travel bills, several expenses classified as company expenses, appear highly questionable with regards to being associated with OT's daily operations, for example purchases of clothing, numerous toll road passing, travels to places where OT has no operations (e.g. Verbier, San Remo), helicopter rental expenses in Monaco and dining expenses with no information about participants, the purpose of the meal or the relation to OT's operations.

**Table 11.1a:** Fraud investigation reports.

| Year | Country | Corporate Investigator | Client Organization | White-Collar Person |
|---|---|---|---|---|
| 2018 | Denmark | Bruun Hjejle | Danske Bank | Thomas Borgen |
| 2018 | Moldova | Kroll | Moldova Banks | Ilan Shor |
| 2019 | Netherlands | Sands | Oceanteam | Hessel Halbesma |
| 2019 | Denmark | PwC | Socialstyrelsen | Britta Nielsen |
| 2020 | Denmark | Kammeradvokaten | Banedanmark | Several individuals |
| 2020 | Denmark | Plesner | Danske Bank | Chris Vogelzang |
| 2020 | Denmark | Kammeradvokaten | Ejendomsstyrelse | Dennis Engmann |
| 2020 | Congo | Smith | Mercy Corp | Several individuals |
| 2020 | Sweden | Clifford Chance | Swedbank | Birgitte Bonnesen |
| 2020 | USA | State Auditor | UC Berkley | Lori Loughlin |
| 2020 | USA | U.S. House | Wells Fargo | Carrie Tolstedt |
| 2020 | Germany | KPMG | Wirecard | Markus Braun |
| 2021 | USA | Dechert | Apollo Global | Leon Black |
| 2021 | Austria | Commission | IBU | Anders Besseberg |
| 2021 | Sweden | Finansinspektionen | Nasdaq Clearing | Einar Aas |

Table 11.1b: Attribution by corporate investigators.

| Year | Client Organization | Punishment | Responsibility | Knowledge | Intention | Seriousness |
|---|---|---|---|---|---|---|
| 2018 | Danske Bank | 6 | 2 | 2 | 8 | 9 |
| 2018 | Moldova Banks | 7 | 11 | 11 | 11 | 9 |
| 2019 | Oceanteam | 2 | 11 | 11 | 11 | 3 |
| 2019 | Socialstyrelsen | 10 | 11 | 11 | 11 | 8 |
| 2020 | Banedanmark | 1 | 5 | 6 | 6 | 2 |
| 2020 | Danske Bank | 2 | 2 | 3 | 1 | 4 |
| 2020 | Ejendomsstyrelse | 10 | 9 | 10 | 11 | 4 |
| 2020 | Mercy Corp | 1 | 8 | 7 | 10 | 8 |
| 2020 | Swedbank | 2 | 2 | 3 | 8 | 9 |
| 2020 | UC Berkley | 8 | 9 | 7 | 9 | 3 |
| 2020 | Wells Fargo | 2 | 11 | 4 | 10 | 7 |
| 2020 | Wirecard | 5 | 8 | 7 | 11 | 6 |
| 2021 | Apollo Global | 4 | 4 | 2 | 2 | 1 |
| 2021 | IBU | 5 | 5 | 9 | 4 | 3 |
| 2021 | Nasdaq Clearing | 1 | 5 | 8 | 1 | 4 |

The punishment for Hessel Halbesma is at stage 2 since the only consequence was for him to avoid private expenses paid for by Oceanteam. He was considered completely responsible for the misconduct, he had complete knowledge of the misconduct, and the misconduct was intentional, therefore stage 11 for all three issues in the table. The wrongdoing was not considered that serious and thus assigned stage 3.

The fourth entry in Table 11.1 is concerned with the investigation report by audit firm PwC in Denmark regarding fraud at the national social security agency Socialstyrelsen. Socialstyrelsen aims at actively contributing to social initiatives for the benefit of citizens. Socialstyrelsen is responsible for a variety of tasks and projects in the social area, including children, young people, and families, disabilities, aids, and psycho-social initiatives, and adults with social problems. Socialstyrelsen does not only support vulnerable groups such as unemployed and homeless people, it provides social benefits to a large fraction of the Danish population. Britta Nielsen embezzled funds intended for vulnerable and disabled people by creating fake receivers of social benefits (BBC, 2020; Newth, 2018; NTB, 2019). She received a sentence of six and a half years in prison for embezzling 117 million Danish kroner of government funding intended for social security needs (Ottermann, 2020). A sentence of six and a half years in prison is a very serious conviction in Scandinavia and thus at stage 10 on the punishment scale in Table 1. Corporate examiners at PwC (2019) found her completely responsible, knowledgeable, and intentional in her wrongdoing and thus stage 11 seems appropriate for all three issues. The seriousness of violating trust in public office is very high and assigned stage 8 in the table.

The fifth entry in Table 11.1 is concerned with the investigation report by law firm Kammeradvokaten in Denmark. In the summer of 2018, Banedanmark noticed an article in the Danish newspaper Berlingske that there were rumors of financial crime by some employees in the public railroad maintenance organization for several years. Banedanmark is a state-owned company that is responsible for operating and maintaining the entire Danish railway network. The company outsources several service functions to outside vendors. The newspaper article was based on journalists having received a number of anonymous tips related to twenty-three named employees who were still or had previously been employed by Banedanmark. The tips suggested that employees were guilty of misconduct and illegal activities such as bribery and abuse of power when cooperating with subcontractors over several years (Jessen and Jung, 2020; Jung and Jessen, 2020). The suspected fraud was concerned with employee receipt of bribes. The investigation report by Kammeradvokaten has 191 pages. After initial chapters on rules and regulations, the report reviews all of the 23 individuals from page 79 to page 185. For each individual, various email messages between employees and vendors are reviewed. The payments and benefits are modest, but seem to fit into the picture of a corrupt culture that existed for many years (Kammeradvokaten, 2020a: 187):

> On the basis of the above review of the material concerning the 23 persons who were selected for the present investigation, Kammeradvokaten has made a number of general observations, which are described in more detail below.

Based on the overall review of the material included in this study, it is Kammeradvokaten's assessment that in a number of areas there has been negative behavior among a number of Banedanmark employees. At the same time, the documentation shows that a number of suppliers have also shown reprehensible behavior. As can be seen from the report, the overall picture is that the problems have clearly diminished over the entire period examined from 2011 to March 2020. Thus, the vast majority of the negative circumstances that appear in the reviewed material took place in the period from 2011 to 2015.

As indicated by stage 1 for punishment, there were no consequences for employees after the completed investigation. Employees carried some responsibility for the misconduct (stage 5), had knowledge of deviance (stage 6), and accepted favors with some intention (stage 6). However, the deviance was not at all considered serious (stage 2).

The sixth entry in Table 11.1 is concerned with the investigation report by law firm Plesner in Denmark. The law firm conducted a corporate investigation into wrongdoing at Danske Bank. The bank admitted in September 2020 that they had known for years about the bank's practice of collecting outdated and excessive debt from customers. Denmark's financial watchdog Finanstilsynet (2020) launched the previous month an inquiry into how Danske Bank had wrongly collected debt from up to 106,000 customers since 2004. The bank blamed IT system errors (Reuters, 2020):

> "There has been knowledge about at least parts of the problem in different parts and levels of the organization, including leaders, during the years", Denmark's largest bank said in a statement. "Despite attempts to manage the problems, the underlying data flaws were never fully addressed, and unfortunately this has caused the issues to continue for several years", it said.

The investigation report by Plesner (2020) concerning fraudulent debt collection by Danske Bank has 120 pages. The report is addressed to the Danish Financial Supervisory Authority and dated September 10, 2020. The report is a response to the supervisory authority's request for an account of the bank's debt collection system. Chis Vogelzang had to leave the CEO position (Solgård, 2021), but he faced no other consequences at the time of writing, so punishment is at stage 2 in the table. His responsibility for the scandal seems limited (stage 2), his knowledge of the scandal seems limited (stage 3), and his intention of wrongdoing was not present (stage 1). The seriousness of the wrongdoing is assessed at stage 4 since the victims had minor losses.

The seventh entry in Table 11.1 is concerned with the investigation report by law firm Kammeradvokaten in Denmark. Dennis Bechmann Engmann, who was previously head of the building department at Karup Airport, was sentenced by the court in Viborg to two years in prison. The verdict was the end of the case of bribery in the Ministry of Defense's property management agency (Julsgaard, 2020). In 2015 and 2016, Dennis Bechmann Engmann made extensive renovations of his house in Møldrup and an extension of the building at a total value of 1.7 million kroner (about USD 240,000). The building work was completed free of charge by one of the vendors who did construction work for the Ministry of Defense's property management agency (Ritzau, 2020). As a consequence of the detected bribery, law firm Kammeradvokaten (2020b) was hired by the Danish ministry to investigate allegations of financial misconduct in the management of real estate properties (Danish Ministry of Defense's property management agency: "Forsvarsministeriets ejendomsstyrelse"). In particular, examiners had a mandate of investigating Hans J. Høyer who was the chief executive at the Ejendomsstyrelse. The investigation report by Kammeradvokaten (2020b) provides valuable insights into the convenient opportunity structure for Engmann. While Høyer had to leave his position as chief executive because of mismanagement, Engmann ended up in prison. The punishment was thus serious (stage 10), he was responsible (stage 9), he had knowledge of the wrongdoing (stage 10), and his intention of personal benefit was obvious (stage 11). The fraud was occupational crime with limited consequences and thus seriousness at stage 4 in the table.

The eighth entry in Table 11.1 is concerned with the investigation report by the consulting firm Smith in Congo. Mercy Corps is a charity. The international non-government organization (NGO) experienced a scam in the Democratic Republic of Congo (DRC). The scam involved corrupt aid workers, business owners, and community leaders (Kleinfeld, 2020b):

> Together they zeroed in on the humanitarian sector's flagship rapid response programmes – the main mechanism for helping displaced people in Congo, where hundreds of millions of dollars of foreign aid are spent every year.

Some $636,000 was lost by Mercy Corps and partners in just a few months. It was estimated that the charity had lost $6 million in about two years. Kleinfeld (2020b) described the modus operandi in some of the wrongdoing:

> When a conflict or natural disaster occurred, aid groups would receive reports from local community leaders that exaggerated the number of people who had fled their homes. Businesspeople would then pay kickbacks to corrupt aid workers to register hundreds of additional people for cash support who were not actually displaced. The merchants would then receive the aid payments and share with the local leaders. Of the nineteen Mercy Corps aid workers alleged to be involved in the scam, some were using the extra cash to buy new cars, Armani glasses, and iPhones, according to several of their colleagues who spoke to The New Humanitarian (TNH). One even started building a hotel, colleagues said.

UN agencies and aid groups in Congo created an anti-fraud task to conduct an operational review after the NGO Mercy Corps discovered the fraud scheme. The investigating team consisted of three international consultants and two Congolese researchers contracted by Adam Smith International, an aid consultancy. The anti-fraud task was funded with a grant from the UK government (Smith, 2020). There was no punishment (stage 1 in the table), while responsibility for wrongdoing was quite obvious (stage 8), and so was also knowledge (stage 7) and intention (stage 10).

The ninth entry in Table 11.1 is concerned with the investigation report by Clifford Chance in Sweden. Swedbank carried out bank transactions of more than 37 billion Euros (about US$40 billion) with a high risk for money laundering over a five-year period according to private policing in terms of an internal investigation by fraud examiners from law firm Clifford Chance (2020). The investigation report suggests that the Swedish bank actively targeted high-risk individuals in the Baltic region and points to failings from both top management and the board (Milne, 2020). Birgitte Bonnesen was the chief executive officer (CEO) at Swedbank. She had to leave the position in 2019 (Makortoff, 2019). When Clifford Chance (2020) presented their report of investigation, the new Swedbank board decided to withdraw her final compensation of 26 million Swedish kroner (US$2.7 million). At the same time, Swedbank accepted a fine of 4 billion Swedish kroner (US$408 million) from the Swedish finance inspection (Johannessen and Christensen, 2020).

The former chief executive at Swedbank resigned from the position while Clifford Chance was still conducting the internal investigation. Another executive resigned from the position of chief compliance officer when the bank publicized the report of investigation. Two years later, in 2022, the former chief executive at Swedbank, Birgitte Bonnesen, was charged with fraud and market manipulation by the Swedish prosecutor (Ismail, 2022: 7):

> The revelations at that time led to a number of people in senior positions having to leave. The bank also received a record fine of four billion Swedish kroner, according to Swedish public broadcasting. One of those who were fired was Swedbank's top executive Birgitte Bonnesen. In January this year, the Swedish economic crime authority brought charges against Bonnesen for gross fraud and market manipulation.

In addition, the entire former management of Swedbank in Estonia was suspected of money laundering. The Estonian public prosecutor suspected that the management of Swedbank's Estonian bank contributed to laundering of 100 million Euros in the years 2014 to 2016. Some of the suspected money laundering was linked to Mikhail Abyzov, a former minister in the Russian government (Ismail, 2022).

The tenth entry in Table 11.1 is concerned with the investigation report by a State Auditor in the United States. The California state auditor found that qualified students faced an inconsistent and unfair admissions system that had been improperly influence by relationships and monetary donations (State Auditor, 2020). Several rich and mighty people were involved in the corruption scandal. On May 22, 2020, actress Lori Anne Loughlin in Hollywood pleaded guilty to one count of conspiracy to commit wire and mail fraud. Her husband Mossimo Giannulli, an American fashion designer, pleaded guilty to one count of conspiracy to commit wire and mail fraud and honest services wire and mail fraud. On August 21, 2020, Loughlin was sentenced to two months in prison while her husband was sentenced to five months. They had committed federal program corruption by bribing employees of the University of California to facilitate their children's admission. In exchange for the bribes, employees at the university designated the couple's children as athletic recruits with little or no regard for their athletic abilities. The university officials that were bribed claimed that the two daughters were qualified for the women's rowing team although none of them had trained in the sport of rowing nor had plans to do so. Loughlin and Giannulli paid $500,000 in bribes for the corrupt university service (Puente, 2020; Taylor, 2020). While sentenced to prison, the sentence length was very short, thus stage 8 for punishment in the table. Loughlin did not completely know what she was doing (stage 7), but her intention was obvious (stage 9), and she carries responsibility (stage 9). The crime is not that serious compared to other offenses in the table, thus stage 3.

The eleventh entry in Table 11.1 is concerned with the investigation report by the U.S. House of Representatives under the chairwoman Maxine Waters. Carrie Tolstedt was the chief executive at Community Bank, a subsidiary of Wells Fargo (Shichor and Heeren, 2021). She was extremely ambitious and developed a business model that she believed in, and everyone had to follow. Shearman Sterling (2017) found that Tolstedt reinforced a culture of tight control over information about the cummunity bank division, including sales practice issues. She retired before the accounting fraud scandal became public, while later receiving the blame (stage 2 in punishment). Her intention was obvious (stage 10), while her knowledge of actual implementation of her business model was somewhat limited (stage 4).

Nevertheless, she was completely blamed for the scandal in terms of responsibility (stage 11). U.S. House (2020) found that the bank had failed to correct serious deficiencies in its infrastructure for managing risks to consumers and complying with the law. As a result, bank customers had been exposed to countless abuses, including racial discrimination, wrongful foreclosure, illegal vehicle repossession, and fraudulently opened accounts.

The twelfth entry in Table 11.1 is concerned with the investigation report by audit firm KPMG (2020) in Germany. Markus Braun, Wirecard's former chief executive officer, gave himself up to German police and testified in the fall of 2020 in front of the Bundestag commission investigating the bank collapse. Jan Marsalek, former chief operating officer, disappeared to Belarus and was on Interpol's most-wanted list (Storbeck, 2020a, 2020b). As the Wirecard scandal evolved, more elite members in German society got involved. One of them was Alexander Schütz, a Deutsche Bank board member who was accused of insider trading in Wirecard shares (Storbeck and Morris, 2021). At the time of writing, it was expected that Markus Braun would receive a prison sentence (stage 5 for punishment). He carried responsibility for the fraud (stage 8), he had some knowledge of the fraud scheme (stage 7), and he lead the intention of fraud (stage 11). The seriousness is the extent to which Wirecard customers suffered from the bank collapse (stage 6).

The thirteenth entry in Table 11.1 is concerned with the investigation report by law firm Dechert in the United States. The media reported in 2020 that "the billionaire who stood by Jeffrey Epstein", "Dechert's Leon Black investigation: things you may have missed", "what a sad tale of sycophants: Wall Street is not buying Leon Black's Epstein story", "Jeffrey Epstein's deep ties to top Wall Street figures", "billionaire Leon Black is leaving Apollo following scrutiny over ties to Jeffrey Epstein", and "billionaire Leon Black, revealed to pay Jeffrey Epstein $158, is stepping down" (Gara and Voytko, 2021). These headlines emerged as law firm Dechert (2021) concluded an investigation on behalf of Apollo Global Management' board. Jeffrey Epstein committed suicide in jail in August 2019 after conviction as a sex offender abusing underage female prostitutes (Sampson, 2020). The suspected fraud was concerned with Black's involvement with Epstein. While the investigation found no evidence of fraud, the media was still skeptical towards Leon Black, which increased the level of punishment (stage 4) and the level of responsibility (stage 4) compared to the assumption of innocence. Black's knowledge of wrongdoing (stage 2) and his intention of wrongdoing (stage 2) were low. Since there was no evidence of wrongdoing, the seriousness was low (stage 1).

The fourteenth entry in Table 11.1 is concerned with the investigation report by a commission appointed by the International Biathlon Union in Austria. Anders Besseberg was president of the International Biathlon Union (IBU) from 1992 until he was laid off in 2018 on the basis of accusations of wrongdoing (Ellingworth and Dunbar, 2018). During those years, the sport of biathlon evolved from being a sport for people who were particularly interested to becoming one of the most popular winter sports on television. Besseberg is considered the architect of the various successful forms of competition in biathlon such as hunting start, joint start, and mixed relays. He lifted the sport of biathlon to new heights during his period as president. By being in the position of president over such a long time, he became a powerful individual with great influence internationally. There were no restrictions on being the union president and how many periods he could be in such a central position without being replaced. Besseberg has been a central figure in shaping the business, culture, ethics, structure, and compliance of right and wrong at IBU as an organization. The suspected fraud was concerned with the president receiving favors and bribes from Russian biathlon union officials. The investigation report claims that Besseberg received gifts from the former heads of the Russian Biathlon Federation (RBU), Alexander Kravtsov and Alexander Tikhonov, including a cash sum of up to $300,000, hunting trips, and services from prostitutes. In return did Besseberg protect Russia – both public and private – by covering up positive doping results and blocking investigations that could disqualify Russian athletes (Commission, 2021). Being subject to police investigation is a punishment (stage 5), while the alleged offense was not that serious (stage 3). He had knowledge of what he did in Russia (stage 9), but he carried less responsibility (stage 5) and had less intention (stage 4) of participating in wrongdoing.

The fifteenth and final entry in Table 11.1 is concerned with the investigation report by Finansinspektionen in Sweden. Nasdaq Clearing was fined 300 million Swedish crowns ($36 million) by Sweden's financial supervisory authority Finansinspektionen (2021a, 2021b). The fine was over the default of the power trader Einar Aas in 2018 that showed deficiencies in its operations. The default by private trader Einar Aas left a 114 million Euro ($139 million) hole in the clearing house's resources, forcing other members of the market to cover the loss within two business days or face default themselves (Buli, 2021a). Clearing houses are crucial institutions in the proper functioning of markets, standing between trades to prevent a default on one side or the other from spreading out to other participants. Policymakers have treated them as vital for stability since the 2008 financial crises. However, Nasdaq Clearing, a Swedish unit of Nasdaq Inc, not only caused loss to its members. The company also violated European Union regulations by investing its own funds in derivative contracts for too long after the default, the regulator Finansinspektionen said (Buli, 2021b). While Aas suffered from his own gambling, he received no punishment (stage 1). He carried responsibility for harming Nasdaq Clearing (stage 5), he knew what he was doing (stage 8), while his intention was not to cause harm (stage 1). The seriousness of his misconduct is in terms of some losses to members (stage 4).

## Statistical Attribution Analysis

The fifteen recent investigation reports by fraud examiners listed in Table 11.1 are not sufficient for statistical analysis. From previous research, the author has collected a number of reports as listed in Tables 11.2 and 11.3 that can be included and combined with the reports in Table 12.1, thereby having a total sample of 15 + 18 + 16 = 49 cases. Five variables were applied in this research that diverges somewhat from the analysis by Schmidt et al. (2022) since there are three independent variables (knowledge, intention, and seriousness) and two dependent variables (responsibility and punishment):

- Knowledge – was the actor aware or could foresee consequences, was aware of the potential consequences for what happened, was able to foresee the harm of own action, and recognized the seriousness of own action.
- Intentionality – was the action intentional, the actor intended to commit wrongdoing, the action was no accident, and the actor planned the action in advance.
- Seriousness – how wrong was the action, what the actor did was wrong, the actor was not acting morally, the actor was deceitful in the action, the actor was not justified in the action, the action was serious.
- Responsibility – the person acted of own will, the person is blameworthy, and the person is responsible for what happened.
- Punishment – the extent of negative reaction towards the actor.

While information about fraud examiners' assessment of actor knowledge, actor intentionality, action seriousness, and action responsibility can be derived from the investigation reports, the information about the extent of punishment that typically occurred after investigation completion was retrieved from media coverage of the cases. Similar to Schmidt et al. (2022), 11-point Likert-type scales were applied where the scores ranged

**Table 11.2a:** Fraud investigation reports from previous sample.

| Year | Country | Corporate Investigator | Client Organization | White-Collar Person |
|---|---|---|---|---|
| 2002 | USA | Wilmer Cutler Pickering | Enron Energy | Kenneth Lay |
| 2003 | USA | Wilmer Cutler Pickering | WorldCom | Bernard Ebbers |
| 2008 | USA | Wilmer Cutler Pickering | Tax Office | Henriette Walters |
| 2010 | USA | Sidley Austin | CTO Washington | Yusuf Acar |
| 2010 | USA | Jenner Block | Lehman Brothers | Richard Fuld |
| 2011 | Japan | Deloitte | Olympus | Tsuyoshi Kikukawa |
| 2012 | USA | Hastings | Texas University | Kern Wildenthal |
| 2013 | USA | Freeh | BP Deepwater | Dion Sutton |
| 2014 | Switzerland | Garcia | FIFA World Cup | Joseph Blatter |
| 2014 | USA | Jenner Block | General Motors | Mary Barra |
| 2015 | USA | BDO | Coatesville School | Richard Como |
| 2015 | Nigeria | PwC | NNPC Petroleum | Emmanuel Kachikwu |
| 2015 | Denmark | Kromann Reumert | Syddanmark Region | Carl Holst |
| 2015 | Japan | Deloitte | Toshiba | Hisao Tanaka |
| 2016 | Sweden | Mannheimer Swartling | Nordea Bank | Gunn Wærsted |
| 2017 | New Zealand | Deloitte | FujiFilm | Neil Whittaker |
| 2017 | Canada | KPMG | Pelham Project | Cari Pupo |
| 2017 | USA | Shearman Sterling | Wells Fargo | Carrie Tolstedt |

from low (1) to high (11). Complete knowledge of the incident, complete intention of the incident, and a very serious incident all result in a high score. Similarly, complete responsibility for the incident results in a high score. Punishment including prison sentence results in a high score. In Table 11.2, Kenneth Lay, Henriette Walters, Yusuf Acar, Tsuyoshi Kikukawa, Hisao Tanaka, and Neil Whittaker were all sentenced to prison.

**Table 11.2b:** Attribution by corporate investigators from previous sample.

| Year | Client Organization | Punishment | Responsibility | Knowledge | Intention | Seriousness |
|---|---|---|---|---|---|---|
| 2002 | Enron Energy | 11 | 9 | 8 | 7 | 9 |
| 2003 | WorldCom | 9 | 7 | 11 | 6 | 9 |
| 2008 | Tax Office | 11 | 11 | 11 | 11 | 11 |
| 2010 | CTO Washington | 10 | 11 | 11 | 11 | 8 |
| 2010 | Lehman Brothers | 2 | 4 | 6 | 4 | 7 |
| 2011 | Olympus | 11 | 9 | 11 | 11 | 7 |
| 2012 | Texas University | 2 | 10 | 9 | 8 | 1 |
| 2013 | BP Deepwater | 1 | 2 | 7 | 7 | 2 |
| 2014 | FIFA World Cup | 1 | 8 | 11 | 7 | 3 |
| 2014 | General Motors | 1 | 8 | 2 | 3 | 9 |
| 2015 | Coatesville School | 3 | 4 | 3 | 3 | 2 |
| 2015 | NNPC Petroleum | 1 | 2 | 5 | 3 | 8 |
| 2015 | Syddanmark Reg. | 3 | 3 | 2 | 1 | 2 |
| 2015 | Toshiba | 11 | 9 | 1 | 1 | 7 |
| 2016 | Nordea Bank | 3 | 8 | 5 | 3 | 3 |
| 2017 | FujiFilm | 10 | 4 | 11 | 11 | 7 |
| 2017 | Pelham Project | 3 | 4 | 5 | 2 | 2 |
| 2017 | Wells Fargo | 2 | 8 | 7 | 8 | 4 |

**Table 11.3a:** Fraud investigation reports from Norway.

| Year | Country | Corporate Investigator | Client Organization | White-Collar Person |
|---|---|---|---|---|
| 2019 | Norway | Ernst & Young | Bergen Clinics | Kari Lossius |
| 2019 | Norway | Kluge | Ferde Toll | Trond Juvik |
| 2019 | Norway | Deloitte | Oslo Housing | Geir Fredriksen |
| 2019 | Norway | Ernst & Young | Oslo Environmental | Thorstein Skjaker |
| 2019 | Norway | PwC | Oslo Energy | Per Kristiansen |
| 2019 | Norway | PwC | Oslo Care | Per Johansen |
| 2019 | Norway | DLA Piper | XXL Sports | Tolle Grøterud |
| 2020 | Norway | PwC | Equinor Energy | Helge Lund |
| 2020 | Norway | Ernst & Young | Born Free | Shabana Rehman |
| 2020 | Norway | Wiersholm | Hurtigruten Cruises | Daniel Skjeldam |
| 2020 | Norway | PwC | Norfund Aid | Unknown Perpetrator |
| 2020 | Norway | PwC | Rema Grocery | Unknown Perpetrator |
| 2020 | Norway | Salten | Stamina Health | Marious Øksenvåg |
| 2021 | Norway | KPMG | Obos Housing | Daniel Siraj |
| 2021 | Norway | Grimstad | Nittedal Municipality | Hilde Thorkildsen |
| 2021 | Norway | PwC | Bergen University | Dag Olsen |

**Table 11.3b:** Attribution by corporate investigators from Norway.

| Year | Client Organization | Punishment | Responsibility | Knowledge | Intention | Seriousness |
|---|---|---|---|---|---|---|
| 2019 | Bergen Clinics | 3 | 2 | 5 | 2 | 2 |
| 2019 | Ferde Toll | 1 | 2 | 2 | 1 | 1 |
| 2019 | Oslo Housing | 5 | 8 | 9 | 5 | 6 |
| 2019 | Oslo Environmental | 10 | 8 | 6 | 8 | 5 |
| 2019 | Oslo Energy | 2 | 4 | 2 | 2 | 1 |
| 2019 | Oslo Care | 3 | 4 | 5 | 2 | 2 |
| 2019 | XXL Sports | 2 | 7 | 5 | 8 | 2 |
| 2020 | Equinor Energy | 1 | 3 | 1 | 1 | 2 |
| 2020 | Born Free | 3 | 1 | 1 | 1 | 1 |
| 2020 | Hurtigruten Cruises | 1 | 5 | 3 | 2 | 4 |
| 2020 | Norfund Aid | 1 | 11 | 11 | 11 | 5 |
| 2020 | Rema Grocery | 4 | 2 | 1 | 1 | 1 |
| 2020 | Stamina Health | 1 | 5 | 8 | 3 | 3 |
| 2021 | Obos Housing | 1 | 4 | 5 | 1 | 2 |
| 2021 | Nittedal Municip. | 4 | 2 | 6 | 3 | 2 |
| 2021 | Bergen University | 1 | 5 | 7 | 3 | 1 |

Table 11.4 lists correlation coefficients among the five variables. All variables are significantly correlated with each other. For example, a harsher punishment is significantly correlated with higher attribution of responsibility, higher knowledge assumption, stronger intention, and more serious act.

**Table 11.4:** Correlation coefficients.

| | Punishment | Responsibility | Knowledge | Intention | Seriousness |
|---|---|---|---|---|---|
| Punishment | 1 | .443** | .402** | .463** | .517** |
| Responsibility | | 1 | .638** | .705** | .441** |
| Knowledge | | | 1 | .711** | .349* |
| Intention | | | | 1 | .536** |
| Seriousness | | | | | 1 |

The research model is shown in Figure 11.1, where knowledge, intention and seriousness are predictors of responsibility, while responsibility is a predictor of punishment. From the correlation analysis it is already evident that the latter relationship between responsibility and punishment is significant. In terms of regression analysis, the extent of responsibility attribution to the offender can explain 20 % of the variation in punishment as the statistical R square has the value of .198, while the adjusted R square has a value of .179. In the regression equation, responsibility has a standardized positive coefficient of .443 that is significant at $p<.01$.

When multiple regression analysis is applied to knowledge, intention, and seriousness as predictors of responsibility, then the set of three predictors explain more than half of the variation in responsibility with an R square of .542 and adjusted R square of .512. Among the three predictor variables, only intention is statistically significant with a p-value of .007, while knowledge and seriousness have not sufficient significance with p-values of .055 and .406 respectively. Intentionality, that is, was the action intentional, the actor intended to commit wrongdoing, the action was no accident, and the actor planned the action in advance. Based on this sample, it is possible to conclude that the attribution of responsibility increases significantly when fraud examiners found that the offender committed the act intentionally.

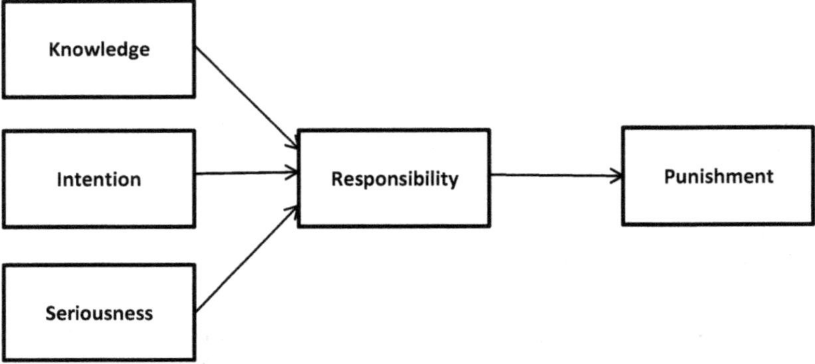


**Figure 11.1:** Research model for attribution of responsibility and punitiveness.

# Conclusion

This book has presented a bottom-up approach to corporate control of white-collar crime based on the theory of convenience. The concept of white-collar crime was coined by Edwin Sutherland in his 1939 speech to the American Sociological Society. Convenience theory for white-collar crime expressly works within the paradigm of Sutherland's white-collar crime definition. White-collar crime is financial crime committed by privileged individuals who have legitimate access to resources based on the power and trust inherent through their professional position. Convenience theory proposes that motive, opportunity, and willingness are the three dimensions that underlie white-collar crime, and it is dependent on crime that occurs in an organizational context. This book contributes to the study of white-collar criminality through a blend of theoretical discussions and practical materials that illuminate and support the use of convenience theory. The book introduced the difficulty of detecting white-collar crime. The power and organizational opportunities that white-collar criminals possess facilitate escaping detection in various ways. Whistleblowers serve as the confidential informants that are paramount towards detection, but the retaliation they often face serves as a substantial deterrent. Norway is one of the few countries in the world that introduced a law on the protection of whistleblowers against retaliation, though it is not being implemented effectively. Further, the concept of symbolic defense shows that, even when detected, white-collar criminals still have an arsenal of resources at their fingertips to avoid or mitigate consequences. Symbolic defense refers to the robust access that white-collar criminals have to effective defense attorneys and resources that enable information control and mobilization of sympathy to frame them as victims.

Fraud examinations are often conducted once white-collar crime is detected. While the usefulness of fraud examination reports has to be acknowledged, it is important to realize that these examinations often fail and require more policing. Aside from fraud examinations running the risk of assigning blame without being confined by the rules and protections of the justice system, the individuals customarily conducting these examinations may lack the appropriate knowledge and background to interpret the facts accurately—for instance, accountants may not know enough about the psychology or sociology of white-collar criminals, and lawyers may not know how to interpret facts requiring specialized accounting knowledge.

The theory of convenience puts such elements from various situations into perspective. The theory proposes that the triangle of motive, opportunity, and willingness are the three dimensions that underlie white-collar crime. With each dimension, the theory differentiates between white-collar crime and street crime to further shed light on its underpinnings. In the economic dimension (motive), it is suggested that Maslow's hierarchy of needs is a starting point that sheds light on both the motivations for and differences between white-collar and street crime.

https://doi.org/10.1515/9783110986686-013

While street crime finds its motivation in the lower levels of this hierarchy, such as to satisfy basic needs like food and housing, white-collar crime concerns itself with the higher levels, such as needs for respect and self-actualization. As such, the motivation for white-collar crime is found not only in accumulating financial wealth, but also in garnering respect and admiration. In the organizational dimension (opportunity), the theory emphasizes how organizational settings offer white-collar criminals access to resources, legitimacy, and power that street criminals do not similarly enjoy. This very setting and status facilitate the concealment and execution of white-collar crime. Finally, within the behavioral dimension (willingness), the theory sets forth how white-collar offenders engage in blame games and employ neutralization techniques which, combined with oftentimes narcissistic tendencies, can lead an individual on a slippery slope from right to wrong. Common neutralization techniques consist of condemning the condemners and claiming that the law itself is unreasonable. The presentation of these neutralization techniques ties harmoniously with symbolic defense where attempts at offender victimization are made. White-collar criminals rationalize their behavior, which both facilitates and helps cope with committing crime, by believing that when faced with the relevant possibilities and threats, deviant behavior was the rational choice, and anyone would have proceeded similarly. White-collar criminals oftentimes display narcissistic tendencies which lead to entitlement feelings and narcissistic identification. In fact, research supports that many white-collar criminals identify so strongly with their organization, which enables the mindset that there really is no difference between the personal wallet and the wallet of the business. This entitlement can make white-collar criminals feel that they are above the law, and lead to the creation of a world where right and wrong are redefined in their minds. Interestingly, and on par with the neutralization mindset, white-collar criminals seldom think of themselves as "real criminals". Indeed, a convicted white-collar criminal from Norway stated; "we are all mixed in the same soup . . . one should never look at convicts as a homogenous group". In a similar vein, Thomas Middelhoff, a former German CEO and convicted fraudster, expressed feelings that exemplify precisely the rationalization and neutralization explored in the behavioral dimension: "[t]hought that certain rules did not apply to me . . . I don't regard myself as a criminal in the legal sense, but I do accept my sentence".

In the process of detecting wrongdoing and making misconduct information internally and externally available, the powerful will tend to try to silence information sources. This is in line with corporate efforts to silence researchers who publish their findings in academic journals (Haan, 2022: 30):

> It is not uncommon for researchers to be the bearers of unwelcome messages. It is also not unusual that efforts are made to censure the publication of their research (. . .) The current state of affairs raises some pertinent questions about the freedom of research and the chances that researchers are being silenced by legal means. Can researchers prevent lawsuits for libel

or defamation without compromising the integrity of their research? Should they even try when their publishers require them to do so?

The bottom-up approach in this book serves to prevent and detect white-collar crime. The bottom-up approach to executive compliance focuses on organizational measures to make white-collar crime less convenient for potential offenders. Control is concerned with a negative discrepancy between the desired and current state of affairs. Control mechanisms attempt to reduce the discrepancy through adaptive action in the form of behavioral reactions. Control mechanisms attempt to influence and manage the process, content, and outcome of work. Control involves processes of negotiation in which various strategies are developed to produce particular outcomes. Control is therefore a dynamic process that regulates behavior through a set of modes, rules, or strategies. This book has documented where control mechanisms might be most effective based on the theory of convenience.

# Bibliography

Adler, P.S. and Kwon, S.W. (2002). Social capital: Prospects for a new concept, *Academy of Management Review*, 27 (1), 17–40.

Agnew, R. (2014). Social concern and crime: Moving beyond the assumption of simple self-interest, *Criminology*, 52 (1), 1–32.

Aguilera, R.V. and Vadera, A.K. (2008). The dark side of authority: Antecedents, mechanisms, and outcomes of organizational corruption, *Journal of Business Ethics*, 77, 431–449.

Aguilera, R.V., Judge, W.Q. and Terjesen, S.A. (2018). Corporate governance deviance, *Academy of Management Review*, 43 (1), 87–109.

Akers, R.L. (1985). *Deviant Behavior: A Social Learning Approach*, 3rd edition, Belmont, CA: Wadsworth.

Al-Suwaidi, N.A. and Nobanee, H. (2021). Anti-money laundering and anti-terrorism financing: A survey of the existing literature and a future research agenda, *Journal of Money Laundering Control*, 24 (2), 396–426.

Alcadipani, R. and Medeiros, C.R.O. (2020). When corporations cause harm: A critical view of corporate social irresponsibility and corporate crimes, *Journal of Business Ethics*, 167, 285–297.

Alon, A., Mennicken, A. and Samsonova-Taddei, A. (2019). Dynamics and limits of regulatory privatization: Reorganizing audit oversight in Russia, *Organization Studies*, 40 (8), 1217–1240.

Alvarez, S.A. and Parker, S.C. (2009). Emerging firms and the allocation of control rights: A bayesian approach, *Academy of Management Review*, 34 (2), 209–227.

Amjad, R.M., Rafay, A., Arshed, N., Munir, M. and Amjad, M.M. (2021). Non-linear impact of globalization on financial crimes: A case of developing economies, *Journal of Money Laundering Control*, published online doi 10.1108/JMLC-032021-0023.

Amry, M.A. and Meliala, A. (2021). Lifestyle-related shaming: The significance of reintegrative shaming on drug relapse offenders in Indonesia, *Journal of Social and Political Sciences*, 4 (1), 145–153.

Amundsen, B. (2021). Politiet overlater etterforskning av økonomisk kriminalitet til de mistenkte (The police leave investigation of economic crime to the suspects), web-based research journal *Forskning*, www.forskning.no, published April 19.

Anderson, P.D. (2022). On moderate and radical government whistleblowing: Edward Snowden and Julian Assange as theorists of whistleblowing ethics, *Journal of Media Ethics*, 37 (1), 38–52.

Arrigo, B.A. and Bernard, T.J. (1997). Postmodern criminology in relation to radical and conflict criminology, *Critical Criminology*, 8 (2), 39–60.

Artello, K. and Albanese, J.S. (2021). Culture of corruption: Prosecutions, persistence, and desistence, *Public Integrity*, pages 1–21, published online doi 10.1080/10999922.2021.1881300.

Ashforth, B.E., Gioia, D.A., Robinson, S.L. and Trevino, L.K. (2008). Re-reviewing organizational corruption, *Academy of Management Review*, 33 (3), 670–684.

Associated Press (2016). The latest: Ex-PM for Georgia said to have 'nothing to hide', *The Associated Press*, April 4, https://infoweb.newsbank.com/apps/news/document-view?p=AWNB&t=&sort=YMD_date%3AD&page=8&maxresults=20&f=advanced&val-base-0=nordea&fld-base-0=alltext&bln-base-1=and&val-base-1=panama%20papers&fld-base-1=all text&bln-base-3=and&val-base-3=2016&fld-base-3=YMD_date&docref=news/15C0ADA08E6FFBE0.

Asting, C. and Gottschalk, P. (2022). Attorney fraud in the law firm: A case study of crime convenience theory and crime signal detection theory, *Deviant Behavior*, published online doi 10.1080/01639625.2022.2071657.

https://doi.org/10.1515/9783110986686-014

Baird, J.E. and Zelin, R.C. (2009). An examination of the impact of obedience pressure on perceptions of fraudulent acts and the likelihood of committing occupational fraud, *Journal of Forensic Studies in Accounting and Business*, 1 (1), 1–14.

Balakrishnan, K., Blouin, J.L. and Guay, W.R. (2019). Tax aggressiveness and corporate transparency, *The Accounting Review*, 94 (1), 45–69.

Bamvik, B.S. (2022). -De vil klare seg uansett (-They will manage anyway), daily Norwegian newspaper *VG*, Friday, March 4, page 18.

Bandura, A. (1999). Moral disengagement in the perpetration of inhumanities, *Personality and Social Psychology Review*, 3 (3), 193–209.

Bao, D., Kim, Y., Mian, G.M. and Su, L. (2019). Do managers disclose or withhold bad news? Evidence from short interest, *The Accounting Review*, 94 (3), 1–26.

Barak, M.P. (2021). Family separation as state-corporate crime, *Journal of White Collar and Corporate Crime*, 2 (2), 109–121.

Barton, H. (2004). Cultural reformation: a case for intervention within the police service, *International Journal of Human Resources Development and Management*, 4 (2), 191–199.

BBC (2020). Britta Nielsen: Danish social worker accused of stealing millions, *British Broadcasting Corporation*, www.bbc.com, published February 18.

BDO (2014). *Gransking av Stiftelsen Betanien i Bergen (Examination of the Foundation Betanien in Bergen) – Anonymisert og revidert sammendrag (Anonymised and revised summary)*, auditing firm BDO, Oslo, Norway.

BDO (2016). *Rapport til kontrollutvalget. Undersøkelse av kjøp av helsetjenester i Grimstad kommune (Report to the control committee. Review of health services procurement in Grimstad municipality)*, audit firm BDO, Oslo, Norway.

Beckett, L. (2020). Older people would rather die than let Covid-19 harm US economy – Texas official, *The Guardian*, www.theguardian.com, published March 24.

Beji, R., Yousfi, O., Loukil, N. and Omri, A. (2021). Board diversity and corporate social responsibility: Empirical evidence from France, *Journal of Business Ethics*, 173, 133–155.

Bendiktsson, M.O. (2010). The Deviant organization and the bad apple CEO: Ideology and accountability in media coverage of corporate scandals, *Social Forces*, 88 (5), 2189–2216.

Benson, M.L. (2021). Theoretical and empirical advances in the study and control of white-collar offenders, *Justice Evaluation Journal*, 4 (1), 1–20.

Benson, M.L. and Chio, H.L. (2020). Who commits occupational crimes, in: Rorie, M. (editor), *The Handbook of White-Collar Crime*, Hoboken, NJ: John Wiley & Sons, chapter 7, pages 97–112.

Benson, M.L. and Simpson, S.S. (2018). *White-Collar Crime: An Opportunity Perspective*, Third Edition, New York, NY: Routledge.

Benson, M.L., Feldmeyer, B., Gabbidon, S.L. and Chio, H.L. (2021). Race, ethnicity, and social change: The democratization of middle-class crime, *Criminology*, 59 (1), 10–41.

Berg, P.Y. (2016). Fikk nei til dypere graving i helsekjøpssaken (Got no to dig deeper into the health care case), local daily newspaper *Agderposten*, www.agderposten.no, published December 23.

Berg, P.Y. (2017). Ber politiet etterforske (Asks the police to investigate), local Norwegian newspaper *Agderposten*, Tuesday, July 4, page 13.

Berg, P.Y. (2021). Inngikk avtale – Hemmeligholder profilert varslers skjebne (Entered into an agreement – Secrets the fate of the profiled whistleblower), local Norwegian newspaper *Agderposten*, www.agderposten.no, published May 14.

Berge, I. (2011). Utga seg for å være Spetalens lillebror (Pretended to be Spetalen's younger brother), web-based Norwegian newspaper *Nettavisen*, www.nettavisen.no, published March 30.

Berghoff, H. (2018). "Organised irresponsibility?" The Siemens corruption scandal of the 1990s and 2000s, *Business History*, 60 (3), 423–445.

Berghoff, H. and Spiekermann, U. (2018). Shady business: On the history of white-collar crime, *Business History*, 60 (3), 289–304.

Bernal, C., Forero, A. and Rivera, I. (2014). Corporate crime and social harm in the Spanish crisis, *State Crime Journal*, 3 (2), 220–236.

Bernat, I. and Whyte, D. (2020). State-corporate crimes, in: Rorie, M.L. (editor), *The Handbook of White-Collar Crime*, Hoboken, NJ: Wiley & Sons, chapter 9, pages 191–208.

Berry, L.L., Seiders, K. and Grewal, D. (2002). Understanding service convenience, *Journal of Marketing*, 66, 1–17.

Bertrand, O. and Lumineau, F. (2016). Partners in crime: The effects of diversity on the longevity of cartels, *Academy of Management Journal*, 59 (3), 983–1008.

BHR Resource Center (2018). Lundin Energy lawsuit (re compplcity in war crimes, Sudan), *Business & Human Rights Resource Centre*, www.business-humanrights.org, published October 18.

Bigley, G.A. and Wiersma, M.F. (2002). New CEOs and corporate strategic refocusing: How experience as heir apparent influences the use of power, *Administrative Science Quarterly*, 47, 707–727.

Bjørkelo, B., Einarsen, S., Nielsen, M.B. and Matthiesen, S.B. (2011). Silence is golden? Characteristics and experiences of self-reported whistleblowers, *European Journal of Work and Organizational Psychology*, 20 (2), 206–238.

Bjørklund, I. (2018). Må betale over 137 mill I erstatning (Must pay over 137 million in compensation), daily Norwegian business newspaper *Dagens Næringsliv*, www.dn.no, published January 19.

Blix, N.T. (2021). Nå har hyttemilliardæren fjernet sanda (Now the summerhouse billionaire has removed the sand), local Norwegian newspaper *Øyene*, www.oyene.no, published January 4.

Blickle, G., Schlegel, A., Fassbender, P. and Klein, U. (2006). Some personality correlates of business white-collar crime, *Applied Psychology: An International Review*, 55 (2), 220–233.

BMJ (2019). The whistleblowing drama behind Astellas's suspension from the ABPI, *BMJ*, www.bmj.com, published July 2.

Boghossian, J. and Marques, J.C. (2019). Saving the Canadian fur industry's hide: Government's strategic use of private authority to constrain radical activism, *Organization Studies*, 40 (8), 1241–1268.

Borgarting (2015). Court of appeals case number 14-181913AST-BORG/02, *Borgarting lagmannsrett (Borgarting Court of Appeals)*, July 8.

Bosse, D.A. and Phillips, R.A. (2016). Agency theory and bounded self-interest, *Academy of Management Review*, 41 (2), 276–297.

Braaten, C.N. and Vaughn, M.S. (2019). Convenience theory of cryptocurrency crime: A content analysis of U.S. federal court decisions, *Deviant Behavior*, published online https://doi.org/10.1080/01639625.2019.1706706.

Bradshaw, E.A. (2014). State-corporate environmental cover-up: The response to the 2010 Gulf of Mexico oil spill, *State Crime Journal*, 3 (2), 163–181.

Bradshaw, E.A. (2015). "Obviously, we're all oil industry": The criminogenic structure of the offshore oil industry, *Theoretical Criminology*, 19 (3), 376–395.

Braithwaite, J. (2020). Regulatory mix, collective efficacy, and crimes of the powerful, *Journal of White Collar and Corporate Crime*, 1 (1), 62–71.

Brandvol, I. (2016). AF-gruppen dumpet kloakk på nye E6 (The AF group dumped sewage on the new E6 road), daily Norwegian newspaper *VG*, www.vg.no, published December 17.

Brightman, H.J. (2009). *Today's White-Collar Crime: Legal, Investigative, and Theoretical Perspectives*, Routledge, Taylor & Francis Group, NY: New York.

Brown, J.O., Hays, J. and Stuebs, M.T. (2016). Modeling accountant whistleblowing intentions: Applying the theory of planned behavior and the fraud triangle, *Accounting and the Public Interest*, 16 (1), 28–56.

Bruun Hjejle (2018). *Report on the Non-Resident Portfolio at Danske Bank's Estonian branch*, law firm Bruun Hjejle, Copenhagen, Denmark, 87 pages.

Buanes, F. (2015). Aktor krever fire års fengsel for tidligere Stavanger-pastor (The prosecutor requires four years in prison for previous Stavanger pastor), daily Norwegian newspaper *Stavanger Aftenblad*, www.aftenbladet.no, published January 27.

Bucy, P.H., Formby, E.P., Raspanti, M.S. and Rooney, K.E. (2008). Why do they do it? The motives, mores, and character of white collar criminals, *St. John's Law Review*, 82, 401–571.

Budo, M.N. (2021). Corporate crime and the use of science in the case of asbestos: Producing harm through discursive shields, *Journal of White Collar and Corporate Crime*, 2 (2), 81–96.

Buli, N. (2021a). Nasdaq Clearing fined $36 million in Sweden over 2018 trader default, *Reuters*, www.reuters.com, published January 27.

Buli, N. (2021b). Nasdaq Clearing appeals $36 million fine by Swedish financial watchdog, *Reuters*, www.reuters.com, published February 16.

Bundy, J. and Pfarrer, M.D. (2015). A burden of responsibility: The role of social approval at the onset of a crisis, *Academy of Management Review*, 40 (3), 345–369.

Bussmann, K.D., Niemeczek, A. and Vockrodt, M. (2018). Company culture and prevention of corruption in Germany, China and Russia, *European Journal of Criminology*, 15 (3), 255–277.

Button, M. (2020). The "new" private security industry, the private policing of cyberspace and the regulatory questions, *Journal of Contemporary Criminal Justice*, 36 (1), 39–55

Böhm, M.L. (2020). Criminal business relationships between commodity regions and industrialized countries: The hard road from raw material to new technology, *Journal of White Collar and Corporate Crime*, 1 (1), 34–49.

Bøe, E. (2022). Tidligere Danske Bank-sjef var fortsatt siktet i hvitvaskingssak da han fikk ny jobb (Former Danske Bank chief executive was still charged in a money laundering case when he got a new job), Norwegian web-based newspaper *E24*, www.e24.no, published January 12.

Campbell, J.L. and Göritz, A.S. (2014). Culture corrupts! A qualitative study of organizational culture in corrupt organizations, *Journal of Business Ethics*, 120 (3): 291–311.

Chamlin, M.B. (2009). Threat to whom? Conflict, consensus, and social control, *Deviant Behavior*, 30, 539–559.

Chan, F. and Gibbs, C. (2020). Integrated theories of white-collar and corporate crime, in: Rorie, M.L. (editor), *The Handbook of White-Collar Crime*, Hoboken, NJ: Wiley & Sons, chapter 13, pages 191–208.

Chan, F. and Gibbs, C. (2022). When guardians become offenders: Understanding guardian capability through the lens of corporate crime, *Criminology*, 1–21, published online doi 10.1111/1745-9125.12300.

Chang, J.J., Lu, H.C. and M. Chen (2005). Organized crime or individual crime? Endogeneous size of a criminal organization and the optimal law enforcement, *Economic Inquiry*, 43 (3), 661–675.

Chatterjee, A. and Pollock, T.G. (2017). Master of puppets: How narcissistic CEOs construct their professional worlds, *Academy of Management Review*, 42 (4), 703–725.

Chazan, G. and Storbeck, O. (2020a). Wirecard: the scandal spreads to German politics, *Financial Times*, www.ft.com, published September 29.

Chazan, G. and Storbeck, O. (2020b). Wirecard's Markus Brown says regulators not to blame in scandal, *Financial Times*, www.ft.com, published November 20.

Chen, J. and Nadkarni, S. (2017). It's about time! CEOs' temporal dispositions, temporal leadership, and corporate entrepreneurship, *Administrative Science Quarterly*, 62 (1), 31–66.

Chen, Y. and Moosmayer, D.C. (2020). When guilt is not enough: Interdependent self-construal as moderator of the relationship between guilt and ethical consumption in a Confucian context, *Journal of Business Ethics*, 161, 551–572.

Chown, J. (2021). The unfolding of control mechanisms inside organizations: Pathways of customization and transmutation, *Administrative Science Quarterly*, 66 (3), 711–752.

Chrisman, J.J., Chua, J.H., Kellermanns, F.W. and Chang, E.P.C. (2007). Are family managers agents or stewards? An exploratory study in privately held family firms, *Journal of Business Research*, 60 (10), 1030–1038.

Christian, M.S., Eisenkraft, N. and Kapadia, C. (2015). Dynamic associations among somatic complaints, human energy, and discretionary behaviors: Experiences with pain fluctuations at work, *Administrative Science Quarterly*, 60 (1), 66–102.

Clifford Chance (2020). *Report of Investigation on Swedbank*, law firm Clifford Chance, Washington, DC, USA, 218 pages.

Cohen, S. (2001). *States of Denial: Knowing about Atrocities and Suffering*, Cambridge, UK: Polity Press.

Cohen, L.E. and Felson, M. (1979). Social change and crime rate trends: A routine activity approach. *American Sociological Review*, 44, 588–608.

Coleman, J. (1987). Toward an integrated theory of white-collar crime, *American Journal of Sociology*, 93 (2), 406–439.

Collier, J.E. and Kimes, S.E. (2012). Only if it is convenient: Understanding how convenience Influences self-service technology evaluation, *Journal of Service Research*, 16 (1), 39–51.

Commission (2021). *Final Report of the IBU External Review Commission*, IBU External Review Commission: Jonathan Taylor, Vincent Defrasne, Christian Dorda, Tanja Haug, Anja Martin, and Lauren Pagé, January 28, 220 pages.

Corteen, K. (2018). In plain sight – examining the harms of professional wrestling as state-corporate crime, *Journal of Criminological Research, Policy and Practice*, 4 (1), 46–59.

Council (2021). *Human Rights Violations and Related Economic Crimes in the Republic of South Sudan*, Conference room paper of the commission on human rights in South Sudan, Human rights council, Agenda item 4, 13 September – 08 October.

Craig, J.M. and Piquero, N.L. (2016). The effects of low self-control and desire-for-control on white-collar offending: A replication, *Deviant Behavior*, 37 (11), 1308–1324.

Craig, J.M. and Piquero, N.L. (2017). Sensational offending: An application of sensation seeking to white-collar and conventional crimes, *Crime & Delinquency*, 63 (11), 1363–1382.

Cropanzano, R. and Mitchell, M.S. (2005). Social exchange theory: An interdisciplinary review, *Journal of Management*, 31 (6), 874–900.

Crosina, E. and Pratt, M.G. (2019). Toward a model of organizational mourning: The case of former Lehman Brothers bankers, *Academy of Management Journal*, 62 (1), 66–98.

Cullen, F.T., Chouhy, C. and Jonson, C.L. (2020). Public opinion about white-collar crime, in: Rorie, M.L. (editor), *The Handbook of White-Collar Crime*, Hoboken, NJ: Wiley & Sons, chapter 14, pages 211–228.

Dahle, D.Y. (2011). Christer Tromsdal var politiagent (Christer Tromsdal was police agent), daily Norwegian newspaper *Aftenposten*, publisched October 19.

Darian-Smith, E. (2020). Dying for the economy: Disposable people and economies of death in the global north, *State Crime Journal*, 10 (1), 61–79.

Darian-Smith, D. (2021). Dying for the economy: Disposable people and economies of death in the global north, *State Crime*, 10 (1), 61–79.

Davidson, R.H., Dey, A. and Smith, A.J. (2019). CEO materialism and corporate social responsibility, *The Accounting Review*, 94 (1), 101–126.

Davies, J. (2021). Criminogenic dynamics of the construction industry: A state-corporate crime perspective, *Journal of White-Collar and Corporate Crime*, published online doi 10.1177/2631309X211023055.

Davies, J. and Malik, H. (2022). Challenging existing regulatory approaches for white-collar and corporate crimes, *Journal of White Collar and Corporate Crime*, 3 (1), 3–6.

Davis, G.F. and DeWitt, T. (2021). Organization theory and the resource-based view of the firm: The great divide, *Journal of Management*, 47 (7), 1684–1697.

Dearden, T.E. and Gottschalk, P. (2020). Gender and white-collar crime: Convenience in target selection, *Deviant Behavior*, published online doi 10.1080/01639625.2020.1756428, pages 1–9.

Dechert. (2021). *Investigation of Epstein/Black Relationship and Any Relationship between Epstein and Apollo Global Management*, law firm Dechert, report of investigation, New York, 21 pages.

Deloitte (2011). *Investigation Report. Olympus Corporation. Third Party Committee*. Kainaka, T., Nakagome, H., Arita, T., Sudo, O., Katayama, E. and Takiguchi, K., https://www.olympus-global.com/en/common/pdf/if111206corpe_2.pdf, published December 6, retrieved September 10, 2018.

Deloitte (2015). *Investigation Report, Summary Version, Independent Investigation Committee for Toshiba Corporation*, audit firm Deloitte, Tokyo, Japan, 90 pages.

Deloitte (2016). *Review – Ownership Vimpelcom Telenor*, audit firm Deloitte, Oslo, Norway, 54 pages.

Deloitte (2017). *Investigation Report*, Independent Investigation Committee, by global auditing firm Deloitte, published June 10, Ito, T., Sato, K. and Nishimura, K., https://www.fujifilmholdings.com/en/pdf/investors/finance/materials/ff_irdata_investigation_001e.pdf, downloaded September 8, 2018, 89 pages.

Demetriades, P and Owusu-Agyei, S. (2021). Fraudulent financial reporting: An application of fraud diamond to Toshiba's accounting scandal, *Journal of Financial Crime*, published online doi 10.1108/JFC-05-2021-0108.

Deng, Z., Yan, J. and Sun, P. (2020). Political status and tax haven investment of emerging market firms: Evidence from China, *Journal of Business Ethics*, 165, 469–488.

Desmond, S.A., Rorie, M. and Sohoni, T. (2022). Working for God: Religion and occupational crime and deviance, *Deviant Behavior*, published online doi 10.1080/01639625.2021.2022968.

Dewan, Y. and Jensen, M. (2020). Catching the big fish: The role of scandals in making status a liability, *Academy of Management Journal*, 63 (5), 1652–1678.

Dion, M. (2008). Ethical leadership and crime prevention in the organizational setting, *Journal of Financial Crime*, 15 (3), 308–319.

Dion, M. (2019). A Gadamerian perspective on financial crimes, *Journal of Financial Crime*, 26 (3), 836–860.

Dion, M. (2020). Bribery, extortion and "morally ambiguous" leadership in organizations, *Journal of Financial Crime*, 27 (4), 1027–1046.

Dion, M. (2021). Conscious capitalism and the organizational propensity to fight corruption, *Journal of Financial Crime*, 28 (3), 686–701.

Direnzo, M.S. and Greenhaus, J.H. (2011). Job search and voluntary turnover in a boundaryless world: A control theory perspective, *Academy of Management Review*, 36 (3), 567–589.

Dodge, M. (2009). *Women and white-collar crime*, Saddle River, NJ: Prentice Hall.

Dodge, M. (2020). Who commits corporate crime? in: Rorie, M. (editor), *The Handbook of White-Collar Crime*, Hoboken, NJ: John Wiley & Sons, chapter 8, pages 113–126.

Donk, D.P. and Molloy, E. (2008). From organizing as projects, to projects as organizations, *International Journal of Project Management*, 26, 129–137.

Downing, S.T., Kang, J.S., and Markman, G.D. (2019). What you don't see can hurt you: Awareness cues to profile indirect competitors, *Academy of Management Journal*, 62 (6), 1872–1900.

Drammen tingrett (2015). Dom avsagt 02.02.2015 i Drammen tingrett med saksnummer 15-002674ENE-DRAM (Sentence announced on February 2, 2015 in Drammen district court with case number 15-002674ENE-DRAM), *Drammen tingrett (Drammen district court)*, Drammen, Norway.

Dunne, N.J., Brennan, N.M. and Kirwan, C.E. (2021). Impression management and big four auditors: Scrutiny at a public inquiry, *Accounting, Organizations and Society*, 88, 1–20.

Durand, R., Hawn, O. and Ioannou, I. (2019). Willing and able: A general model of organizational responses to normative pressures, *Academy of Management Review*, 44 (2), 299–320.

Duriau, V.J., Reger, R.K. and Pfarrer, M.D. (2007). A content analysis of the content analysis literature in organization studies: Research themes, data sources, and methodological refinements, *Organizational Research Methods*, 10 (1), 5–34.

Dyreng, S.D., Hanlon, M. and Maydew, E.L. (2019). When does tax avoidance result in tax uncertainty? *The Accounting Review*, 94 (2): 179–203.

EBA. (2021). EBA consults on new Guidelines on the role of AML/CFT compliance officers, *European Banking Authority*, Paris, France, www.eba.europa.eu, published August 2.

Eberl, P., Geiger, D. and Assländer, M.S. (2015). Repairing trust in an organization after integrity violations. The ambivalence of organizational rule adjustments, *Organization Studies*, 36 (9), 1205–35.

Eberlein, B. (2019). Who fills the global governance gap? Rethinking the roles of business and government in global governance, *Organization Studies*, 40 (8), 1125–1146.

Eberly, M.B., Holley, E.C., Johnson, M.D. and Mitchell, T.R. (2011). Beyond internal and external: a dyadic theory of relational attributions, *Academy of Management Review*, 36 (4), 731–753.

Edelman, J. (2021). Reviving antitrust enforcement in the airline industry, *Michigan Law Review*, 120 (1), 125–155.

Eisenhardt, K.M. (1989). Agency theory: An assessment and review, *Academy of Management Review*, 14 (1), 57–74.

Ekroll, H.C., Breian, Å. and NTB. (2019). Økokrim starter etterforskning av DNB i forbindelse med islandsk fiskerisak (Økokrim is launching an investigation into DNB related to the Icelandic fisheries case), daily Norwegian newspaper *Aftenposten*, www.aftenposten, published November 29.

Ellingsen, K.A. (2015). *Gud med oss (God with us): Tilsynsmennenes rapport til årskonferansen I Halden 2015 (Trustee report to the annual conference in Halden)*, Metodistkirken i Norge (The Methodist Church in Norway), www.metodistkirken.no, published June 16.

Ellingworth, J. and Dunbar, G. (2018). Biathlon president steps down after police raid in Austria, *AP News*, www.apnews.com, published April 12.

Engdahl, O. (2015). White-collar crime and first-time adult-onset offending: Explorations in the concept of negative life events as turning points, *International Journal of Law, Crime and Justice*, 43 (1), 1–16.

EU. (2021). Anti-money laundering and countering the financial of terrorism legislative package, *European Commission*, Brussels, Belgium, www.ec.europa.eu, published July 20.

EY (2019). *Rapport Stiftelsen Bergensklinikkene (Report Foundation Bergen Clinics)*, report of investigation, audit firm Ernst & Young, Oslo, Norway, February 5, 59 pages.

Farquhar, J.D. and Rowley, J. (2009). Convenience: a services perspective, *Marketing Theory*, 9 (4), 425–438.

FATF. (2021). Opportunities and challenges of new technologies for AML/CFT, *The Financial Action Task Force*, Paris, France, www.fatf-gafi.org, published in July, 76 pages.

Feratovic, L. (2021). Færder kommune avdekket flere ulovligheter på Pernille Sørensen og Dagfinn Lyngbøs hytteeiendom (Færder municipality detected more illegalities on the summerhouse property of Pernille Sørensen and Dagfinn Lyngbø), daily Norwegian business newspaper *Dagens Næringsliv*, www.dn.no, published January 11.

Ferraro, F., Pfeffer, J. and Sutton, R.I. (2005). Economics language and assumptions: How theories can become self-fulfilling, *Academy of Management Review*, 30 (1), 8–24.

Finansinspektionen (2021a). *Warning and administrative fine – Finansinspektionen's decision (to be announced 27 January 2021 at 8:00)*, Swedish financial supervisory authority, Stockholm, Sweden, January 27, 46 pages.

Finansinspektionen (2021b). *Varning och sanktionsavgift – Finansinspektionens beslut (att meddeleas den 27 januari 2021 kl. 08.00)*, Swedish financial supervisory authority, Stockholm, Sweden, January 27, 46 pages.

Finanstilsynet (2020). *Anmodning om redegørelse om Danske Bank A/S' gældsinddrivelsessystem (Request for account concerning Danske Bank Inc.'s debt collection system)*, Finanstilsynet (The Danish Financial Supervisory Authority), Copenhagen, Denmark, 3 pages.

Fisse, B. and Braithwaite, J. (1988). The allocation of responsibility for corporate crime: Individualism, collectivism and accountability, *Sydney Law Review*, 11, 468–513.

Fleckenstein, M.P. and Bowes, J.C. (2000). When trust is betrayed: Religious institutions and white collar crime, *Journal of Business Ethics*, 23 (1), 111–115.

Forti, G. and Visconti, A. (2020). From economic crime to corporate violence: The multifaceted harms of corporate crime, in: Rorie, M.L. (editor), *The Handbook of White-Collar Crime*, Hoboken, NJ: John Wiley & Sons, chapter 5, pages 64–80.

Fowler, T. (2014). BP's new tactic in oil spill claims: Go after he 'special master', *The Wall Street Journal*, https://blogs.wsj.com/corporate-intelligence/2014/01/27/bps-new-tactic-in-oil-spill-claims-go-after-the-special-master/, published January 27, retrieved September 14, 2018.

Freeh, L.J. (2013). *Independent external investigation of the Deepwater Horizon court supervised settlement program, report of special master Louis J. Freeh*, September 6, http://www.laed.us courts.gov/sites/default/files/OilSpill/Orders/Report11287.pdf, retrieved September 14, 2018.

Freiberg, A. (2020). Researching white-collar crime: An Australian perspective, in: Rorie, M.L. (editor), *The Handbook of White-Collar Crime*, Hoboken, NJ: Wiley & Sons, chapter 26, pages 418–436.

Friedrichs, D.O. and Weis, V.V. (2021). Covid-19 and the U.S. health care industry: Towards a "critical health criminology" within state crime studies, *State Crime Journal*, 10 (1), 126–146.

Friedrichs, D.O., Schoultz, I. and Jordanoska, A. (2018). *Edwin H. Sutherland, Routledge Key Thinkers in Criminology*, Routledge, UK: London.

Furnham, A. (2021). Just world beliefs, personnel success and beliefs in conspiracy theories, *Current Psychology*, published online doi 10.1007/s12144-021-01576-z.

Furnham, A. and Grover, S. (2021). Do you have to be mad to believe in conspiracy theories? Personality disorders and conspiracy theories, *International Journal of Social Psychiatry*, doi 10.1177/00207640211031614.

Füss, R. and Hecker, A. (2008). Profiling white-collar crime. Evidence from German-speaking countries, *Corporate Ownership & Control*, 5 (4), 149–161.

Gailey, J.A. and Lee, M.T. (2005). An integrated model of attribution of responsibility for wrongdoing in organizations, *Social Psychology Quarterly*, 68, 338–358.

Galvin, B.M., Lange, D. and Ashforth, B.E. (2015). Narcissistic organizational identification: Seeing oneself as central to the organization's identity, *Academy of Management Review*, 40 (2), 163–181.

Gamache, D.L. and McNamara, G. (2019). Responding to bad press: How CEO temporal focus influences the sensitivity to negative media coverage of acquisitions, *Academy of Management Journal*, 62 (3), 918–943.

Gangloff, K.A., Connelly, B.L. and Shook, C.L. (2016). Of scapegoats and signals: Investor reactions to CEO succession in the aftermath of wrongdoing, *Journal of Management*, 42, 1614–1634.

Gara, A. and Voytko, L. (2021). Billionaire Leon Black, revealed to pay Jeffrey Epstein $158 million, is stepping down, *Forbes*, www.forbes.com, published January 25.

Garcia (2014). *Report on the Inquiry into the 2018/2019 Fifa World Cup Bidding Process*, Investigatory Chamber, FIFA Ethics Committee, Zürich, Switzerland.

Garcia-Rosell, J.C. (2019). A discursive perspective on corporate social responsibility education: A story co-creation exercise, *Journal of Business Ethics*, 154, 1019–1032.

Garoupa, N. (2007). Optimal law enforcement and criminal organization, *Journal of Economic Behaviour & Organization*, 63, 461–474.

Gedde-Dahl, S., Magnussen, A.E. and Hafstad, A. (2007). Peab får bot på 15 millioner (Peab will be fined 15 million), Norwegian daily newspaper *Aftenposten*, www.aftenposten.no, published February 22.

Geest, V.R., Weisburd, D. and Blokland, A.A.J. (2017). Developmental trajectories of offenders convicted of fraud: A follow-up to age 50 in a Dutch conviction cohort, *European Journal of Criminology*, 14 (5), 543–565.

Ghannam, S., Bugeja, M., Matolcsy, Z.P. and Spiropoulos, H. (2019). Are qualified and experienced outside directors willing to join fraudulent firms and if so, why? *The Accounting Review*, 94 (2): 205–227.

Gill, M.J. (2019). The significance of suffering in organizations: Understanding variation in workers' responses to multiple modes of control, *Academy of Management Review*, 44 (2), 377–404.

Gilmour, P.M. (2020). Exploring the barriers to policing financial crime in England and Wales, *Policing: A Journal of Policy and Practice*, published online doi 10.1093/police/paaa081.

Goldstraw-White, J. (2012). *White-collar crime: Accounts of offending behavior*, London, UK: Palgrave Macmillan.

Gomulya, D. and Mishina, Y. (2017). Signaler credibility, signal susceptibility, and relative reliance on signals: How stakeholders change their evaluative processes after violation of expectations and rehabilitative efforts, *Academy of Management Journal*, 60 (2), 554–583.

Goncharov, I. and Peter, C.D. (2019). Does reporting transparency affect industry coordination? Evidence from the duration of international cartels, *The Accounting Review*, 94 (3), 149–175.

Goodhand, J. (2005). Frontiers and war: The opium economy in Afghanistan, *Journal of Agrarian Change*, 5 (2), 191–216.

Gorecki, M.A. and Letki, N. (2021). Social norms moderate the effect of tax system on tax evasion: Evidence from a large-scale survey experiment, *Journal of Business Ethics*, 172, 727–746.

Gottfredson, M.R. and Hirschi, T. (1990). *A General Theory of Crime*, Stanford University Press, CA: Stanford.

Gottschalk, P. (2014). *Financial Crime and Knowledge Workers – An Empirical Study of Defense Lawyers and White-Collar Criminals*, New York, NY: Palgrave Macmillan.

Gottschalk, P. and Benson, M.L. (2020). The evolution of corporate accounts of scandals from exposure to investigation, *British Journal of Criminology*, 60, 949–969.

Gottschalk, P. and Gunnesdal, L. (2018). *White-Collar Crime in the Shadow Economy: Lack of Detection, Investigation, and Conviction Compared to Social Security Fraud*, UK, London: Palgrave Pivot, Palgrave Macmillan, Springer publishing.

Gottschalk, P. and Tcherni-Buzzeo, M. (2017). Reasons for gaps in crime reporting: The case of white-collar criminals investigated by private fraud examiners in Norway, *Deviant Behavior*, 38 (3), 267–281.

Granda, M.L. (2021). Tax haven ownership and business groups: Tax avoidance incentives in Ecuadorian firms, *Journal of Business Research*, 130, 698–708.

Grønningsæter, F. (2022). Russlands svarte økonomi (Russia's black economy), Norwegian business magazine *Kapital*, 5, 16–23.

Guenther, D.A., Wilson, R.J. and Wu, K. (2019). Tax uncertainty and incremental tax avoidance, *The Accounting Review*, 94 (2): 229–247.

Guiso, L., Sapienza, P. and Zingales, L. (2015). The value of corporate culture, *Journal of Financial Economics*, 117, 60–76.

Gupta, V.K., Mortal, S., Chakrabarty, B., Guo, X. and Turban, D.B. (2020). CFO gender and financial statement irregularities, *Academy of Management Journal*, 63 (3), 802–831.

Gustafsson, K. (2015). Tviler på at styret ikke visste (Doubts that the board did not know), Norwegian web newspaper *Dagen*, www.dagen.no, published March 17.

Gyõry, C. (2020). The institutional context of financial fraud in a post-transition economy: The Quaestor scandal, *European Journal of Criminology*, 17 (1), 31–49.

Haack, P., Martignoni, D. and Schoeneborn, D. (2021). A bait-and-switch model of corporate social responsibility, *Academy of Management Review*, 46 (3), 440–464.

Haan, W. (2022). Do lawsuits silence? Legal harassment in corporate crime research, in: Davis, K. and Irvine, J. (editors), *Silences, Neglected Feelings, and Blind-Spots in Research Practice*, Routledge, UK: Abingdon, chapter 4.

Hagan, J. (1980). The legislation of crime and delinquency: A review of theory, method, and research, *Law and Society Review*, 14 (3), 603–628.

Haines, F. (2014). Corporate fraud as misplaced confidence? Exploring ambiguity in the accuracy of accounts and the materiality of money, *Theoretical Criminology*, 18 (1), 20–37.

Haines, F. and Macdonald, K. (2021). Grappling with injustice: Corporate crime, multinational business and interrogation of law in context, *Theoretical Criminology*, 25 (2), 284–303.

Haines, F., Bice, S., Einfeld, C. and Sullivan, H. (2022). Countering corporate power through social control: What does a social licence offer? *The British Journal of Criminology*, 62, 184–199.

Hambrick, D.C., Misangyi, V.F. and Park, C.A. (2015). The quad model for identifying a corporate director's potential for effective monitoring: Toward a new theory of board sufficiency, *Academy of Management Review*, 40 (3), 323–344.

Hamilton, S. and Micklethwait, A. (2006). *Greed and Corporate Failure: The Lessons from Recent Disasters*, Basingstoke, UK: Palgrave Macmillan.

Hamish, M. (2016). SFO closes Fuji Xerox probe, *The Press*, December 24, https://infoweb.newsbank.com/apps/news/document-view?p=AWNB&t=&sort=YMD_date%3AD&maxresults=20&f=advanced&val-base-0=fuji%20xerox&fld-base-0=alltext&bln-base-2=and&val-base-2=new%20zealand&fld-base-2=alltext&bln-base-3=and&val-base-3=2016&fld-base-3=YMD_date&docref=news/16175F5693A0BFF0, retrieved November 3, 2018.

Hanrahan, C. (2021). *Antiquities Acquisitions in U.S. Museums: A Qualitative Study of Non-Compliance and Extra-Legal Behavior*, Master of Science Thesis, UK: University of Glasgow.

Harvin, O. and Killey, M. (2021). Do "superstar" CEOs impair auditor's judgement and reduce fraud detection opportunities? *Journal of Forensic and Investigative Accounting*, 13 (3), 500–514.

Hatch, M.J. (1997). *Organizational Theory – Modern, Symbolic, and Postmodern Perspectives*, Oxford University Press.

Hecklen, A., Ussing, J. and Sommer, M. (2020). 'Beskidte milliarder': Sådan blev hvidvask-sag til Danske Banks største krise. Se tidslinjen over hvidvaskskandalen i Danske Bank ('Dirty billions': This is how money laundering became Danske Bank's biggest crisis), *Danmarks Radio (Danish Public Broadcasting)*, www.dr.dk, published September 21.

Helgheim, A.E. (2021). Streik til retten (Strike in court), daily Norwegian newspaper *Klassekampen*, www.klassekampen.no, published February 15.

Hellerud, S.S. (2022). Fullsatt kirke tok et siste farvel med Rune Hvidsten: -En vanskelig tid for alle (Full church said a final goodbye to Rune Hvidsten: -A difficult time for everyone), local Norwegian newspaper *Smaalenenes Avis*, Tuesday, April 12, pages 4–5.

Henning, P.J. (2017). Why it is getting harder to prosecute executives for corporate misconduct, *Vermont Law Review*, 41 (3), 503–522.

Herron, E.T. and Cornell, R.M. (2021). Creativity amidst standardization: Is creativity related to auditors' recognition of and responses to fraud risk cues? *Journal of Business Research*, 132, 314–326.

Hestnes, M. (2017). *Hvorfor avdekket ikke revisor underslaget i Hadeland og Ringerike Bredbånd? (Why did the auditor not detect the embezzlement at Hadeland and Ringerike Broadband?)*, Master of Science thesis, BI Norwegian Business School, Oslo, Norway.

Hirschi, T. (1989). Exploring alternatives to integrated theory, in: Messner, S.F., Krohn, M.D. and Liska, A.E. (editors), *Theoretical Integration in the Study of Deviance and Crime*, Albany, NY: State University of New York Press, chapter 2, pages 37–50.

Hoffmann, J.P. (2002). A contextual analysis of differential association, social control, and strain theories of delinquency, *Social Forces*, 81 (3), 753–785.

Holmquist, T. (2011). Skandale avdekket i privat omsorg (Scandal detected in private care), Norwegian magazine for municipalities *Kommunal Rapport*, www.kommunal-rapport.no, published November 23.

Holmøy, E. (2021). Hermine Midelfart og hennes mann vil også søke om ettergodkjenning: Villig til å rive noe (Hermine Midelfart and her husband will also apply for post-approval: Willing to tear something down), local daily newspaper *Tønsbergs Blad*, Wednesday, June 30, page 4.

Holt, R. and Cornelissen, J. (2014). Sensemaking revisited, *Management Learning*, 45 (5), 525–539.

Hovland, K.M. and Gauthier-Villars, D. (2015). VimpelCom bribery investigations spark Telenor review, *The Wall Street Journal*, www.wsj.com, published November 5.

Hovland, K.M., Høgseth, M.H. and Lorentzen, M. (2019). Regjeringen vil ikke lenger selge seg ned i Telenor (The government will no longer sell down at Telenor), web-based Norwegian business newspaper *E24*, www.e24.no, published November 22.

Högseth, M.H. (2019). Thomas Borgen siktet i hvitvaskingssaken (Thomas Borgen charged in the money laundering case), webbased Norwegian newspaper *E24*, www.e24.no, published May 7.

Hsieh, H. and Shannon, S.E. (2005). Three approaches to qualitative content analysis, *Qualitative Health Research*, 15 (9): 1277–1288.

Huang, L. and Knight, A.P. (2017). Resources and relationships in entrepreneurship: An exchange theory of the development and effects of the entrepreneur-investor relationship, *Academy of Management Review*, 42 (1), 80–102.

Huff, M.J. and Bodner, G.E. (2013). When does memory monitoring succeed versus fail? Comparing item-specific and relational encoding in the DRM paradigm, *Journal of Experimental Psychology: Learning, Memory, and Cognition*, 39 (4), 1246–1256.

Huisman, W. and Erp, J. (2013). Opportunities for environmental crime, *British Journal of Criminology*, 53, 1178–1200.

Hultgreen, G. (2012). Seks års fengsel for Christer Tromsdal (Six years prison for Christer Tromsdal), daily Norwegian newspaper *Dagbladet*, published November 2.

Hultgreen, G., Mogen, T. and Meldalen, S.G. (2019). -En Donald Duck-historie (-A Donald Duck story), daily Norwegian newspaper *Dagbladet*, www.dagbladet.no, published October 8.

Hunter, B. (2022). Exiting an offender role: White-collar offenders' sense of self and the demonstration of change, in: Hardie-Blick, J. and Scott, S. (editors), *Ex-treme Identities and Transitions Out of Extraordinary Roles*, Palgrave Macmillan, Switzerland: Cham.

Hurley, P.J., Mayhew, B.W. and Obermire, K.M. (2019). Realigning auditors' accountability: Experimental evidence, *The Accounting Review*, 94 (3), 233–250.

Hurrell, S.A. (2016). Rethinking the soft skills deficit blame game: Employers, skills withdrawal and the reporting of soft skills gaps, *Human Relations*, 69 (3), 605–628.

Inagati, K. (2015). Toshiba scraps dividend after finding accounting irregularities, *Financial Times*, May 8, https://infoweb.newsbank.com/apps/news/document-view?p=AWNB&t=&sort=YMD_date%3AD&page=43&maxresults=20&f=advanced&val-base-0=toshiba&fld-base-0=all

text&bln-base-1=and&val-base-1=accounting%20scandal&fld-base-1=alltext&bln-base-2=and&val-base-2=2015&fld-base-2=YMD_date&docref=news/1553B56CCE48DC40, retrieved November 3, 2018.

Iannacci, F., Seepma, A.P., Blok, C., and Resca, A. (2019). Reappraising maturity models in e-government research: The trajectory-turning point theory, *Journal of Strategic Information Systems*, 28, 310–329.

Ionescu, L. (2021). Corporate environmental performance, climate change mitigation, and green innovation behavior in sustainable finance, *Economics, Management, and Financial Markets*, 16 (3), 94–106.

Iordachescu, I. and Rodina, M. (2019). Israeli-born convicted fraudster on track for seat in Moldovan parliament, *The Times of Israel*, www.timesofisrael.com, published February 20.

Ismail, K. (2022). Swedbanks tidligere ledelse i Estland mistenkt for hvitvasking (Swedbank's former management in Estland suspected of money laundering), daily Norwegian business newspaper *Dagens Næringsliv*, Monday, March 28, page 7.

Jardine, M.R., Marti, E. and Durand, R. (2020). Why activist hedge funds target socially responsible firms: The reaction costs of signaling corporate social responsibility, *Academy of Management Journal*, 64 (3), 851–872.

Jaspers, J.D. (2020). Leniency in exchange for cartel confessions, *European Journal of Criminology*, 17 (1), 106–124.

Jayasekara, S.D. (2021). How effective are the current global standards in combating money laundering and terrorist financing? *Journal of Money Laundering Control*, 24 (2), 257–267.

Jenner Block (2010). *In regard Lehman Brothers Holdings Inc. to United States Bankruptcy Court in Southern District of New York*, law firm Jenner & Block, A.R. Valukas, https://jenner.com/lehman/VOLUME%203.pdf.

Jenner Block (2014). *Report to board of directors of General Motors company regarding ignition switch recalls*, law firm Jenner Block, Chicago, IL, USA, 325 pages.

Jessen, C.K. and Jung, E. (2020). Banedanmark mistænker medarbeidere for bestikkelse og ulovlige forhold (Banedenmark suspects Employees for Bribe and illegal circumstances), Danish daily newspaper *Berlingske*, www.berlingske.dk, published March 7.

Johannessen, S.Ø. and Christensen, J. (2020). Swedbank vil ikke betale sluttpakke til toppsjef som måtte gå av etter hvitvaskingsskandale (Swedbank will not pay final package to top executive who had to leave after money laundering scandal), daily Norwegian business newspaper *Dagens Næringsliv*, www.dn.no, published March 23.

Johansen, L. (2015). Hele styret trekker seg etter pastor-skandalen (The whole board resigns after pastor scandal), daily Norwegian newspaper *VG*, www.vg.no, published April 14.

Johnsen, L. (2013). Drammensprest siktet for underslag av nesten 15 millioner (Drammen priest charged for embezzlement of nearly 15 million), daily Norwegian newspaper *Drammens Tidende*, www.dt.no, published November 21.

Johnson, D. (2022). What are the merits of taking a hybrid regulatory approach toward the enforcement of corporate financial crime in the United Kingdom and United States of America? *Journal of White Collar and Corporate Crime*, 3 (1), 23–32.

Jonnergård, K., Stafsudd, A. and Elg, U. (2010). Performance evaluations as gender barriers in professional organizations: A study of auditing firms, *Gender, Work and Organization*, 17 /6), 721–747.

Jordanoska, A. (2018). The social ecology of white-collar crime: Applying situational action theory to white-collar offending, *Deviant Behavior*, 39 (11), 1427–1449.

Josephson, M. (1962). *The Robber Barons: The Classic Account of the Influential Capitalists who Transformed America's Future*, Harcourt, FL: Orlando.

Julsgaard, R.E. (2020). Svindel i Forsvarsministeriets ejendomsstyrelse: Tidligere leder idømt to års fængsel (Fraud in the Ministry of Defense's property management: Former leader sentenced to two years in prison), Danish local TV station *TV Midtvest*, www.tvmidtvest.dk, published December 2.

Jung, E. and Jessen, C.K. (2020). Politikere kommer med hård kritik af forhold i Banedanmark: «Skræmmende», «uhyre alvorligt» og «komplet uacceptabelt» (Politicians come with harsh criticism of conditions in Banedanmark: "Scary", "extremely serious" and "completely unacceptable"), daily Danish newspaper *Berlingske*, www.berlingske.dk, published June 8.

Jung, J.C. and Sharon, E. (2019). The Volkswagen emissions scandal and its aftermath, *Global Business & Organizational Excellence*, 38 (4), 6–15.

Kakkar, H., Sivanathan, N., and Globel, M.S. (2020). Fall from grace: The role of dominance and prestige in punishment of high-status actors, *Academy of Management Journal*, 63 (2), 530–553.

Kammeradvokaten. (2020a). *Undersøgelse af forholdet mellem visse ansatte hos Banedanmark og private virksomheder (Investigation of the relationship between certain employees at Banedanmark and private companies)*, law firm Poul Schmith Kammeradvokaten, Copenhagen, Denmark, October 5, 191 pages.

Kammeradvokaten (2020b). *Advokatundersøgelse af det økonomiske kontrolmiljø i forsvarsministeriets ejendomsstyrelse (Lawyer investigation of the economic control regime in the ministry of defense's property management)*, law firm Poul Schmith Kammeradvokaten, Copenhagen, Denmark, October 6, 270 pages.

Kane, R.J. (2003). Social control in the metropolis: A community-level examination of the minority group-threat hypothesis, *Justice Quarterly*, 20 (2), 265–295.

Kang, P. (2015). 3 Deepwater attys disqualified over improper referral fees, *Law360*, https://www.law360.com/articles/625822/3-deepwater-attys-disqualified-over-improper-referral-fees, published February 26, retrieved September 15, 2018.

Kang, E. and Thosuwanchot, N. (2017). An application of Durkheim's four categories of suicide to organizational crimes, *Deviant Behavior*, 38 (5), 493–513.

Kaptein, M. and Helvoort, M. (2019). A model of neutralization techniques, *Deviant Behavior*, 40 (10), 1260–1285.

Karim, K.E. and Siegel, P.H. (1998). A signal detection theory approach to analyzing the efficiency and effectiveness of auditing to detect management fraud, *Managerial Auditing Journal*, 13 (6), 367–375.

Karlsen, T.K. (2018). Sosiale nettverk, maktmisbruk og korrupsjon (Social networks, abuse of power and corruption), local Norwegian newspaper *Agderposten*, Thursday, January 18, page 21.

Karlsen, K. (2020). Advokater mener kommunen gjorde et ulovlig innkjøp (Attorneys believe the municipality made an illegal purchase), local Norwegian newspaper *Grimstad Adressetidende*, Saturday, February 15, pages 12–13.

Katz, J. (1979). Concerted ignorance: The social construction of cover-up, *Urban Life*, 8 (3), 295–316.

Katz, J.P. (1999). The new global leaders: Richard Branson, Percy Barnevik, David Simon and the remaking of international business, *Academy of Management Executive*, 13 (3), 119–120.

Kawasaki, T. (2020). Review of comparative studies on white-collar and corporate crime, in: Rorie, M.L. (editor), *The Handbook of White-Collar Crime*, Hoboken, NJ: Wiley & Sons, chapter 27, pages 437–447.

Keaveney, S.M. (2008). The blame game: An attribution theory approach to marketer-engineer conflict in high-technology companies, *Industrial Marketing Management*, 37, 653–663.

Keil, M., Tiwana, A., Sainsbury, R. and Sneha, S. (2010). Toward a theory of whistleblowing intentions: A benefit-cost differential perspective, *Decision Sciences*, 41 (4), 787–812.

Kempa, M. (2010). Combating white-collar crime in Canada: Serving victim needs and market integrity, *Journal of Financial Crime*, 17 (2), 251–264.

Ken, I. and León, K.S. (2021). Necropolitical governance and state-corporate harms: Covid-19 and the U.S. pork packing industry, *Journal of White Collar and Corporate Crime*, published online doi 10.1177/2631309X211011037, pages 1–14.

Kennedy, J.P. (2020). Organizational and macro-level corporate crime theories, in: Rorie, M.L. (editor), *The Handbook of White-Collar Crime*, Hoboken, NJ: Wiley & Sons, chapter 12, pages 175–190.

Kennedy, J.P., Rorie, M. and Benson, M.L. (2021). Covid-19 frauds: An exploratory study of victimization during a global crisis, *Criminology & Public Policy*, published online doi 10.1111/1745-9133.12554.

Kessler, G. and Reinecke, J. (2021). Dynamics of the causes of crime: A life-course application of situational action theory for the transition from adolescence to adulthood, *Journal of Developmental and Life-Course Criminology*, published online 10.1007/s40865-021-00161-z.

Khanna, V., Kim, E.H. and Lu, Y. (2015). CEO connectedness and corporate fraud, *The Journal of Finance*, 70, 1203–1252.

Kibar, O. (2020a). Varsleren (The whistleblower), daily Norwegian business newspaper *Dagens Næringsliv*, Saturday, August 8, pages 32–37.

Kibar, O. (2020b). Både ryddet opp for og gransket fiskerikjempe (Both cleaned up and investigated fishing giant), daily Norwegian business newspaper *Dagens Næringsliv*, Tuesday, September 1, pages 18–19.

Kim, P.H., Dirks, K.T. and Cooper, C.D. (2009). The repair of trust: A dynamic bilateral perspective and multilevel conceptualization, *Academy of Management Review*, 34 (3), 401–422.

King, M. (2020a). What makes a successful corporate investigator – An exploration of private investigators attributes, *Journal of Financial Crime*, published online doi: 10.1108/JFC-02-2020-0019.

King, M. (2020b). Out of obscurity: The contemporary private investigator in Australia, *International Journal of Police Science and Management*, published online doi: 10.1177/1461355720931887.

King, M. (2021). Profiting from a tainted trade: Private investigators' views on the popular culture glamorization of their trade, *Journal of Criminological Research Policy and Practice*, published online doi 10.1108/JCRPP-07-2020-0050.

Kjeldsen, A.M. and Jacobsen, C.B. (2013). Public service motivation and employment sector: Attraction or socialization? *Journal of Public Administration Research and Theory*, 23 (4), 899–926.

Kleinewiese, J. (2020). Situational action theory and the particular case of settings including a group, *European Journal of Criminology*, pages 1–17, doi 10.1177/1477370820953088.

Kleinfeld, J. (2019). Anatomy of a Bribe: A deep dive into an underworld of corruption, news organization *Al Jazeera*, www.aljazeera.com, published December 1.

Kleinfeld, J. (2020a). Corruption allegations in Namibian 5G deal with Huawei, news organization *Al Jazeera*, www.aljazeera.com, published July 15.

Kleinfeld, P. (2020b). Congo aid scam triggers sector-wide alarm, *The New Humanitarian*, www.thenewhumanitarian.org, published June 11.

Kleppe, M.K. (2015). Tromsdal: -Der er han skurken som lurte de gamle menneskene (There is the crock who cheated the old people), daily Norwegian business newspaper *Dagens Næringsliv*, published January 8.

Klevstrand, A. (2021). Tidligere Danske Bank-toppsjef Thomas Borgen er ikke lenger siktet i hvitvaskingssak (Former Danske Bank CEO Thomas Borgen is no longer charged in a money laundering case), daily Norwegian business newspaper *Dagens Næringsliv*, www.dn.no, published April 29.

Kolthoff, E. (2020). Criminological responses to corruption, in *Handbook on Corruption, Ethics and Integrity in Public Administration*, edited by Graycar, A., Cheltenham, UK: Edward Elgar Publishing, chapter 30, 434–448.

Koppen, M.V., Poot, C.J. and Blokland, A.A.J. (2010). Comparing criminal careers of organized crime offenders and general offenders, *European Journal of Criminology*, 7 (5), 356–374.

Kostova, T., Roth, K. and Dacin, M.T. (2008). Institutional theory in the study of multinational corporations: A critique and new directions, *Academy of Management Review*, 33 (4), 994–1006.

Kourula, A., Moon, J., Salles-Djelic, M.L. and Wicker, C. (2019). New roles of government in the governance of business conduct: Implications for management and organizational research, *Organization Studies*, 40 (8), 1101–1123.

Kownatzki, M., Walter, J., Floyd, S.W. and Lechner, C. (2013). Corporate control and the speed of strategic business unit decision making, *Academy of Management Journal*, 56 (5), 1295–1324.

KPMG (2020). *Report Concerning the Independent Special Investigation at Wirecard AG*, April 27, audit firm KPMG, Munich, Germany, 74 pages.

Kristiansen, T. (2019). Skandale ved kommunalt sykehjem: Gjør ikke forsøk på å gjenopplive pasienter (Scandal at a municipal nursing home: Do not try to revive patients), web-based Norwegian magazine *Document*, www.document.no, published July 20.

Krohn, M.D. and Eassey, J.M. (2014). Integrated theories of crime, in: Miller, J.M. (editor), *The Encyclopedia of Theoretical Criminology*, Chichester, UK: John Wiley & Sons, pages 458–463.

Kroll. (2018). *Project Tenor II – Detailed Report, Report Prepared for The National Bank of Moldova*, investigation firm Kroll, 25 Farringdon Street, London, UK, 154 pages.

Kroneberg, C. and Schultz, S. (2018). Revisiting the role of self-control in situational action theory, *European Journal of Criminology*, 15 (1), 56–76.

Kuhn, B.M. (2020). Sustainable finance in Germany: Mapping discourses, stakeholders, and policy initiatives, *Journal of Sustainable Finance & Investment*, published online doi 10.1080/20430795.2020.1783151.

Kundro, T.G. and Nurmohamed, S. (2021). Understanding when and why cover-ups are punished less severly, *Academy of Management Journal*, 64 (3), 873–900.

Kværnes, M. (2022). Banksjef Rune Hvidsten i Askim og Spydeberg Sparebank får sparken på dagen (Bank executive Rune Hvidsten at Askim and Spydeberg Savings Bank gets fired the same day), daily Norwegian business newspaper *Dagens Næringsliv*, www.dn.no, published February 7.

König, A., Graf-Vlachy, L., Bundy, J. and Little, L.M. (2020). A blessing and a curse: How CEOs' trait empathy affects their management of organizational crises, *Academy of Management Review*, 45 (1), 130–153.

Landre, E. (2006). Millionbøter fra Økokrim (Millions in fines from the Norwegian national authority for investigation and prosecution of economic and environmental crime), Norwegian web-based newspaper *Nettavisen*, www.nettavisen.no, published June 30.

Lange, D. (2008). A multidimensional conceptualization of organizational corruption control, *Academy of Management Journal*, 33 (3), 710–29.

Langton, L. and Piquero, N.L. (2007). Can general strain theory explain white-collar crime? A preliminary investigation of the relationship between strain and select white-collar offenses, *Journal of Criminal Justice*, 35, 1–15.

Lanier, M.M. and Henry, S. (2009a). Chapter 3: Conflict and Radical Theories,in: *Essential Criminology*, Third Edition, Westview, Member of the Perseus Books Group, Colorado: Boulder.

Lanier, M.M. and Henry, S. (2009b). Chapter 10: Capitalism as a Criminogenic Society – Conflict, Marxist, and Radical Theories of Crime, in: *Essential Criminology*, Third Edition, Westview, Member of the Perseus Books Group, Colorado: Boulder.

Laughland, O. (2017). Fifa official took bribes to back Qatar's 2022 world cup bid, court hears, *The Guardian*, www.theguardian.com, published November 15.

Lawler, E.J. and Hipp, L. (2010). Corruption as social exchange, *Advances in Group Processes*, 27, 269–296.

Lee, F. and Robinson, R.J. (2000). An attributional analysis of social accounts: Implications of playing the blame game, *Journal of Applied Social Psychology*, 30 (9), 1853–1879.

Lehman, D.W., Cooil, B. and Ramanujam, R. (2020). The effects of rule complexity on organizational noncompliance and remediation: Evidence from restaurant health inspections, *Journal of Management*, 46 (8), 1436–1468.

Leigh, A.C., Foote, D.A., Clark, W.R. and Lewis, J.L. (2010). Equity sensitivity: A triadic measure and outcome/input perspectives, *Journal of Managerial Issues*, 22 (3), 286–305.

Li, S., og Ouyang, M. (2007). A dynamic model to explain the bribery behavior of firms, *International Journal of Management*, 24 (3), 605–618.

Liang, L.H., Lian, H., Brown, D.J., Ferris, D.J., Hanig, S. and Keeping, L.M. (2016). Why are abusive supervisors abusive? A dual-system self-control model, *Academy of Management Journal*, 59 (4), 1385–1406.

Lilleås, H.S. (2011). -Mafiavirksomhet (Mafia activity), Norwegian web-based newspaper *Nettavisen*, www.nettavisen.no, published January 26.

Linder, S., Leca, B., Zicari, A. and Casarin, V. (2021). Designing ethical management control: Overcoming the harmful effect of management control systems on job-related stress, *Journal of Business Ethics*, 172, 747–764.

Liphshiz, C. (2019). Moldova Jews bear anti-semitic brunt as corrupt lawmaker flees, maybe to Israel, *The Times of Israel*, www.thetimesofisrael.com, published August 30.

Liska, A.E., Krohn, M.D. and Messner, S.F. (1989). Strategies and requisites for theoretical integration in the study of crime and deviance, in: Messner, S.F., Krohn, M.D. and Liska, A.E. (editors), *Theoretical Integration in the Study of Deviance and Crime*, Albany, NY: State University of New York Press, pages 1–20.

Liu, W., Qiu, G. and Zhang, S. (2020). Situational action theory and school bullying: Rethinking the moral filter, *Crime & Delinquency*, published online doi: 10.1177/0011128720974318.

Locatelli, G., Mariani, G., Sainati, T. and Greco, M. (2017). Corruption in public projects and megaprojects: There is an elephant in the room! *International Journal of Project Management*, 35 (3), 252–268.

Locke, S.L. and Blomquist, G.C. (2016). The cost of convenience: Estimating the impact of communication antennas on residential property values, *Land Economics*, 92 (1), 131–147.

Locke, E.A. and Latham, G.P. (2013). Goal setting theory: The current state, in: Locke, E.A. and Latham, G.P. (editors), *New Developments in Goal Setting and Task Performance*, New York, NY: Routledge, 623–630.

Long, C.P., Bendersky, C. and Morrill, C. (2011). Fairness monitoring: Linking managerial controls and fairness judgments in organizations, *Academy of Management Review*, 54 (5), 1045–1068.

Lopez-Rodriguez, S. (2009). Environmental engagement, organizational capability and firm performance, *Corporate Governance*, 9 (4), 400–408.

Lord, N., Van Wingerde, K. and Campbell, L. (2018). Organising the monies of corporate financial crimes via organizational structures: Ostensible legitimacy, effective anonymity, and third-party facilitation, *Administrative Sciences*, 8 /17), 1–17.

Lorentzen, M. (2020). Alex Schneiter går av som Lundin Energy-sjef: Nick Walker tar over 1. januar (Alex Schneiter resigns as Lundin Energy chief: Nick Walker takes over on January 1, web-based Norwegian newspaper *E24*, www.e24.no, published August 18.

Loyens, K., Claringbould, I., Heres-van Rossem, L. and Eekeren, Frank van. (2021). The social construction of integrity: A qualitative case study in Dutch football, *Sports in Society*, published online doi 10.1080/17430437.2021.1877661.

Lynch, M.J. (2020). Green criminology and environmental crime: Criminology that matters in the age of global ecological collapse, *Journal of White Collar and Corporate Crime*, 1 (1), 50–61.

Lynn, A. (2021). Why "doing well by doing good" went wrong: Getting beyond "good ethics pays" claims in managerial thinking, *Academy of Management Review*, 46 (3), 512–533.

Lønnebotn, L. (2021). Venninnen om Lan Marie Berg: -Lei meg når jeg ser hvor mye dritt hun må tåle (The friend about Lan Marie Berg: -I'm sad when I see how much shit she has to endure), web-based Norwegian newspaper *E24*, www.e24.no, published June 19.

Maas, V.S. and Yin, H. (2021). Finding partners in crime? How transparency about managers' behavior affects employee collusion, *Accounting, Organizations, and Society*, published online doi 10.106/j.aos.2021.101293.

Maher, R., Valenzuela, F., and Böhm, S. (2019). The enduring state: An analysis of governance-making in three mining conflicts, *Organization Studies*, 40 (8), 1169–1192.

Mai, H.T.X. and Olsen, S.O. (2016). Consumer participation in self-production: The role of control mechanisms, convenience orientation, and moral obligation, *Journal of Marketing Theory and Practice*, 24 (2), 209–223.

Makortoff, K. (2019). Swedbank chief sacked amid money laundering scandal, *The Guardian*, www.theguardian.com, published March 28.

Malmi, T., Bedford, D.S., Brühl, R., Dergård, J., Hoozée, S., Janschek, O., Willert, J., Ax, C., Bednarek, P., Gosselin, M., Hanzlick, M., Israelsen, P., Johanson, D., Johanson, T., Madsen, D.Ø., Rohde, C., Sandelin, M., Strömsten, T., and Toldbod, T. (2020). Culture and management control interdependence: An analysis of control choices that compelement the delegation of authority in Western cultural regions, *Accounting, Organizations and Society*, 86, 1–16.

Mannheimer Swartling (2016). *Report on Investigation of Nordea Private Banking in Relation to Offshore Structures*, law firm Mannheimer Swartling, Stockholm, Sweden, 42 pages.

Manning, L. and Kowalska, A. (2021). Illicit alcohol: Public health risk of methanol poisoning and policy mitigation strategies, *Foods*, 10, 1625, doi 10.3390/foods10071625.

Mannucci, P.V., Orazi, D.C. and Valck, K. (2021). Developing improvisation skills: The influence of individual orientations, *Administrative Science Quarterly*, 66 (3), 612–658.

Marmo, M. and Bandiera, R. (2021). Modern slavery as the new moral asset for the production and reproduction of state-corporate harm, *Journal of White Collar and Corporate Crime*, published online doi 10.1177/2631309X211020994.

Martin, P.R. (2021). Corporate social responsibility and capital budgeting, *Accounting, Organizations and Society*, 92, published online doi 10.1016/j.aos.2021.101236.

Martinsen, Ø.L., Furnham, A. and Hærem, T. (2016). An integrated perspective on insight, *Journal of Experimental Psychology*, 145 (10), 1319–1332.

Maslow, A.H. (1943). A theory of human motivation, *Psychological Review*, 50 (4), 370–396.

Masood, T. (2020). A machine learning approach for performance-oriented decision support in service-oriented architecture, *Journal of Intelligent Information Systems*, published online doi 10.1007/s10844-020-00617-6.

Mawritz, M.B., Greenbaum, R.L., Butts, M.M. and Graham, K.A. (2017). I just can't control myself: A self-regulation perspective on the abuse of deviant employees, *Academy of Management Journal*, 60 (4), 1482–1503.

McCarthy, N. (2021). 6,500 migrant workers have died in Qatar since it was named Fifa world cup host, *The Wire*, www.thewire.in, published February 25.

McClean, E.J., Martin, S.R., Emich, K.J. and Woodruff, T. (2018). The social consequences of voice: An examination of voice type and gender on status and subsequent leader emergence, *Academy of Management Journal*, 61 (5), 1869–1891.

McClelland, P.L., Liang, X. and Barker, V.L. (2010). CEO commitment to the status quo: Replication and extension using content analysis, *Journal of Management*, 36 (5), 1251–1277.

McCrum, D. (2019). Wirecard's suspect accounting practices revealed, *Financial Times*, www.ft.com, published October 15.

McCrum, D. (2020). Wirecard: the timeline, *Financial Times*, www.ft.com, published June 25.

McElwee, G. and Smith, R. (2015). Towards a Nuanced Typology of Illegal Entrepreneurship: A Theoretical and Conceptual Overview, in: McElwee, G. and Smith, R. (editors), *Exploring Criminal and Illegal Enterprise: New Perspectives on Research, Policy & Practice: Contemporary Issues in Entrepreneurship* Research *Volume 5*, Emerald, Bingley.

McKinley, J. (2015). Settlement in Suit Against Ex-Lawmaker, *The New York Times*, Friday, February 6, page A20.

Meerts, C. (2020). Corporate investigations: Beyond notions of public-private relations, *Journal of Contemporary Criminal Justice*, 36 (1), 86–100.

Megaw, N. and Neville, S. (2017). Drugmaker Astellas handed further ABPI suspension, *Financial Times*, www.ft.com, published June 23.

Mehrpouya, A. and Salles-Djelic, M.L. (2019). Seeing like the market; Exploring the mutual rise of transparency and accounting in transnational economic and market governance, *Accounting, Organizations and Society*, 76, 12–31.

Meldalen, S.G. (2015). –Når noen hører ordet «stråmann», høres det skummelt ut (When someone hears the word «straw man», it sounds scary), daily Norwegian newspaper *Dagbladet*, published January 8.

Melgård, M. and Oterholm, G. (2020). Norge brukte 17 millioner kroner på Sikkerhetsrådet-kampanje i 2019 (Norway spent NOK 17 million on the Security Council campaign in 2019), daily Norwegian business newspaper *Dagens Næringsliv*, www.dn.no, published February 13.

Menon, S. and Siew, T.G. (2012). Key challenges in tackling economic and cybercrimes – Creating a multilateral platform for international co-operation, *Journal of Money Laundering Control*, 15 (3), 243–256.

Mesmer-Magnus, J.R. and Viswesvaran, C. (2005). Whistleblowing in an organization: An examination of correlates of whistleblowing intentions, actions, and retaliation, *Journal of Business Ethics*, 62 (3), 266–297.

Miceli, M.P. and Near, J.P. (2013). An international comparison of the incidence of public sector whistle-blowing and the prediction of retaliation: Australia, Norway, and the US, *Australian Journal of Public Administration*, 72 (4), 433–446.

Michel, C. (2016). Violent street crime versus harmful white-collar crime: A comparison of perceived seriousness and punitiveness, *Critical Criminology*, 24, 127–143.

Milne, R. (2019a). Prosecutors charge ex-Danske Bank chief in money laundering probe, *Financial Times*, www.ft.com, published May 7.

Milne, R. (2019b). Body of Danske Bank's former Estonian chief found, *Financial Times*, www.ft.com, published September 25.

Milne, R. (2020). Swedbank failings on E37bn of transactions revealed in report, *Financial Times*, www.ft.com, published March 23.

Milne, R. and Binham, C. (2018). Danske Bank chief Thomas Borgen quits over money laundering scandal, *Financial Times*, www.ft.com, published September 19.

Mitnick, B.M., Windsor, D. and Wood, D.J. (2021). CSR: Undertheorized or essentially contested? *Academy of Management Review*, 40 (3), 623–629.

Mohliver, A. (2019). How misconduct spreads: Auditors' role in the diffusion of stock-option backdating, *Administrative Science Quarterly*, 64 (2), 310–336.

Moore, C. (2015). Moral disengagement, *Current Opinion in Psychology*, 6, 199–204.

Mpho, B. (2017). Whistleblowing: What do contemporary ethical theories say? *Studies in Business and Economics*, 12 (1), 19–28.

Mulinari, S., Davis, C. and Ozieranski, P. (2021). Failure of responsive regulation? Pharmaceutical marketing, corporate impression management and off-label promotion of enzalutamide in Europe, *Journal of White Collar and Corporate Crime*, 2 (2), 69–80.

Murphy, P.R. and Dacin, M.T (2011). Psychological pathways to fraud: Understanding and preventing fraud in organizations, *Journal of Business Ethics*, 101, 601–618.

Murphy, P.R. and Free, C. (2015). Broadening the fraud triangle: Instrumental climate and fraud, *Behavioral Research in Accounting*, 28 (1), 41–56.

Müller, S.M. (2018). Corporate behavior and ecological disaster: Dow Chemical and the Great Lakes mercury crisis, 1970-1972, *Business History*, 60 (3), 399–422.

Nakamoto, M. (2011). Olympus turns focus on Japan's governance, *Financial Times*, November 8, https://infoweb.newsbank.com/apps/news/document-view?p=AWNB&t=&sort=YMD_date%3AD&maxresults=20&f=advanced&val-base-0=tobashi&fld-base-0=alltext&bln-base-1=and&val-base-1=olympus&fld-base-1=alltext&bln-base-2=and&val-base-2=fraud&fld-base-2=alltext&bln-base-3=and&val-base-3=2011&fld-base-3=YMD_date&docref=news/13AE854CE15B17D0, retrieved October 31, 2018.

Nakling, A. (2015). Lærdomen frå Betanien (Lessons learned from Betanien), daily Norwegian newspaper *Bergens Tidende*, www.bt.no, published March 20.

Naylor, R.T. (2003). Towards a general theory of profit-driven crimes, *British Journal of Criminology*, 43, 81–101.

Neate, R. (2012). Michael Woodford: The man who blew whistle on £1bn fraud, *The Guardian*, https://www.theguardian.com/business/2012/nov/23/michael-woodford-olympus-whistleblower, published November 23, downloaded September 10, 2018.

Nechepurenko, I. (2015). Moldova parliament dismisses government amid bank scandal, *The New York Times*, www.nytimes.com, published October 29.

Nesti, L. (2014). The 2010 "Agreement on mutual enforcement of debarments decisions" and its impact for the fight against fraud and corruption in public procurement, *Journal of Public Procurement*, 14 (1), 62–95.

Newth, M. (2018). Britta Nielsen (64) mistenkt for å ha stjålet 140 millioner (Britta Nielsen (64) suspected of having stolen 140 million), daily Norwegian newspaper *VG*, www.vg.no, published November 5.

Nichol, J.E. (2019). The effects of contract framing on misconduct and entitlement, *The Accounting Review*, 94 (3), 329–344.

Nielsen, R.P. (2003). Corruption networks and implications for ethical corruption reform, *Journal of Business Ethics*, 42 (2), 125–149.

NTB (2015). Økokrim ber om seks års fengsel for Tromsdal (Økokrim asks for six years prison for Tromsdal), daily Norwegian newspaper *Klassekampen*, published March 20.

NTB (2019). Dansk kvinne for retten i storstilt svindelsak (Danish women prosecuted in court in a big fraud case), ABC *nyheter*, www.abcnyheter.no, published October 24.

Nurse, A. (2022). *Cleaning Up Greenwash: Corporate Environmental Crime and the Crisis of Capitalism*, UK, London: Lexington Books.

O'Leary, S. and Smith, D. (2020). Moments of resistance: An internally persuasive view of performance and impact reports in non-governmental organizations, *Accounting, Organization and Society*, 85, 1–21.

Obodaru, O. (2017). Forgone, but not forgotten: Toward a theory of forgone professional identities, *Academy of Management Journal*, 60 (2), 523–553.

OECD (2021). *Ending the Shell Game: Checking down on the Professionals who enable Tax and White Collar Crimes*, OECD Publishing, Organization for Economic Co-operation and Development, Paris, www.oecd.org, 57 pages.

Oh, J.J. (2004). How (Un)ethical Are You? Letters to the Editor, *Harvard Business Review*, March, 122.

Olav, H.E. (2014). *Det store selvbedraget: Hvordan statsmakt ødelegger menneskeverd og velferd (The grand self-deception: How state power harms human dignity and welfare)*, Kolofon publishing, Oslo, Norway.

Olav, H.E. (2015). *The Grand Self-Deception: A Libertarian Manifesto Against the Deep State – The Failed Welfare-Taxation Model of Norway*, Kindle Edition, printed in Great Britain by Amazon.

Oliveira, C.R. and Silveira, R.A. (2020). An essay of corporate crimes in the post-colonial perspective: Challenging traditional literature, *Journal of Contemporary Administration*, 25 (4), 1–17.

Onna, J.H.R. and Denkers, A.J.M. (2019). Social bonds and white-collar crime: A two-study assessment of informal social controls in white-collar offenders, *Deviant Behavior*, 40 (10), 1206–1225.

Onna, J.H.R., Geest, V.R., Huisman, W. and Denkers, J.M. (2014). Criminal trajectories of white-collar offenders, *Journal of Research in Crime and Delinquency*, 51, 759–784.

Oosterman, N., Mackenzie, S. and Yates, D. (2021). Regulating the wild west: Symbolic security bubbles and white collar crime in the art market, *Journal of White Collar and Corporate Crime*, published online doi 10.1177/2631309X211035724.

Oslo tingrett (2015a). Case number 14-067448MED-OTIR/06, *Oslo tingrett* (Oslo district court), January 12.

Oslo tingrett (2015b). Case number 14-035631MED-OTIR/05, *Oslo tingrett* (Oslo district court), June 19.

Osoria, J.A. (2021). The Covid-19 pandemic in Puerto Rico: Exceptionality, corruption and state-corporate crimes, *State Crime Journal*, 10 (1), 104–125.

Ottermann, P. (2020). Danish social worker jailed for stealing £13m of government funds, *The Guardian*, www.theguardian.com, published February 18.

Oyerogba, E.O. (2021). Forensic auditing mechanism and fraud detection: The case of Nigerian public sector, *Journal of Accounting in Emerging Economies*, published online doi 10.1108/JAEE-04-2020-0072.

Papadimitri, P., Pasiouras, F. and Tasiou, M. (2021). Do national differences in social capital and corporate ethical behavior perceptions influence the use of collateral? Cross-country evidence, *Journal of Business Ethics*, 172, 765–784.

Paruchuri, S., Han, J.H. and Prakash, P. (2021). Salient expectations? Incongruence across capability and integrity signals and investor reactions to organizational misconduct, *Academy of Management Journal*, 64 (2), 562–586.

Patel, P.C. and Cooper, D. (2014). Structural power equality between family and nonfamily TMT members and the performance of family firms, *Academy of Management Journal*, 57 (6), 1624–1649.

Paternoster, R., Jaynes, C.M. and Wilson, T. (2018). Rational choice theory and interest in the "fortune of others", *Journal of Research in Crime and Delinquency*, 54 (6), 847–868.

Patrucco, A.S., Luzzini, D. and Ronchi, S. (2017). Research perspectives on public procurement: Content analysis of 14 years of publications in the Journal of Public Procurement, *Journal of Public Procurement*, 16 (2), 229–269.

Paun, T. and Pinzaru, F. (2021). Advancing strategic management through sustainable finance, *Management Dynamics in the Knowledge Economy*, 9 (2), 279–291.

Perry, J., Hondeghem, A.and Wise, L. (2010). Revisiting the motivational bases of public service, *Public Administration Review*, 70 (5), 681–690.

Pertiwi, K. (2018). Contextualizing corruption: A cross-disciplinary approach to studying corruption in organizations, *Administrative Sciences*, 8 (12), 1–19.

Petrocelli, M., Piquero, A.R. and Smith, M.R. (2003). Conflict theory and racial profiling: An empirical analysis of police traffic stop data, *Journal of Criminal Justice*, 31 (1), 1–11.

Pettrem, M.T. (2021). Langt dyrere enn først antatt (Far more expensive than first thought), daily Norwegian newspaper *Aftenposten*, Tuesday, September 21, page 14.

Piazza, A. and Jourdan, J. (2018). When the dust settles: The consequences of scandals for organizational competition, *Academy of Management Journal*, 61 (1), 165–190.

Piening, E.P., Salge, T.O., Antons, D. and Kreiner, G.E. (2020). Standing together or falling apart? Understanding employees' responses to organizational identity threats, *Academy of Management Review*, 45 (2), 325–351.

Pillay, S. and Kluvers, R. (2014). An institutional theory perspective on corruption: The case of a developing democracy, *Financial Accountability & Management*, 30 (1), 95–119.

Pinto, J., Leana, C.R. and Pil, F.K. (2008). Corrupt organizations or organizations of corrupt individuals? Two types of organization-level corruption, *Academy of Management Review*, 33 (3), 685–709.

Piquero, N.L. (2012). The only thing we have to fear is fear itself: Investigating the relationship between fear of falling and white-collar crime, *Crime and Delinquency*, 58 (3), 362–379.

Pitelis, C.N. and Wagner, J.D. (2019). Strategic shared leadership and organizational dynamic capabilities, *The Leadership Quarterly*, 30, 233–242.

Plesner (2020). *Response to DFSA-letter: Anmodning om redegørelse om Danske Bank A/S' gældsinddrivelsessystem (Response to DFSA letter: Request for account concerning Danske Bank Inc.'s debt collection system)*, investigation report by Danske Bank, law firm Plesner, Copenhagen, Denmark, 120 pages.

Podgor, E.S. (2007). The challenge of white collar sentencing, *Journal of Criminal Law and Criminology*, 97 (3), 1–10.

Pontell, H.N., Black, W.K. and Geis, G. (2014). Too big to fail, too powerful to jail? On the absence of criminal prosecutions after the 2008 financial meltdown, *Crime, Law and Social Change*, 61 (1), 1–13.

Pontell, H.N., Ghazi-Tehrani, A.K. and Burton, B. (2020). White-collar and corporate crime in China, in: Rorie, M.L. (editor), *The Handbook of White-Collar Crime*, Hoboken, NJ: Wiley & Sons, chapter 22, pages 347–362.

Pontell, H.N., Tillman, R. and Ghazi-Tehrani, A.K. (2021). In-your-face Watergate: Neutralizing government lawbreaking and the war against white-collar crime, *Crime, Law and Social Change*, published online doi 10.1007/s10611-021-09954-1, 19 pages.

Porter, M.E., Lorsch, J.W. and Nohria, N. (2004). Seven surprises for new CEOs, *Harvard Business Review*, October, 62–72.

Power, M. (2021). Modelling the micro-foundations of the audit society: Organizations and the logic of the audit trail, *Academy of Management Review*, 46 (1), 6–32.

Pratt, T.C. and Cullen, F.T. (2005). Assessing macro-level predictors and theories of crime: A meta-analysis, *Crime and Justice*, 32, 373–450.

Puente, M. (2020). Lori Loughlin released from prison after serving 2-month sentence in college bribery scheme, *USA Today*, www.eu.usatoday.com, published December 28.

Puranam, P., Alexy, O. and Reitzig, M. (2014). What's «new» about new forms of organizing? *Academy of Management Review*, 39 (2), 162–180.

PwC (2003). *Report of investigation by the special investigative committee of the Board of Directors of WorldCom Inc.*, Wilmer Cutler Pickering, https://www.concernedshareholders.com/CCS_WCSpecialReportExc.pdf.

PwC (2015). *Auditor-General for the Federation. Investigative Forensic Audit into the Allegations of Unremitted Funds into the Federation Accounts by the NNPC*, engagement leader Pedro Omontuemhen, PricewaterhouseCoopers, Lagos, Nigeria, https://www.premiumtimesng.com/docs_download/Full%20report–20billion%20dollars%20missing%20oil%20money.pdf?cf=1.

PwC. (2019). *Ekstern undersøgelse af tilskudsadministrationen 1977-2018 – Udarbeijdet for Socialstyrelsen (External examination of the benefits administration 1977-2018 – Prepared for the Social security administration)*, audit firm PwC, Copenhagen, Denmark, February, 80 pages.

Qiu, B. and Slezak, S.L. (2019). The equilibrium relationships between performance-based pay, performance, and the commission and detection of fraudulent misreporting, *The Accounting Review*, 94 (2), 325–356.

Qu, J. (2021). The challenge against economic regulation ethics under the Covid-19 epidemic: An analysis of unethical behavior of convenience, *Converter Magazine*, volume 2021, no. 5, 74–79.

Ragothaman, S.C. (2014). The Madoff debacle: What are the lessons? *Issues in Accounting Education*, 29 (1), 271–285.

Ramoglou, S. and Tsang, E.W.K. (2016). A realist perspective of entrepreneurship: Opportunities as propensities, *Academy of Management Review*, 41, 410–434.

Randers, J. (2019). The great challenge for system dynamics on the path forward: Implementation and real impact, *System Dynamics Review*, 35 (2), 19–24.

Rashbaum, W.K. and Kaplan, T. (2015). U.S. says assembly speaker took millions in payoffs, abusing office, *The New York Times*, Friday, January 23, pages A1 and A24.

Rashid, A., Al-Mamun, A., Roudaki, H. and Yasser, Q.R. (2022). An overview of corporate fraud and its prevention approach, *Australasian Accounting, Business and Finance Journal*, 16 (1), Article 6,101–118.

Rehg, M.T., Miceli, M.P., Near, J.P. and Scotter, J.R.V (2009). Antecedents and outcomes of retaliation against whistleblowers: Gender differences and power relationships, *Organization Science*, 19 (2), 221–240.

Resodihardjo, S.L., Carroll, B.J., Eijk, C.J.A. and Maris, S. (2015). Why traditional responses to blame games fail: The importance of context, rituals, and sub-blame games in the face of raves gone wrong, *Public Administration*, 94 (2), 350–363.

Reuters (2019). Norway's DNB investigates allegedly improper Samherji payments to Namibia, *Under Current News*, www.undercurrentnews.com, published November 15.

Reuters (2020). Danske Bank admits it knew of erroneous debt collection for years, *Financial Post*, www.financialpost.com, published September 11.

Reyns, B.W. (2013). Online routines and identity theft victimization: Further expanding routine activity theory beyond direct-contact offenses, *Journal of Research in Crime and Delinquency*, 50, 216–238.

Riis, C. and Øverland, K.J. (2018). *Økonomisk kriminalitet i religiøse miljøer: Hva er spesielle kjennetegn ved mulighet, motiv og villighet når økonomisk kriminalitet begås av hvitsnipper i religiøse miljøer? (Economic crime in religious environments: What are special characteristics of opportunity, motive and willingness when economic crime is committed by white-collars in religious environments?)*, Master thesis, BI Norwegian Business School, Oslo, Norway.

Riisnæs, M.G. (2018). Advokat gransker Oceanteam videre (Attorney continues Oceanteam investigation), daily Norwegian business newspaper *Dagens Næringsliv*, www.dn.no, published September 26.

Ritzau. (2020). Forsvarsansat skal i fængsel for at modtage bestikkelse (Defense employee shall in prison for receipt of bribe), Danish daily newspaper *Nordjyske Stiftsdiende*, www.nordjyske.dk, published December 2.

Rodriguez, P., Uhlenbruck, K. and Eden, L. (2005). Government corruption and the entry strategies of multinationals, *Academy of Management Review*, 30 (2), 383–396.

Rorie, M. (2015). An integrated theory of corporate environmental compliance and overcompliance, *Crime, Law and Social Change*, 64 (2-3), 65–101.

Rorie, M. and West, M. (2022). Can "focused deterrence" produce more effective ethics codes? An experimental study, *Journal of White Collar and Corporate Crime*, 3 (1), 33–45.

Rosca, M. (2015). Vanishing act: How global auditor failed to spot theft of 15% of Moldova's wealth, *The Guardian*, www.theguardian.com, published July 1.

Rothacker, R. (2016). Banking – Wells Fargo gives few details about firings, *Charlotte Observer*, published September 10, https://infoweb.newsbank.com/apps/news/document-view?p=AWNB&t=&sort=YMD_date%3AD&maxresults=20&f=advanced&val-base-0=rothacker&fld-base-0=Author&bln-base-1=and&val-base-1=wells%20fargo&fld-base-1=alltext&bln-base-2=and&val-base-2=eshet&fld-base-2=alltext&docref=news/15F5B3B95E914970.

Rothe, D.L. (2020). Moving beyond abstract typologies? Overview of state and state-corporate crime, *Journal of White-Collar and Corporate Crime*, 1 (1), 7–15.

Rothe, D.L. and Medley, C. (2020). Beyond state and state-corporate crime typologies: The symbiotic nature, harm, and victimization of crimes of the powerful and their continuation, in: Rorie, M. (editor), *The Handbook of White-Collar Crime*, Hoboken, NJ: John Wiley & Sons, chapter 6, pages 81–94.

Röglinger, M., Pöppelbuss, J. and Becker, J. (2012). Maturity model in business process management, *Business Process Management Journal*, 18 (2), 328–346.

Sale, H.A. (2021). The corporate purpose of social license, *Sothern California Law Review*, 94 (4), 785–842.

Samherji (2019a). *Statement from Samherji: Press release*, www.samherji.is, published November 11 by Margrét Ólafsdóttir, margret@samherji.is.

Samherji (2019b). *Samherji CEO steps aside while investigations are ongoing*, www.samherji.is, published November 14 by Margrét Ólafsdóttir, margret@samherji.is.

Samherji (2020a). *Samherji's Namibia investigation finalized*, Samherji ice fresh seafood, website https://www.samherji.is/en/moya/news/samherjis-namibia-investigation-finalized, Akureyri, Iceland, published July 29 by Margrét Ólafsdóttir, margret@samherji.

Samherji (2020b). *Fees for quotas were in line with market prices in Namibia*, Samherji seafood, www.samherji.is, published September 25 by Margrét Ólafsdóttir, margret@samherji.is.

Samherji (2021). Statement and apology from Samherji, published June 22 by Margrét Ólafsdóttir, margret@samherji.is.

Sampson, A. (2020). Art billionaire and collector Leon Black investigated over financial dealings with Epstein, *Tatler*, www.tatler.com, published August 25.

Sands. (2019). *Factual report: Oceanteam ASA Investigation of related party transactions*, law firm Sands, Oslo, Norway, November 4, 256 pages.

Sanger, S.W., Duke, E.A., James, D.M. and Hernandez, E. (2017). *Independent Directors of the Board of Wells Fargo & Company: Sales Practices Investigation Report*, April 10, 113 pages, https://www08.wellsfargomedia.com/assets/pdf/about/investor-relations/presentations/2017/board-report.pdf, downloaded September 7, 2018.

Saunders, M., Lewis, P. and Thornhill, A. (2007). *Research Methods for Business Students*, 5th edition, London, UK: Pearson Education.

Scheaf, D.J. and Wood, M.S. (2021). Entrepreneurial fraud: A multidisciplinary review and synthesized framework, *Entrepreneurship: Theory and Practice*, published online doi 10.1177/0422587211001818, pages 1–36.

Schjelderup, G. (2020). Skatteparadis (Tax paradise), *Store Norske Leksikon (Large Norwegian Encyclopedia)*, www.snl.no/skatteparadis, published February 1.

Schjelderup, G. and Sævold, K. (2021). Skatteplanlegging i sentralbankens blindsoner (Tax planning in the central bank's blind zones), daily Norwegian business newspaper *Dagens Næringsliv*, www.dn.no, published August 19.

Schlabach, M. (2019). Feds allege coaches bribed for school admisstion, *ESPN*, www.espn.com, published March 12.

Schmal, F., Sasse, K.S. and Watrin, C. (2021). Trouble in paradise? Disclosure after tax haven leaks, *Journal of Accounting, Auditing & Finance*, pages 1–22 published online 10.1177/0148558X20986348.

Schmidt, M.R., McGrimmon, T.S. and Dilks, L.M. (2022). Social roles and organizational culture: Attributions of responsibility and punitiveness for financial crime, *Journal of White Collar and Corporate Crime*, 3 (1), 46–55.

Schnatterly, K., Gangloff, K.A. and Tuschke, A. (2018). CEO wrongdoing: A review of pressure, opportunity, and rationalization, *Journal of Management*, 44 (6), 2405–2432.

Schneider, A. and Scherer, A.G. (2019). State governance beyond the 'shadow of hierarchy': A social mechanisms perspective on governmental CSR policies, *Organization Studies*, 40 (8), 1147–1168.

Schoen, J.L., DeSimone, J.A., Meyer, R.D., Schnure, K.A. and LeBreton, J.M. (2021). Identifying, defining, and measuring justification mechanisms: The implicit biases underlying individual differences, *Journal of Management*, 47 (3), 716–744.

Schoepfer, A. and Piquero, N.L. (2006). Exploring white-collar crime and the American dream: A partial test of institutional anomie theory, *Journal of Criminal Justice*, 34 (3), 227–235.

Schoultz, I. and Flyghed, J. (2016). Doing business for a 'higher loyalty' How Swedish transnational corporations neutralize allegations of crime, *Crime, Law and Social Change*, 66 (2), 183–198.

Schoultz, I. and Flyghed, J. (2019). From "we didn't do it" to "we've learned our lesson": Development of a typology of neutralizations of corporate crime, *Critical Criminology*, published online doi.org/10.1007/s10612-019-09483-3.

Schoultz, I. and Flyghed, J. (2020a). From "we didn't do it" to "we've learned our lesson": Development of a typology of neutralizations of corporate crime, *Critical Criminology*, 28, 739–757.

Schoultz, I. and Flyghed, J. (2020b). Denials and confessions: An analysis of the temporalization of neutralizations of corporate crime, *International Journal of Law, Crime and Justice*, 62, September, Article 100389.

Schoultz, I. and Flyghed, J. (2021a). "We have been thrown under the bus": Corporate versus individual defense mechanisms against transnational corporate bribery charges, *Journal of White Collar and Corporate Crime*, 2 (1), 24–35.

Schoultz, I. and Flyghed, J. (2021b). Performing unbelonging in court: Observations from a transnational corporate bribery trial – A dramaturgical approach, *Crime, Law and Social Change*, published online doi 10.1007/s10611-021-09990-x.

Schultz, J. (2019). Wikborg Rein-gransker om Samherji: -Planen er å være ute av Namibia innen få måneder (Wikborg Rein investigator about Samherji: -The plan is to be out of Namibia within a few months, daily Norwegian business newspaper *Dagens Næringsliv*, www.dn.no, published December 1.

Schultz, J. and Trumpy, J. (2019a). NRK: DNB brukte mer enn et år på å stenge Samherji-kontoer (NRK: DNB spent more than a year to close Samherji accounts), Norwegian daily business newspaper *Dagens Næringsliv*, www.dn.no, published August 26.

Schultz, J. and Trumpy, J. (2019b). Björgolfur Johannsson ble Samherji-sjef etter hvitvaskingsavsløring: -Jeg tror ikke det har vært noen bestikkelser, Norwegian daily business newspaper *Dagens Næringsliv*, www.dn.no, published December 13.

Schwendinger, H. and Schwendinger, J. (2014). Defenders of order or guardians of human rights? *Social Justice*, 40 (1/2), 87–117.

Seiders, K., Voss, G.B., Godfrey, A.L. and Grewal, D. (2007). SERVCON: Development and validation of a multidimensional service convenience scale, *Journal of the Academy of Marketing Science*, 35, 144–156.

Seljan, H., Kjartansson, A. and Drengsson, S.A. (2019). What Samherji wanted hidden, Kveikur at *RUV*, public broadcasting in Iceland, www.ruv.is/kveikur/fishrot/fishrot.

Seron, C. and Munger, F. (1996). Law and inequality: Race, Gender . . . and, of Course, Class, *Annual Review of Sociology*, 22, 187–212.

Shadnam, M. and Lawrence, T.B. (2011). Understanding widespread misconduct in organizations: An institutional theory of moral collapse, *Business Ethics Quarterly*, 21 (3), 379–407.

Shah, S. (2002). ABB demands Barnevik repay part of pension, *Independent*, www.independent.co.uk, published February 14.

Shawver, T. and Clements, L.H. (2019). The impact of value preferences on whistleblowing intentions of accounting professionals, *Journal of Forensic and Investigative Accounting*, 11 (2), 232–247.

Shearman Sterling (2017). *Independent Directors of the Board of Wells Fargo & Company: Sales Practices Investigation Report*, law firm Shearman & Sterling, New York, NY, 113 pages.

Shen, W. (2003). The dynamics of the CEO-board relationship: An evolutionary perspective, *Academy of Management Review*, 28 (3), 466–476.

Shepardson, D. and Burden, M. (2014). GM recalls 778K cars to replace ignition switches after fatal crashes, *Detroit News*, February 13, https://infoweb.newsbank.com/apps/news/document-view?p=AWNB&t=&sort=YMD_date%3AA&maxresults=20&f=advanced&val-base-0=ignition%20switch%20failure&fld-base-0=alltext&bln-base-1=and&val-base-1=GM&fld-base-1=alltext&bln-base-2=and&val-base-2=cobalt&fld-base-2=alltext&bln-base-3=and&val-base-3=2014&fld-base-3=YMD_date&bln-base-4=and&val-base-4=learned&fld-base-4=alltext&docref=news/14BF79CC1AB3B180.

Shepherd, D. and Button, M. (2019). Organizational inhibitions to addressing occupational fraud: A theory of differential rationalization, *Deviant Behavior*, 40 (8), 971–991.

Shichor, D. and Heeren, J.W. (2021). Reflecting on corporate crime and control: The Wells Fargo banking saga, *Journal of White Collar and Corporate Crime*, 2 (2), 97–108.

Siegel, L.J. (2011). *Criminology*, 11th edition, CA, Belmont: Wadsworth Publishing.

Simmons, A. (2018). Why students cheat and what to do about it, *Edutopia*, www.edutopia.org.

Singh, C. and Lin, W. (2021). Can artificial intelligence, RegTech and CharityTech provide effective solutions for anti-money laundering and counter-terror financing initiatives in charitable fundraising, *Journal of Money Laundering Control*, 24 (3), 464–482.

Skatteetaten. (2021). *Trusselvurdering Covid-19: Hvilke alvorlige kriminalitetstrusler vil Skatteetaten stå overfor ved en normalisering? (Threat Assessment Covid-19: What Serious Crime Threats will the Tax Administration face at normalization?)*, report issued by the Norwegian tax administration, www.skatteetaten.no, September.

Skurdal, M. (2020a). Dårlige jobber (Bad jobs), daily Norwegian newspaper *Klassekampen*, www.klassekampen.no, published September 18.

Skurdal, M. (2020b). Tåkelagt profit (Hazy profit), daily Norwegian newspaper *Klassekampen*, www.klassekampen.no, published December 17.

Sleesman, D.J., Conlon, D.E., McNamara, G. and Miles, J.E. (2012). Cleaning up the big muddy: A meta-analysis review of the determinants of escalation of commitment, *Academy of Management Journal*, 55 (3), 541–562.

Sleesman, D.J., Lennard, A.C., McNamara, G. and Conlon, D.E. (2018). Putting escalation of commitment in context: A multilevel review and analysis, *Academy of Management Annals*, 12 (1), 178–207.

Slyke, S.R.V. and Bales, W.D. (2013). Gender dynamics in the sentencing of white-collar offenders, *Criminal Justice Studies*, 26 (2), 168–196.

Smets, M., Morris, T. and Greenwood, R. (2012). From practice to field: A multilevel model of practice-driven institutional change, *Academy of Management Journal*, 55 (4), 877–904.

Smith, R. (2009). Understanding entrepreneurial behavior in organized criminals, *Journal of Enterprising Communities: People and Places in the Global Economy*, 3 (3), 256–268.

Smith, G. (2009). Citizen oversight of independent police services: Bifurcated accountability, regulation creep, and lessons learning, *Regulation & Governance*, 3, 421–441.

Smith. (2020). *Operational Review of Exposure to Corrupt Practices in Humanitarian Aid Implementation Mechanisms in the DRC*, Adam Smith International, www.reliefweb.int, written by N. Henze, F. Grünewald, and S. Parmar, published in July.

Smith, R., Manning, L. and McElwee, G. (2022). The anatomy of 'so-called food-fraud scandals' in the UK 1970-2018: Developing a contextualized understanding, *Crime, Law and Social Change*, published online doi 10.1007/s10611-021-10000-3.

Soble, J. and Nakamoto, M. (2012). Former Olympus executives arrested, *Financial Times*, https://www.ft.com/content/15bb88de-5850-11e1-ae89-00144feabdc0, published February 16, retrieved September 10, 2018.

Sohoni, T. and Rorie, M. (2021). The whiteness of white-collar crime in the United States: Examining the role of race in a culture of elite white-collar offending, *Theoretical Criminology*, 25 (1), 66–87.

Solgård, J. (2021). Danske Banks toppsjef Chris Vogelzang går på dagen (Danske Bank's top executive Chris Vogelzang leaves on the day), daily Norwegian business newspaper *Dagens Næringsliv*, www.dn.no, published April 19.

Solli-Sæther, H. and Gottschalk, P. (2015). Stages-of-growth in outsourcing, offshoring and backsourcing: Back to the future? *Journal of Computer Information Systems*, 55 (2), 88–94.

Sonnier, B.M., Lassar, W.M. and Lassar, S.S. (2015). The influence of source credibility and attribution of blame on juror evaluation of liability of industry specialist auditors, *Journal of Forensic & Investigative Accounting*, 7 (1), 1–37.

Sorour, M.K., Boadu, M. and Soobaroyen, T. (2021). The role of corporate social responsibility in organizational identity communication, co-creation and orientation, *Journal of Business Ethics*, 173, 89–108.

Spector, J. (2015). Lawmaker accused in graft scheme, *USA Today*, Friday, January 23, page 4A.

Srivastava, S.B. and Goldberg, A. (2017). Language as a window into culture, *California Management Review*, 60 (1), 56–69.

Stadler, W.A., Benson, M.L., and Cullen. F.T. (2013). Revisiting the special sensitivity hypothesis: The prison experience of white-collar inmates, *Justice Quarterly*, 30 (6), 1090–1114.

Stadler, W.A. and Gottschalk, P. (2021). Testing convenience theory for white-collar crime: Perceptions of potential offenders and non-offenders, *Deviant Behavior*, published online doi 10.1080/01639625.2021.1919037, pages 1–11

Standing, A. (2015). Mirage of pirates: State-corporate crime in West Africa's Fisheries, *State Crime Journal*, 4 (2), 175–197.

State Auditor (2020). *University of California*, California State Auditor, 621 Capitol Mall, Sacramento, Calfornia, USA, report of investigation 82 pages.

Steffensmeier, D., Schwartz, J., and Roche, M. (2013). Gender and twenty-first-century corporate crime: Female involvement and the gender gap in Enron-era corporate frauds, *American Sociological Review*, 78 (3), 448–476.

Sterman, J.D. (2018). System dynamics at sixty: The path forward, *System Dynamics Review*, 34 (1), 5–47.

Storbeck, O. (2020a). Wirecard: The frantic final months of a fraudulent operation, *Financial Times*, www.ft.com, published August 25.

Storbeck, O. (2020b). Whistleblower warned EY of Wirecard fraud four years before collapse, *Financial Times*, www.ft.com, published September 30.

Storbeck, O. and Morris, S. (2021). BaFin files insider trading complaint against Deutsche Bank board member, *Financial Times*, www.ft.com, published April 19.

Strandli, A. (2019). Oceanteam vil stanse granskningen av selskapet (Oceanteam wants to stop the investigation of the company), daily Norwegian financial newspaper *Finansavisen*, www.finan savisen.no, published May 5.

Strøm, O.K. (2021). Økokrim-sjefen: -Norge bør boikotte Qatar-VM (The head of Økokrim: -Norway should boycott the Qatar World Cup), daily Norwegian newspaper *Aftenposten*, www.aftenpos ten.no, published October 28.

Sundström, M. and Radon, A. (2015). Utilizing the concept of convenience as a business opportunity in emerging markets, *Organizations and Markets in Emerging Economies*, 6 (2), 7–21.

Sutherland, E.H. (1939). White-collar criminality, *American Sociological Review*, 5 (1), 1–12.

Sutherland, E.H. (1983). *White Collar Crime – The Uncut Version*, New Haven, CT: Yale University Press.

Sved, R. (2018). Anmeldelse mot rådmann henlagt (Notification against councilor dropped), magazine for municipalities *Kommunal Rapport*, www.kommunal-rapport.no, published April 3.

Sved, R. and Frigård, T. (2020). Omstridt kommunedirektør må gå (Controversial municipal councilor must go), magazine for municipalities *Kommunal Rapport*, www.kommunal-rapport. no, published September 16.

Swart, J. and Kinnie, N. (2003). Sharing knowledge in knowledge-intensive firms, *Human Resource Management Journal*, 13 (2), 60–75.

Sykes, G. and Matza, D. (1957). Techniques of neutralization: A theory of delinquency, *American Sociological Review*, 22 (6), 664–670.

Szalma, J.L. and Hancock, P.A. (2013) A signal improvement to signal detection analysis: fuzzy SDT on the ROCs, *Journal of Experimental Psychology: Human Perception and Performance*, 39 (6), 1741–1762.

Tankebe, J. (2019). Cooperation with the police against corruption: Exploring the roles of legitimacy, deterrence and collective action theories, *British Journal of Criminology*, 59, 1390–1410.

Tang, Y., Qian, C., Chen, G. and Shen, R. (2015). How CEO hubris affects corporate social (ir) responsibility, *Strategic Management Journal*, 36, 1338–1357.

Taylor, K. (2020). Lori Loughlin released from federal prison, *New York Times*, www.nytimes.com, published December 28.

Teiss. (2020). Hackers conned Norwegian investment fund out of $10m through email scam, *The Cambodia Daily*, www.cambodiadaily.com, published May 20.

Tombs, S. (2012). State-corporate symbiosis in the production of crime and harm, *State Crime Journal*, 1 (2), 170–195.

Tombs, S. and Whyte, D. (2020). The shifting imaginaries of corporate crime, *Journal of White-Collar and Corporate Crime*, 1 (1), 16–23.

Tonoyan, V., Strohmeyer, R., Habib, M. and Perlitz, M. (2010). Corruption and entrepreneurship: How formal and informal institutions shape small firm behavior in transition and mature market economies, *Entrepreneurship: Theory & Practice*, 34 (5), 803–831.

Toolami, B.N., Roodposhti, F.R., Nikoomaram, H., Banimahd, B. and Vakilifard, H. (2019). The survey of whistleblowing intentions for accounting frauds based on demographic individual differences among accounting staff, *International Journal of Finance and Managerial Accounting*, 4 (14), 1–13.

Transparency (2018). Corruption perceptions index 2018, *Transparency International*, www.transparency.org/cpi2018.

Trumpy, J. (2016). Avgått Telenor-direktør i ny havn (Resigned Telenor executive in new harbor), daily Norwegian business newspaper *Dagens Næringsliv*, Thursday, July 14, page 16.

Ulvin, P.B. (2021). Danske Bank-sjefer kan havne i fengsel for å ha løyet for domstoler (Danske Bank bosses can end up in prison for lying in court), Norwegian public broadcasting *NRK*, www.nrk.no, published August 6.

U.S. House (2020). *The Real Wells Fargo: Board & Management Failures, Consumer Abuses, and Ineffective Regulatory Oversight*, U.S. House of Representatives, Report prepared by chairwoman Maxine Waters, Washington D.C.

Vadera, A.K. and Aguilera, R.V. (2015). The evolution of vocabularies and its relation to investigation of white-collar crimes: An institutional work perspective, *Journal of Business Ethics*, 128, 21–38.

Valentine, S.R., Hanson, S.K. and Fleischman, G.M. (2019). The presence of ethics codes and employees' internal locus of control, social aversion/malevolence, and ethical judgment of incivility: A study of smaller organizations, *Journal of Business Ethics*, 160, 657–674.

Veblen, T. (1899). *The Theory of the Leisure Class: An Economic Study of Institutions*, Macmillan, NY: New York.

Vega, T. (2015). Ex-State Senate Chief Is Guilty of Bribery, *The New York Times*, Friday, February 6, page A20.

Veltrop, D.B., Bezemer, P.J., Nicholson, G. and Pugliese, A. (2021). Too unsafe to monitor? How board-CEO cognitive conflict and chair leadership shape outside director monitoring, *Academy of Management Journal*, 64 (1), 207–234.

Vienola, S.A. (2021). *The Significance of CSR from the Customer's View – Case Nordea Finland*, Bacholor's thesis in business and governance, School of Business and Governance, Tallinn University of Technology, Tallinn, Finland.

Vries, K. (1998). Charisma in action: The transformational abilities of Virgin's Richard Branson and ABB's Percy Barnevik, *Organizational Dynamics*, 26 (3), 7–21.

Wang, Y., Stuart, T. and Li, J. (2021). Fraud and innovation, *Administrative Science Quarterly*, 66 (2), 267–297.

Waters, M. (2020). *The Real Wells Fargo: Board & Management Failures, Consumer Abuses, and Ineffective Regulatory Oversight*, U.S. House of Representatives, Washington, 113 pages.

Weick, K.E. (1995). What theory is not, theorizing Is, *Administrative Science Quarterly*, 40, 385–390.

Welsh, D.T. and Ordonez, L.D. (2014). The dark side of consecutive high performance goals: Linking goal setting, depletion, and unethical behavior, *Organizational Behavior and Human Decision Processes*, 123, 79–89.

Welsh, D.T., Ordonez, L.D., Snyder, D.G. and Christian, M.S. (2014). The slippery slope: How small ethical transgressions pave the way for larger future transgressions, *Journal of Applied Psychology*, 100 (1), 114–127.

Welsh, D., Bush, J., Thiel, C. and Bonner, J. (2019). Reconceptualizing goal setting's dark side: The ethical consequences of learning versus outcome goals, *Organizational Behavior and Human Decision Processes*, 150, 14–27.

Welsh, D.T., Baer, M.D:, Session, H. and Garud, N. (2020). Motivated to disengage: The ethical consequences of goal commitment and moral disengagement in goal setting, *Journal of Organizational Behavior*, 1–15, published online doi 10.1002/job.2467.

Welter, F., Baker, T., Audretsch, D.B. and Gartner, W.B. (2017). Everyday entrepreneurship: A call for entrepreneurship research to embrace entrepreneurial diversity, *Entrepreneurship: Theory and Practice*, 41 (3), 323–347.

Wheelock, D., Semukhina, O. and Demidov, N.N. (2011). Perceived group threat and punitive attitudes in Russia and the United States, *British Journal of Criminology*, 51, 937–959.

Whyte, D. (2014). Regimes of permission and state-corporate crime, *State Crime Journal*, 3 (2), 237–246.

Wieczner, J. (2017). How Wells Fargo's Carrie Tolstedt went from Fortune most powerful woman to villain, *Fortune*, http://fortune.com/2017/04/10/wells-fargo-carrie-tolstedt-clawback-net-worth-fortune-mpw/, published April 10, 2017.

Wikstrom, P.O.H., Mann, R.P. and Hardie, B. (2018). Young people's differential vulnerability to criminogenic exposure: Bridging the gap between people- and place-oriented approaches in the study of crime causation, *European Journal of Criminology*, 15 (1), 10–31.

Williams, J.W. (2008). The lessons of Enron: Media accounts, corporate crimes, and financial markets, *Theoretical Criminology*, 12 (4), 471–499.

Williams, M.L., Levi, M., Burnap, P. and Gundur, R.V. (2019). Under the corporate radar: Examining insider business cybercrime victimization through an application of routine activities theory, *Deviant Behavior*, 40 (9), 1119–1131.

Wilmer Cutler Pickering (2003). *Report of Investigation by the Special Investigative Committee of the Board of Directors of Enron Corp.*, William C. Powers, Raymond S. Troubh, Herbert S. Winokur, law firm Wilmer, Cutler & Pickering, http://i.cnn.net/cnn/2002/LAW/02/02/enron.report/powers.report.pdf.

Wingerde, K. and Lord, N. (2020). The elusiveness of white-collar and corporate crime in a globalized economy, in: Rorie, M.L. (editor), *The Handbook of White-Collar Crime*, Hoboken, NJ: Wiley & Sons, chapter 29, pages 469–483.

Wingerde, K. and Merz, A. (2021). Responding to money laundering across Europe: What we know and what we risk, in: Lord, N., Inzelt, E., Huisman, W. and Faria, R. (editors), *European White-Collar Crime – Exploring the Nature of European Realities*, UK: Bristol University Press, chapter 7, pages 103–124.

Witt, M.A., Fainshmidt, S. and Aguilera, R.V. (2021). Our board, our rules: Nonconformity to global corporate governance norms, *Administrative Science Quarterly*, published online doi 10.1177/00018392211022726, pages 1–36.

Wood, J.D. (2020). Private policing and public health: A neglected relationship, *Journal of Contemporary Criminal Justice*, 36 (1), 19–38.

Wright, B.E. (2007). Public service and motivation: Does mission matter? *Public Administration Review*, 67 (1), 54–64.

Xie, Y. and Keh, H.T. (2016). Taming the blame game: Using promotion programs to counter product-harm crises, *Journal of Advertising*, 45 (2), 211–226.

Yam, K.C., Christian, M.S., Wei, W., Liao, Z. and Nai, J. (2018). The mixed blessing of leader sense of humor: Examining costs and benefits, *Academy of Management Journal*, 61 (1), 348–369.

Yoo, C.S., Fetzer, T., Jiang, S. and Huang, Y. (2021). Due process in antitrust enforcement: Normative and comparative perspectives, *Southern California Law Review*, 94, (4), 843–926.

Yue, L.Q., Luo, J. and Ingram, P. (2013). The failure of private regulation: Elite control and market crises in the Manhattan banking industry, *Administrative Science Quarterly*, 58 (1), 37–68.

Zahra, S.A., Priem, R.L. and Rasheed, A.A. (2005). The antecedents and consequences of top management fraud, *Journal of Management*, 31, 803–828.

Zhang, L., Shan, Y.G. and Chang, M. (2021). Can CSR disclosure protect firm reputation during financial restatements? *Journal of Business Ethics*, 173, 157–184.

Zhong, R. and Robinson, S.L. (2021). What happens to bad actors in organizations? A review of actor-centric outcomes of negative behavior, *Journal of Management*, 47 (6). 1430–1467.

Zhu, D.H. and Chen, G. (2015). CEO narcissism and the impact of prior board experience on corporate strategy, *Administrative Science Quarterly*, 60 (1), 31–65.

Zvi, L. and Elaad, E. (2018). Correlates of narcissism, self-reported lies, and self-assessed abilities to tell and detect lies, tell truths, and believe others, *Journal of Investigative Psychology and Offender Profiling*, 15, 271–286.

Zyglidopoulos, S. (2021). On becoming and being an ethical leader: A Platonic interpretation, *Journal of Business Ethics*, 173, published online doi 10.1007/s10551-020-04544-y.

Zysman-Quirós, D. (2020). White-collar crime in South and Central America: Corporate-state crime, governance, and the high impact of the Odebrecht corruption case, in: Rorie, M.L. (editor), *The Handbook of White-Collar Crime*, Hoboken, NJ: Wiley & Sons, chapter 23, pages 363–380.

Økokrim (2021). *Temarapport: Profesjonelle aktører (Theme Report: Professional Actors)*, Økokrim, Norwegian National Authority for Investigatoin and Prosecution of Economic and Environmental Crime, Oslo, Norway.

# Index



https://doi.org/10.1515/9783110986686-015

www.ingramcontent.com/pod-product-compliance
Lightning Source LLC
Chambersburg PA
CBHW050130290326
R18043500002B/R180435PG41927CBX00020B/3

* 9 7 8 3 1 1 1 5 3 6 7 8 1 *